I YELLED AT GOD!

BARKING AT THE MOON

"Dream"

I Yelled at God!

DEDICATION

I dedicate this to my children, Kerry-Ann and Adam, who have walked alongside me during these trials, enduring traumas of their own due to the fallout of these events.

To my faithful and long-suffering husband, Tony, for his ongoing tolerance and support.

Introduction

Once I was asked, *"Why have you written a book?"*
I couldn't help but wonder if they were implying it was merely a vanity project…. *No Way!!*
This unvarnished memoir recounts how God intervened in my life, and it holds immense personal and cultural value, serving as a legacy for my children and future generations.
God inspired me to write it, and I have received supernatural confirmation of this more than once, even during the writing

I YELLED AT GOD!

process. I'm excited about my book, …
If Almighty God reached down and spoke to a wayward rebel like me, He can also communicate with you!
No one goes through life alone or without challenges.
Our challenges can become obstacles or be turned into stepping stones for growth. The choice is ours.
My aim is for readers to gain valuable insights from my cross-cultural experiences, including a journey through the mental health system and other key milestones in my life.

My story has an international dimension and carries a meaningful message to encourage and remind those who already have faith that they matter to God.

For anyone who doesn't know Him, I hope and pray it inspires you to reach out to Him and explore further. He loves you more than you know.

I was born and raised in a culture where the primary concern is whether you are either a Catholic or a Protestant. I didn't receive any legitimate Christian guidance, though we did have Religious Education at School.

Being less than a year younger than my sister, I knew I wasn't planned and felt like a mistake. I didn't fit in. However, I now appreciate that God doesn't make mistakes!

I yelled at God *when* things became unbearable, *like a dog barking at the moon. God* awakened a sense of purpose and direction that guided me through uncertainty, betrayal, and doubt.

God told me in a dream that :

- ***I would be put through the fire seven times and refined and shaped into the person He wanted me to be.***

I hope you enjoy my story, can relate to my mistakes, and feel reassured that you can call upon God in times of trouble.

Oh, and God doesn't mind if we yell at Him! …

His shoulders are more than broad enough to handle it!

He prefers that we do that, rather than shut Him out.

Prologue

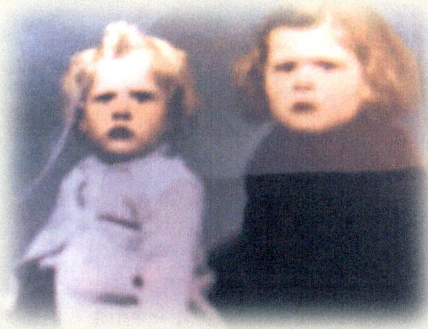

Me & Violet (my sister)

I stood defiantly outside our small, terraced house, leaning against the wall, digging my heels into the ground. I was seven years old. My mother had made me wear THAT dress.
I hated it!
It was a dull, dirty yellow colour she called mustard, and made of coarse wool that rubbed against my skin.
My sister yanked me by the arm pulling me along to go to school with her. A three-mile walk through the Catholic area of the Bogside in our hometown of Derry, where we were taunted by Catholic children who sang bawdy sectarian songs at us and occasionally threw missiles, knowing we were Protestants. As a result, I grew to dread that part of the journey to school.
Christ Church was the Primary School we attended. My family weren't churchgoers, but they sent my sister and me to a church school and Christian Endeavour, a non-denominational

Christian organisation, so we had some religious input in our early years.

Two years later, my dad made a career change, and we relocated to Belfast, where he began working as a prison officer in the Crumlin Road Gaol.

At our new school, we were mocked for our Derry accents, but I suppose over time they turned into Belfast accents, as no one ever mentioned it again.

We attended Sunday School and learnt the Catechism, and occasionally attended church services, but there was no real connection. It was all very cold and formal. The only thing that seemed to matter in our culture was whether we were Catholic or Protestant.

Our parents took my sister and me to the biannual events organised by the Burma Star Association. These gatherings were enjoyable, as they allowed me to mingle with the children of others who had served in the army. Dad would play haunting ballads such as *'Danny Boy'* or *'The Black Velvet Band'* on his harmonica when he was in a good mood or, as they say in Ireland, 'in good form'. I loved these familiar tunes, felt closer to Dad, and resembled him more than my mum. My parents had vastly different personalities, which made me wonder what drew them to each other.

From what I understood, neither of them held any specific religious beliefs; they identified as Protestant, primarily for historical and cultural reasons rather than genuine spiritual conviction. Their belief system was intertwined with political identity—a reflection of their upbringing in a region where

Protestantism held significant cultural sway—rather than a true engagement with religious teachings or practices. It was common for Protestant homes to have a picture of Queen Elizabeth and the Duke of Edinburgh on the wall.

The Orangemen's March, held annually on 12th July, marks the victory of constitutional forces over anti-Parliamentarian forces at the Battle of the Boyne in Ireland in July 1690. On this day, King William of Orange, the Protestant King of England, defeated the former Catholic King James.

As an Ulsterman and staunch Protestant, my father was always proud to commemorate this momentous event and wore the sash, bowler hat, with white gloves, and a carnation fastened on his lapel for these marches.

Like his comrades, Dad would rather die than miss this occasion. While the bands marched past, we cheered him on when his lodge came into view.

12th July Parade

It was captivating to watch the marchers in their respective lodges, as they proudly carried large banners and flags, and played flutes, rhythmically banging large drums to the march's tempo. This ingrained tradition was a vital part of our culture, embodying the history of the people of Northern Ireland.

The sound of pipes and enormous drums blasting a resounding battle cry evoked emotion that was thrilling and inspirational. I accepted this as a part of our lives and didn't even think about questioning it.

My sister and I were sent to church on Sundays, but I would often skip off and instead spend the time with my biker friends hanging out in the forecourt of a local café. I got caught out when my mum asked if I'd seen a friend of hers at church. When I lied and said I did, she remarked,

"That's funny, she's away on holiday in Spain this week."

Many years later, in 1978, I was invited to attend a small church in North Kensington. A few years after joining, God spoke to me in a dream with a message that made a profound impact on my life…

During this dream, God revealed this reassurance and warning:

- **I would be put through the fire seven times and fashioned into the shape He wanted me to become.**
  (I had no idea what was in store for me, but I knew that whatever happened, God would be there, holding me and guiding me to the next step.)

- **My name is written in The Lamb's Book of Life.**
  (In the dream, I knew supernaturally what this meant, though I'd never heard the term before.)

- **Every tear I shed is like a jewel in a crown.**
  (This will be a very bright crown.)

- **A seat is reserved for me at The Banqueting Table, and Joan, the Pastor's wife, would dust it down for me.**
- *(I had heard about the banqueting table before, and we even sang a chorus about it in church; now it was real...Wow!)*

- **I would have riches beyond measure in this life.**
  (God's riches are spiritual blessings, not material wealth. I was ecstatic and excited about the future!)

My heart and my life were changed by this overwhelming prophetic message this now defines my Christian walk.

The pipes in the castle where we were staying tinkled musically, and I could see the colours of the round walls. It was an inspiring, life-changing experience. The presence of God was tangible.

The following morning, I was still reeling from my experience and carried this precious message in my heart because I didn't want to tarnish it. I needed time to savour and process it. Sharing it at that time didn't feel safe.
It was my treasure, so I locked it away.

The Lamb's Book of Life isn't something I'd heard mentioned before. It meant I had a rightful place in God's Kingdom. My name is written in God's Book, and God specifically gave me this dream to reassure me that I was good enough.

Nothing impure will ever enter it, nor will anyone who does what is shameful or deceitful, but only those whose names are written in the Lamb's Book of Life. Rev. 21:27 NIV

He knew that I would have always doubted my worthiness if I hadn't received this confirmation directly from Him.
I am massively grateful for this precious gift.
The following Sunday morning, I purposefully strode up to the front of the church to the pulpit and shared my dream with the

congregation. There wasn't a dry eye in the place. It was humbling. They were emotional because I had been difficult and cynical, constantly questioning their beliefs. They were enthralled because they knew God had spoken to me.

He graciously gave them a profound answer to their prayers for my salvation.

Years later, despite my doubts about her misinterpretation of this message, I eventually gathered the courage to tell Joan about her role in my dream. To my relief, she responded in a light-hearted and supportive way. She didn't mind at all.

I was eager to see how the dream would pan out in my life…

CONTENTS

PART ONE

THE SEVEN TRIALS

Chapter One

BELFAST ~1957

Our maternal grandmother moved in with us when we relocated
seventy miles from Londonderry to Belfast, as my father, a
carpenter, had secured a new job in the prison service there,
marking a career change for him.

Granny was in her late seventies and widowed following my
grandfather's death several years earlier. She became a
cornerstone in our young lives and was always there to comfort
us when we skidded on the steep hill at the top of our road and

fell off our makeshift skateboards, badly grazing our legs, or when we faced overwhelming amounts of homework.

She bandaged my foot when I stepped on a nail while playing with friends in an abandoned house, and hopped home with a blood-soaked sock.

When we got home from school, a warm meal was always waiting for us. With Granny around, we felt loved and cherished. If we were in trouble with our parents, she would intervene, saying, *"Och, they're only weans!"* (They're just little ones.)

Granny had a few old-fashioned sayings and often used words and expressions that were long since outdated, though we understood her meaning and found them amusing.

When I returned from a Girl Guide camping trip or other event, she would say, *"Are ye back?"* With a giggle and a cuddle, I would sarcastically reply, *"No, Granny, I'm still there."*

Our little black cat, Brandy, went missing just as we were about to move to our new home in Belfast. Dad's impatience and insistence on leaving without letting us search further for her forced us into the car for the long journey ahead, without her. Downcast at the loss of our furry companion, I worried about what would happen to her now that we had gone.

Three weeks after we settled into our new home, we heard a low-pitched meow at the back door. To our astonishment, there stood Brandy. I could barely believe my eyes! How she tracked us down remains a complete mystery, but my heart swelled with joy at her return, and it felt almost like a miracle, a supernatural event.

She must have walked seventy miles from Londonderry to Belfast. Her appearance was thin and ragged, and her paws swollen and bleeding. With tender loving care, I nursed her back to health. Before long, she was back to her old self, frolicking around our new home in Belfast. Her capability to find us remains a mystery.

Six months later, Granny's stroke and hospital admission rocked our world. Mum and the rest of the family visited her often, dismayed when she would only utter one word, *'Yes'*. On our last visit to her, everyone was surprised that she managed to say *'Goodbye'* to me as I was leaving. It broke my heart to see her like this, but I was powerless to make her better.

1965

Dad, a Scoutmaster, asked me to help clean up after a party in a Scout hut in Mallusk, a village about twenty miles away in the township of Antrim. Dad dropped me off outside the hut, where I helped clear up the mess from their party.

A couple of the lads had vomited all over the floor, so this wasn't a pleasant job. My stomach heaved…. *Yuk!*

John, the assistant Scout Master, who was around twenty-two, was a tall, gangly guy with a large gap between his front teeth. He took himself and his life seriously, and although he didn't have much of a sense of humour, he was dependable and responsible and could be relied upon to act nobly and do the right thing in any situation.

John was already on the scene, clearing up. When we finished sorting things out, the hut looked and smelled clean and fresh. He offered to take me home on the back of his motorcycle, but there were dire consequences from that charitable act.

Soon after setting out, we were involved in a terrible accident on one of the single-track roads from Mallusk.

A car hit the motorbike on a narrow road, causing it to topple over and knock us to the ground. It landed on the side of the road, and I was flung onto a bed of nettles. A searing pain shot up my right thigh, and I couldn't understand why the onlookers, who by now had arrived en masse at the scene, pushed me down each time I tried to sit up.

In shock and unaware of how serious my injuries were, I desperately wanted to get out of the nettles I had landed in. The broken bone in my right thigh must have been sticking out and would have looked terrible. They tried to stop me from seeing it, and now I'm so glad they did, as seeing my leg injuries would definitely have left a lasting mental scar.

The pain was excruciating! John got off lightly with just a three-inch cut on his left arm.

Eventually, the ambulance arrived, and the paramedics administered a welcome dose of pain relief. They swiftly transported me to a small hospital in Ballymena, where I received a blood transfusion as the first line of treatment. The surgical staff cut through my jeans to remove them without causing further damage, and following emergency surgery, I was taken to a dark, dismal ward filled with older adults who coughed and groaned all night.

4

My transfer by ambulance to Musgrave Park Hospital, on the outskirts of Belfast, the following day, was a tremendous relief.

Two fractures were found in my right femur at the neck and mid-shaft, and my kneecap had shifted down to the side of my leg and was subsequently put back in place and crudely stitched, but it was never the same and was completely numb.

The medics initially treated the fractures with swift, vigorous, and excruciating manipulation. Suddenly, four men in white coats, on a mission to perform this procedure, surrounded my bed without warning or sedation. I was still in shock when they used traction to stabilise my realigned bones after this torturous, but necessary procedure. A pulley and ropes gently repositioned my fractured bones in the right position. Traumatised by my screams of pain, the others in the ward were filled with empathy and concern.

Every evening, Matron made her rounds of the wards, and since I had a mischievous streak, I would hide under the bedcovers and chew gum, which, of course, she didn't appreciate and would give me a good telling off.

One of my pet tricks was to stand on my other leg at the side of the bed, leaving the injured leg raised in traction. My favourite nurse, Katrina, caught me performing this party trick one day and scolded me harshly, adding that she was deeply disappointed in me for risking further injury to my leg. That hurt; I felt ashamed for letting her down, and never did it again.

At the tender age of seventeen, I did not fully understand the seriousness of my injuries or the long-term impact they would have on my life. Although I was warned that more health issues might appear after I turned forty, which seemed like a lifetime away, I didn't pay it much attention.

Monday was the day the consultants did their rounds, and each time they approached my bed, I genuinely hoped that they would discharge me home, as the seriousness of my injuries had still not registered. Three long months down the line, I was still stuck in that hospital bed.

Anyone who has experienced a long hospital confinement will know it's no fun, especially for a teenager. I was often so bored that I felt listless, and this was compounded by the fact that I was unable to get out of bed. Little did I know this would be the first of a catalogue of hospital admissions, as the ramifications of these injuries would have a huge impact on my body.

Desperate to get out of bed, I would pretend I was religious and ask them to take me in a wheelchair to the church service in the hospital on Sunday mornings, which they did, but the services were mediocre and didn't have much impact on me. I was just glad to get out of the ward for a while.

One day, around 3 pm, I distinctly heard my beloved grandmother say a final *'Goodbye.'* At that moment, I sensed deep down that she was no longer with us. Although heartbroken by the loss, I felt relieved for her because I knew that she was no longer suffering and was finally at peace. She did have faith in God, which she mentioned to us a few times, but didn't try to influence us. Now, I wish she had.

Later, when my father came to visit, he approached the side of my bed with a sorrowful look.

"I've got some bad news," he said.

"I know; Granny has died," was my flat response.

Dad was stunned that I already knew we had lost her and naturally assumed the ward sister had told me.

"No, she didn't; I just knew," I said.

He gave me a strange look but didn't pursue it.

Three months after my final discharge, Dad came to pick me up and take me home. Being out of the hospital after such a lengthy inpatient stay felt disorienting, especially with the fast-moving traffic. When I asked Dad to slow down, he became irritated and insisted that he was driving within the speed limit and at a steady pace. He couldn't relate to my anxious state.

An ugly, heavy steel calliper was strapped to my right leg with a leather binder around my knee, stopping me from bending it. This Draconian device forced me to drag my leg around with this heavy contraption. It became my constant companion for the following year.

Looking back, I'm convinced the weight of this calliper caused further pressure on my spine, resulting in a great deal of pain and suffering in the years that followed. Multiple procedures and surgeries ensued and made an ongoing impact on my life.

When I was eighteen and still figuring out my path in life, my parents separated. I felt it was my destiny to leave Ireland, and I eventually went to London with a friend.

My first temporary job there was waiting at tables at a Wimpy bar in Charing Cross. Unsurprisingly, I got fired a few months later when I dropped a red-hot plate of food, spilling it everywhere, and I frequently showed up late due to my unfamiliarity with the London Underground network.

During this challenging time, I felt irresistibly drawn to a fascinating individual named Joe, a familiar face at the lively Wimpy bar. From the moment our eyes met, I was captivated by his charming manner; he had a remarkable talent for making those around him feel genuinely seen and appreciated. His attention wasn't mere frivolity; it seemed sincere and refreshing, in stark contrast to the emotional deprivation I had endured until that moment.

As we engaged in meaningful conversations, our bond deepened incredibly. We were swept up in a whirlwind romance that coloured my days with vibrant shades of excitement and passion.

Inexperienced in the complexities of life and love, I was easily swayed and led by the intoxicating feelings he stirred within me. Joe was a little older than I was and originally from Trinidad; his father was of Indian heritage, and his mother was American.

Over time, I became deeply immersed in the heady joy of our whirlwind romance, relishing our shared laughter and meaningful conversations. Yet, there were moments when I felt uncertain—a small voice that urged me to think carefully before committing.

Regardless, when he proposed to me, I immediately agreed to marry him, convinced it was what I truly wanted. Reflecting on that decision, I rushed blindly into this commitment, blinded by love, passion and innocence of youth, without fully understanding its implications.

We flew to Belfast, where he met my family, who initially seemed quite taken by him.

Three days after my 21st birthday, we got married at our local church, though neither of us had any faith to speak of at that time. People just assumed our wedding would be in a church.

Before our marriage, he lived in an apartment with his older brother, Monty, who struggled with alcoholism and an unusual addiction to hot pepper sauce, often swigging it directly from the bottle.

Tragically, and perhaps inevitably, Monty passed away at the young age of thirty-eight. We arranged to have his body flown back to San Fernando, their hometown in Trinidad, at their father's request, and we travelled there for his funeral on the same flight. The plane shuddered, and we experienced a rough, bumpy landing that was quite alarming, causing an elderly passenger to have a heart attack.

On our arrival in Port of Spain, the strong odour of pitch from the tar lake was noticeable, but it wasn't unpleasant. Warm air hit us as we stepped off the plane, like a hairdryer that blew directly on our faces. An ambulance crew stood by to take the sick man to the hospital.

We stayed with Joe's family for three weeks, which involved thirteen days of mourning. The casket was open and displayed in one of the rooms of their spacious home, and mourners had travelled from near and far to pay their respects. Their family was well-known and highly regarded throughout the area.

Mourners shuffled reverently around the coffin and placed garlands of flowers on the body.

According to Hindu tradition, he was cremated on a pyre of wood, a strange sight to behold. I avoided the rituals, as I didn't fully understand their significance; however, I was aware of their belief in reincarnation.

His wealthy father had bought us first-class tickets to return to England by boat to Portsmouth. After we docked at this busy port, we took a train back to London and flew from Heathrow to Belfast, eager to reconnect with my family.

Knocking at the back door of my mother's house, we waited eagerly for her to appear, but she didn't recognise me at first because I was suntanned and thinner than before with longer hair bleached white by the sun, so I must have looked different to her. Suddenly, the penny dropped, she recognised me, and swiftly ushered us into the house.

Joe was by now showing increasingly worrying possessive characteristics; for instance, he once gave me a black eye because I went to have a bath without first telling him. When my passport photo was taken, I covered the bruising with makeup, but it was still visible.

During this marriage, I lost two babies in the initial stages of pregnancy. On one occasion, I almost died as I had an incomplete miscarriage, lost a huge amount of blood, and needed emergency surgery to remove the remains of the pregnancy.

Our small flat was above an off-licence in the centre of Belfast. Joe worked as a chef at the Royal Hotel on the renowned Royal Avenue in the city centre, and I had a temporary part-time job at the checkout counter in a local supermarket.

Several times, I turned to my dad for help when Joe was violent with me. Once, he threatened to hit me with an iron bar that was laid across the back door of the off-licence. By that time, Dad had had enough and warned me that if I didn't leave him, he would not help me anymore.

Although I had no religious beliefs or background at that time, my marriage vows had always held great significance for me, and I had fought tirelessly to uphold them. Yet one fateful night, a sobering realisation swept over me like a cold wave:

"That's enough!"

In that moment, I flicked a switch in my mind, resolutely deciding to break free from the suffocating grip of a violent and controlling man. With a heavy heart, I acknowledged the painful truth—there could be no future for me in this tumultuous relationship.

Our marriage endured for a brief and turbulent thirteen months, marked by a growing downward spiral of disillusionment.

Soon after, seeking solace, I left and took refuge with an old friend, Shirley, whose warm presence starkly contrasted with the turmoil I had just escaped.

In retrospect, our union was fraught with complications from the outset. During our time together, I realised we came from totally different backgrounds. Unsettling events unfolded, moments so distressing with vast repercussions, I prefer to leave them unexamined, buried in the recesses of my mind.

It's odd how this chapter of my life feels remote, like a distant memory, as though I'm recounting someone else's story rather than reflecting on personal experiences.

For the subsequent few months, Shirley and I shared a flat. When she decided to move on, she asked if I would join her in heading south to Dublin, which seemed like a fantastic opportunity, so I resigned from my job at the supermarket and travelled down to the south with her.

A Change of Scene ~ Bray Co. Wicklow - 1969

Following a series of unremarkable jobs, an opportunity to work as a children's nurse at a cerebral palsy clinic in Bray, a small town in County Wicklow, presented itself. I was interested, thinking it would be a good experience for me, so I pursued it and secured the job.

The children in our care were unique individuals, and I grew fond of each one of them. However, after two years, I became frustrated with the strict and oppressive way the facility was run.

Each day, these poor children were served up the same disheartening slop each day—a thin, unappetising mixture that resembled pale, lifeless mince. Instead of asking, *'What's for dinner?'*, they innocently asked, *'What's for mince today?'* My heart ached for them. Their limited existence left them unaware of how they should have been treated — they deserved so much better, but they lived in an insular world that offered so little.

The matron, a stern-looking woman in her late fifties, ran this facility with an iron fist, making it reminiscent of a prison camp. The atmosphere was punitive for the children, prompting me to voice my concerns.

When no constructive action was taken, I resolved to take matters into my own hands by writing an anonymous letter to a local newspaper, shedding light on the deplorable conditions and antiquated care system within the clinic.

The governing board regarded me with suspicion and summoned me to a meeting that felt more like an interrogation than a discussion. I sensed their inward smirks, the subtle upward twitch of their lips that betrayed their judgment as they scrutinised my perceived shortcomings. They exchanged knowing glances, convinced that I lacked the intellectual strength and eloquence required to compose such a compelling letter to the newspaper.

As the meeting progressed, I could almost feel the weight of their condescension hanging in the air, thick and suffocating. Yet, when the moment came for them to dismiss me with a wave of their hands and an arrogant flicker of their eyes, a groundswell of triumph washed over me.

Their dismissive judgment, so confidently delivered, ultimately fell flat against the resilience I felt bubbling up inside me. I left that room invigorated and determined to continue my quest for awareness of their plight and to fight for a better environment for these children.

They had underestimated me, as many people seem to do, but this time it worked in my favour. I refused to answer their charges. Although the article I wrote was published, the ripples of change I had hoped for never materialised. Still, I took solace in knowing I had highlighted their appalling conditions, igniting a flicker of hope in the bleak existence of these children trapped within that dreadful residential clinic.

As I was usually assigned to night duty, I was required to wake the children at around 5 am to prepare them for breakfast at 7 am. This routine was often frustrating, especially for the children, some of whom wore callipers. They would kick at me, their legs swinging uncontrollably, shouting in their strong

Southern accents, *"You're not in charge!"* Their resistance stemmed from the discomfort caused by my unfamiliar northern accent. The upshot of this was that they often defied me.

Often, I was accidentally kicked in the mouth by their flailing legs, leaving me with a semi-permanent cut on my bottom lip. In some instances, I had to inject these children with tranquillisers to calm and restrain them, making it easier to dress them.

Two years later, I decided to spread my wings, so left this job and headed for the Channel Islands.

JERSEY

An advertisement I saw for a children's nurse position in St Helier, Jersey, one of the picturesque Channel Islands, piqued my interest.

However, when I began working there, they assigned me menial tasks such as sweeping the hall, cleaning the fireplace and bathrooms, nothing to do with childcare.
Furthermore, the few children living there appeared to receive sufficient care. This was a tactic to exploit slave labour. The advertised job did not exist.

Feeling used, I left quickly and met up with an old friend, Wendy, and a group from Dublin who were incredibly helpful in advising me on the customs and quirks of the island. They even organised suitable accommodation for me and a new temporary job at a local restaurant.

Jersey became my home for two years, but I had to move house several times because rooms were rented out to seasonal workers on short-term lets and a *'sleeping-only'* basis. It was a beautiful island with its own unique culture.

Dad kept in touch by letter while I was in Jersey, and it was comforting to hear from him. I assumed he obtained my address from my sister. Communication with him had to remain secret when I spoke to Mum on the phone, as she would have deemed it disloyal of me, particularly as he now had a new girlfriend called Lily.

Dad had always flirted with the ladies, so I wasn't surprised. Once more, we lost touch due to my frequent address changes.

In Jersey, people are categorised as residents, seasonal workers, or holidaymakers. I found myself in the seasonal workers' group. The traditional dish known as a Jersey bean crock also led to locals being nicknamed *'Jersey Beans.'*

During my time there, I met Peter, an Irish guy from Dublin, who was a coach driver, comedian, and singer. He was quite a popular character who frequently performed at holiday camps, hotels, and various entertainment venues. Having lived there for many years, Peter knew many people on the island, which made spending time with him and his friends quite interesting and enjoyable. We were attracted to one another and began dating, developing a positive, steady, though occasionally volatile, relationship.

When I had to relocate from my lodgings once again, as the short-term lease had ended, he informed me about a room near where he was staying that had become vacant. This room was rented out on a *'sleeping-only'* basis, but I didn't mind. It was better than nothing.

A year later, while still in a relationship with Peter, I miscarried and was admitted to the local hospital for a few days. By now, I was anxious and depressed. I had lost three babies and feared I would never be able to carry a baby to full term. A huge bouquet from my work colleagues arrived while I was an inpatient, and it cheered me up to know they cared enough to arrange this.

Over time, I became pregnant again and moved in with friends, a married couple, Gus and Angie, who took great care of me. My prenatal checks were conducted regularly, and I was booked into the local maternity hospital for the due date of 22nd January 1972.

LONDON 1971

During a pre-Christmas trip back to London with Peter in early December 1971, I was rushed to Central Middlesex Hospital in agony with a suspected urinary infection, but instead was stunned when told, *"You're going to have your baby."*

Kerry-Ann was born the next morning at 7:55 am, seven weeks prematurely, weighing 3 lbs 10 oz. As she was underweight, she had to be placed in an incubator until she reached a healthy weight for a newborn. I wasn't allowed to hold her because she was too fragile—her tiny limbs were almost translucent—it was so painful…I longed to pick her up and cuddle her, but could only look at her in the incubator through a glass pane.

17

I was bereft!

Other mothers in the ward had their babies beside them in their cots, but I did not. Now I had no choice but to stay in London in the run-down bed and breakfast where I lodged, and I walked three miles to the hospital each day, carrying the breast milk I expressed by pump for my baby daughter. I was so happy to be a parent at last, though my baby was premature and needed special care.

Finally, I was a mother, *wow!*

Walking down the street felt different almost like I was floating on air!

She was finally discharged from the hospital into my care at six weeks old. Her delicate, wispy blonde hair, striking blue eyes, and delicate rosebud lips made her adorable, yet she was so tiny that only a doll's clothes would fit her.

My Italian landlady, Maria, was excited to have a baby in the house and couldn't stop fussing, lavishing endless affection on her.

A year later, the Italian couple, Mario and Maria, were selling up, intending to return to Italy, as Maria's mother had died and left them her house in a village outside Naples.

Since I was registered on the Housing List, a place in a halfway house in Harrow was offered, and I lived there for what seemed like an eternity, ensconced in a horrible, tiny attic room.

When I was offered a two-bedroom ground-floor council flat in the notorious White City Estate, I was very excited to see it. Although the estate housed many problem families, I felt grateful for any accommodation I could get. Excited to view it, my joy soon turned to dismay when I discovered the floor covered in sewage that leaked from the toilet; however, the flat was spacious.

The bedrooms were light, airy, and a decent size, while the bathroom, kitchen, and lounge were acceptable.   Therefore, I resolved to do whatever was necessary to transform it into a cosy, compact home for the two of us, considering myself very lucky to be offered a place of my own, despite the less-than-salubrious location.

The large windows overlooked a spacious, grassy area at the back of the flat. On one side was a disused washhouse with old wringers and buckets inside.

Annie, a pleasant old lady, lived in the flat on the other side. We got on well and became friends. I gave her a spare key to keep for me, which came in handy more than once when I unintentionally locked myself out.

With the help of a few supportive friends, the flat was scrubbed, bleached, and disinfected, as I couldn't imagine living there with my little girl if there was any risk of infection. Once I was sure it was spotless and germ-free, we moved in, and it became our home for the following four years.

Painting the kitchen cupboards a cheerful yellow was my next project, and I was thrilled with the vibrant transformation. Peter visited occasionally and hinted that we should get married. I didn't want us to live together, so he rented a room in Harlesden, a few miles away, in a house where he knew the owners from his previous stays in London.

However, my then-husband Joe was still stubbornly refusing to grant me a divorce, ironically quoting our wedding vows.

"Those whom God has joined together shall not be put asunder."

God hates divorce, as I later discovered. Still, it was ironic that Joe disregarded our marriage vows, selectively choosing the ones which served his interests, and it was absurd that he used this scripture, given that he had no genuine faith.

Peter wasn't a suitable candidate for marriage; he drank excessively and acted irresponsibly, and I felt a sense of relief at having a valid reason to avoid such a commitment.

Although he could sometimes be entertaining, his charm was superficial and overshadowed by deep-seated flaws. He was unreliable and, as a long-distance lorry driver, a job he secured while in London, he was prone to lengthy absences. He lacked the stability and substance I hoped for in a partner.

As a father, he fell far short, making no effort to provide financial support for our daughter and rarely spending any meaningful time with her. Her bond with him as a child was so weak that she cried and squirmed whenever he tried to hold her. She didn't know him.

His only act of care towards her, was a £5 note he gave me to *'buy her a pair of shoes'*—an insignificant gesture that revealed his priorities and complete disregard for his responsibilities.

In Jersey, there were more job openings than there were people to fill them. In contrast, London had plenty of jobs available, but there were also many more applicants competing for those positions.

Our relationship had become strained and was rapidly deteriorating. I felt a sense of relief when he returned to Jersey after being offered a suitable job there. I must admit, I was glad to have some peace and freedom, so I didn't miss him.

At that time, I was far from God and lacked any spiritual input, guidance, or grounding in my life. Consequently, like most of my peers, I pursued worldly desires and acted according to what seemed right at the time.

After waiting four years, I was finally offered a two-bedroom terraced house in East Acton, complete with a green play area in front. I eagerly seized this opportunity. Although it was somewhat small, it was sufficient for our needs, and we moved in.

The location was significantly better, and also the environment, compared to where we were living. I noted that the house could benefit from some cosmetic work to bring it up to standard, as the décor was outdated with bright yellow and brown, flowery, old-fashioned wallpaper.

At the front of the house, there was a postage-stamp-sized garden and a decent-sized lawn at the back.

A train line ran behind the house, so we had to adjust to the sounds of trains chugging by at regular intervals.

Over time, the necessary improvements were made, and the trains regularly passing became reassuring, fostering a sense of being home. East Acton Tube Station was just around the corner, and we loved seeing the back of our house go past when we took the tube into Central London.

Margaret Thatcher, then Prime Minister, introduced a welcome new bill that granted council tenants the right to purchase their properties at a discounted rate. I took advantage of this golden opportunity and bought the small house.

The outgoings were not much more than when I was renting, so I felt this was the right decision. One unexpected benefit was the convenient location, just a short walk from Old Oak Primary School, where Kerry-Ann attended, and half a mile from Hammersmith Hospital, where I had recently begun working as a casualty officer.

My duties were particularly challenging, none more so than when I had to deliver the heart-wrenching news of a beloved child's passing to his father. It remains etched in my memory: a little boy no older than six was struck by a car while riding his bike on the main road outside the hospital. When they brought him in, outwardly, his body appeared uninjured, but internal bleeding and severe head trauma from the impact claimed his life instantly.

When I called his dad to come to the hospital and informed him of his son's death, he crumpled under the weight of grief, his sobs raw and unrelenting as he buried his head in his hands.

Steering him into the family room for some much-needed privacy, I will never forget the look of devastation on that poor father's face.

In time, my divorce from Joe was granted because we had been apart for seven years, so I no longer needed his consent.
  Yay! I was free at last!
I felt liberated; finally, my legal status reflected my actual position.
Meanwhile, life revolved around looking after my little daughter and my job, so there wasn't much time left for socialising.

With hindsight, I realise that God's hand was always upon me, even during those times when I was unaware of His existence.

Chapter Two

HAMMERSMITH PALAIS ~ 1975...

Magid and I first crossed paths when I took a second job as a barmaid during the evenings at Hammersmith Palais. As a single parent, I juggled two jobs to make ends meet and support myself and my young daughter.

I felt an inexplicable pull, as if drawn by a magnet, to Hammersmith Palais *(now I believe this was God's plan unfolding),* and I hurriedly walked the four miles to meet with the ballroom manager to discuss the available barmaid position I saw advertised. I was offered the job and began working there for two evenings a week, Wednesdays and Saturdays.

The location of the Palais was fitting, right between a police station and a fire station. Consequently, if things did get serious, the police were always nearby to assist, although such instances were thankfully rare.

Parties were a regular occurrence after the evening shifts, but I had little inclination to join them. My top priority was to get back home to relieve Pauline, my regular babysitter.
I had an early start in the morning and needed to take little Kerry-Ann to Christine, my childminder, before checking in to my main job at Hammersmith Hospital.

Socialising with my Palais colleagues after hours held no attraction for me as I was exhausted after the shifts and was anxious to check on my daughter and get some sleep.

Christine was a reliable childminder who, coincidentally, had a young daughter named Susan, born on the same day as my daughter. They got along well, and I was confident she was content and cared for while I was at work, which gave me peace of mind.

Around three months later, the bar staff finally ground me down, and I succumbed, agreeing to attend one of these parties. Pauline, who lived in one of the flats above us, volunteered to stay overnight.

That's when this charismatic Egyptian made an unexpected and flattering play for me. We dated regularly for the next two years and got on well. He was engaging, loyal, attentive, kind and caring, different in most respects from the men I had previously known.

25

Over time, our relationship developed, although no one at the Palais was aware that we were seeing one another, as we maintained a professional front at work.

However, it eventually leaked out, and soon it became common knowledge that we were an item. He bought Kerry-Ann a giant teddy bear, which she loved. She began calling him Dee-Dee *(his family nickname)* and, eventually, Dad.

Two years later, we were married at Hammersmith Registry Office as neither of us had any religious affiliation. He was a nominal Muslim, and I could probably be described as an Agnostic at that time.

Kerry-Ann looked cute in a beautiful little yellow satin gown with puff sleeves. My mother, sister, extended family, friends and our mutual workmates were there.

A celebration party was held in a local club, where our guests danced the night away.

Our honeymoon was spent in Plymouth. A friend offered to look after Kerry-Ann for the week, but I was uncomfortable leaving her, so she came with us.

Magid formally adopted her and, at first, was an attentive husband and a good father. Charismatic, funny, flamboyant, and very generous, our relationship became solid and rewarding.

During my visit to Ireland, I spent time with my mum and sister, who was expecting her third child at the time. When I returned home, I was excited to discover that I was also pregnant, and I wished we lived closer to support each other.

It had been six years since Kerry-Ann was born, and our new baby would be Magid's first biological child. We were both incredibly excited about this news.

Adam was born two days before the due date, the following January in 1978, in Hammersmith Hospital and was a welcome addition to our family.

Eventually, I took our baby boy home, where he was warmly welcomed and spoiled by all, especially his big sister, who was always eager to help with the daily chores and delighted in assisting me with his care.

A photo of Kerry-Ann holding baby Adam and the giant teddy bear Magid had bought her is one that I treasure, bringing back memories of joyful times.

I recall telling her:
"One day, you and your baby brother will be bigger than that bear!"
I was right, they both tower over me now.
At eight months old, we agreed to have Adam circumcised, a customary practice in Magid's Islamic faith. Though I didn't want it done for religious reasons, I considered it the most hygienic option for him. The circumcision took place at our local Hammersmith Hospital.

1978

"It's your dad!" said my husband, with his arm outstretched, offering me the phone receiver—I froze...

"What! My dad?"

I hadn't seen him in 15 years. With trembling hands, I grasped the receiver and recognised the familiar voice that had been absent in my life for so long. After such a lengthy time without contact, it felt strange talking to Dad, and our conversation was stilted.

By this time, I had grown accustomed to not having a father around, but I was thrilled to hear from him and keen to get to know him again.

He asked how I was and told me he had retired from the prison service and moved to Cardiff to be closer to his brother Davy. His decision to leave Northern Ireland surprised me; although he had travelled quite a lot while in the army, he had never lived in another country, and I didn't think he'd ever leave his beloved Ireland.

However, he explained that he had broken up with Lily, his new lady friend, and had been targeted and threatened by various warring factions in Belfast, making it unsafe for him to remain there. He had been shot at on one occasion and needed to constantly check under his car for bombs before starting the engine, each time he went out, so I couldn't blame him for opting to leave.

Unfortunately, this move marked the beginning of the slow unravelling of our relationship. We lost touch for fifteen years, as we both frequently changed addresses, and with each relocation, finding a way to reach him became increasingly complex.

To cope with the growing distance between us, I sought to push him out of my mind, yet deep down, I couldn't shake the feeling that something essential was missing from my life.

My father was a complex man with a difficult past. He served in the army and later joined a special unit in Northern Ireland that dealt with civil unrest. Eventually, he became the principal prison officer at Crumlin Road Gaol in Belfast.

This facility earned the notorious distinction of being the UK's last prison to abolish the death penalty by hanging. Also known as HM Prison Belfast and The Crum. This former prison boasts a haunting and dark history. The Grade A-listed building has been transformed into a tourist attraction, enabling visitors to explore the former prison quarters at their own pace.

Guests can learn about the executions that took place there and engage in interactive exhibitions that display its intriguing past. With a blood-stained history marked by frequent executions and dreadful living conditions for prisoners, the building itself exudes an eerie and mournful atmosphere. The first execution took place in 1854: Robert Henry O'Neill, a soldier. His body and fourteen others are buried in unmarked graves on the jail grounds.

In 1901, a new stone execution chamber was constructed and used for the first time. The last execution of Robert McGladdery occurred on 20th December 1961. The prison closed in 1996.

During its years of operation, the prison saw seventeen men executed. Suffragettes were also imprisoned in the jail, but fifty-two prisoners managed to escape.

The weight of my dad's experiences in such a grim environment altered his personality and gave him a jaundiced outlook on life. The complexities of our relationship kept us apart in ways I struggled to grasp.

Johnny Cash performed in Belfast with Irish singer Sandy Kelly on five occasions, including once on 2nd April 1986 at the Crumlin Road Gaol. The dates of his other visits were kept under wraps due to the ongoing threat of terrorism. Dad was an avid admirer of his music, and I was also a fan. The prisoners and officers idolised Johnny and eagerly anticipated his visits.

As a former inmate in US prisons, he interacted with the prisoners, and they found it easy to relate to him and his music. Now a Christian, he served as a valuable and influential witness.

When Dad was on duty on death row, he came home looking pale and shaken, yet never spoke of his experiences. This profoundly impacted him, and the repercussions were complex for our family, as the atmosphere in our home became oppressive and tense during these times. As children, my sister and I often had to tread on eggshells to avoid upsetting him.

In 1969, thankfully, the UK abolished capital punishment for murder by hanging, and Northern Ireland followed suit in 1973, shortly after Dad retired.

When I returned to Belfast many years later, I discovered that the prison, locally known as The Crum, was decommissioned and reopened as a museum.

Curious and eager to observe and experience the death cell, I found it a spacious room that didn't seem overly foreboding. When the guide pressed a button on the bookcase that spanned the length of the back wall, however, causing it to swing open to reveal the gallows beyond, my heart skipped a beat, and it took on a much more gruesome setting.

How shocking! — I was horrified!

Ironically, prisoners who were awaiting execution would be oblivious to the fact that they were right next to the death chamber where their lives would soon end.

Dad came from a military background and was a strict disciplinarian. His hair was sandy-coloured, and he had a ruddy complexion; his temper could be quite vile when he was provoked, yet he possessed an integrity and depth of character that I admired and cherished. He maintained a positive outlook on life and was naturally outgoing; he enjoyed a wide circle of friends and frequently attended numerous social gatherings.

The Cub Scouts he led held him in deep affection and esteem. Despite his amiable persona, they understood that he wouldn't tolerate any disrespectful behaviour.

One of the cherished items I have from my father is his pocket-sized King James New Testament, which he carried close to his chest during his time in the Army. This small book, tucked in his shirt pocket, contained a message of encouragement from the king and miraculously saved his life by intercepting a bullet. It still bears the burn mark from that fateful incident, with a personal note from his commanding officer written on the introductory pages.

King George New Testament

I don't know how much of the New Testament my father had read, but I hoped that it brought him peace during his time in the army.

He kept a brass bullet removed from his leg after he was shot during battle, on the mantelpiece as a reminder of his injury, service, and sacrifice.

∞

We arranged to meet with Dad, selecting a date that worked for both of us. As we drove to Wales, I felt a mixture of anticipation and anxiety, uncertain about what to expect.

The thought of seeing him again after so many years was nerve-racking, and I couldn't shake the butterflies in my stomach. Despite my nerves, I was eager to reconnect and introduce him to my husband and children, and I wondered if he, too, was feeling anxious and apprehensive about the reunion after such a long time without contact.

Much of his hair had fallen out, and what was left had turned grey. He looked slightly older but otherwise remained just as I remembered him.

He mentioned he was upset because I hadn't invited him to our wedding, which took me by surprise, as I thought he wouldn't be interested in attending, and I didn't have his contact address anyway. Even if I had invited him, it could have been awkward due to potential tension between him and my mother. Worse, she might have refused to come if he were there. He understood this, but the disappointed look on his face was unmistakable. It was heartwarming to see him interact with the kids, and he got along well with my husband, Magid *(pronounced Majeed)*.

During a visit to their local pub in Cardiff, as soon as he saw my dad with his brother Davy, the barman raised his hands in mock alarm and exclaimed, *"Oh no, there's two of them!"* Dad was the spitting image of Davy, who was around a year older. No one could deny they were brothers, and if anyone dared to taunt them about baldness, Dad quipped,

"Grass doesn't grow on a busy street!"

He frequently visited us at our home in London, calling in on Wormwood Scrubs Prison, a stone's throw from us, to catch up with prison officers he knew there who had been transferred from Belfast. Reconnecting with him was a warm addition to our lives.

About a month later, he unexpectedly handed me a cheque for £1,000 from his pension payout, which was very generous of him and much appreciated, as we were struggling financially. I had an uncanny feeling that I shouldn't spend it, so I deposited it into a savings account. *Boy, was I right!*

Two weeks later, I received a letter from him, asking for his money back, using a feeble excuse about needing to buy a new

bed...*Who does that?* I was gutted and hurriedly wrote out a
cheque for the full amount, enclosing it with a letter, telling him
I didn't need his charity, for as long as I was strong and healthy,
I could work for a living, and it was only dirty pieces of paper
anyway.... *(rant, rant!)*

I was deeply hurt and upset by his behaviour, though not
from the loss of the money. While I appreciated life's comforts, I
was never solely motivated by material possessions. His
generous gesture, quickly followed by a sudden withdrawal,
deeply affected me. It was painful, primarily because it
highlighted a profound mistrust. We had only just reconnected,
and I realised that, in his eyes, I would have to prove myself
worthy of his trust again.

As I tried to comprehend what was going on in his mind, it
became clear that his past experiences in a workplace filled with
deceitful and manipulative individuals had hardened him. These
experiences had made him cynical and inherently distrustful,
always expecting the worst from everyone.

Unfortunately, it was evident that I had become a victim of
that distrust, and it saddened me that he allowed such cynical
views of others' intentions to shape his perception of me.

Any faith he once had in human nature seemed to have long
since vanished, leaving him with little more than a deep sense of
disillusionment. As for any belief in God, it was clear that none
existed. That night, I jumped up and down on the bed and yelled
at God about it!

*Call to me, and I will answer you and reveal great and
hidden things that you have not known.* Jer. 33:3 ESV

The higher, the better, as I was closer to heaven and therefore closer to God… *right?*

Although I was unsure if there was a God and, if so, whether He was listening,

Was God there? Was He listening?

It was a Saturday morning. I was still in my lilac Candlewick dressing gown with a large nappy pin on the front when the sound of the doorbell jolted me from my introspection.

Eight-month-old Adam lay in his crib, and his big sister, Kerry-Ann, was already alert and helping with his care. My face was still red and swollen from the tears I shed the night before, the pain of my dad's actions still fresh and raw.

Kerry-Ann answered the door for me, as I wasn't in any fit state to face anyone. She quickly returned with a message that a man was there and wanted to speak with me. Assuming it was someone collecting for charity, I told her to find out how much he was asking for. However, when she came back in, she told me that he wasn't asking for money and only wanted to talk to me.

Although I was initially wary, something inside me shifted. *(God again?)* Curiosity got the better of me, so I stepped out onto the porch to find out what he wanted.

His name was David, and for over an hour, he shared his beliefs about God, his words thoughtful and measured. Before leaving, he invited me to visit Emmanuel Assembly, a small church he attended regularly in North Kensington, about two miles away.

At that time, I had a loose connection with St. Katherine's, a large local church that I visited occasionally, but I wasn't deeply involved there, so I decided to try Emmanuel Church.

The next day, Dad rang, obviously feeling remorseful after receiving my letter. He had torn up the cheque I enclosed and flushed the pieces down the toilet. Even though I knew it had pricked his conscience, there was still a bitter taste in my mouth.

Since it wasn't my style to hold grudges, I forgave him and decided to put it behind me. We continued to meet whenever we could. *God was listening!*

The following Sunday morning, I took the children to this church, while my husband, a nominal, cultural Egyptian Muslim, stayed home to take care of the housework while we were out. He often prepared lunch for our return.

The small church was cosy and plain, quite distinct from the larger, formal, and cold churches with stained glass windows I had previously encountered. A small hall, lacking any opulence, had a simple yet profound statement on the wall at the front of the church.

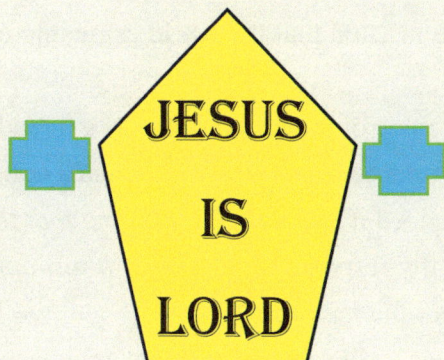

JESUS
IS
LORD

With a warm, homely and friendly atmosphere, a charismatic Welshman named Michael and two of his brothers, Albert and Ralph, who were co-elders, led the church. A piano at the front of the hall was the only musical accompaniment to the congregation's ardent hymn singing.

It was mostly a family church; they seemed sincere, holy and religious. None of the women wore jewellery or makeup and looked plain and proper, if a tad old-fashioned. Despite that, I enjoyed the service, and they seemed genuinely interested in us as a family, so I continued to attend regularly on Sundays.

With my bright clothes, jewellery and make-up, I felt out of place, producing an intense sense of unworthiness to the point where I sometimes felt a sudden urge to run out, ringing a bell proclaiming,

"Unclean, unclean!"

Michael or one of his brothers preached, and often told tales of Metal Box, the nearby company where they both worked. Ralph, Michael's older brother, relished telling the story of the time when he shared his faith in God with one of his work colleagues, who insisted that the world came into existence by osmosis.

A large ball made of silver foil hung by a thread from the ceiling of the works canteen. One day, when a colleague went for lunch, he noticed it and asked, *"Who put that there?"* Ralph sarcastically responded, *"No one., It just appeared!"* His colleague got the message.

At this point, I was still sceptical of it all, and unsure about who Jesus was, and I was vague about what the Bible said about him.

'The Bible as History' by Dr Werner Keller provided some credible answers and assured me that the stories contained in the Bible were indeed valid. I learned that he was a real person who had walked the earth 2,000 years ago.

The frequent use of prophecy, later fulfilled to the letter in the Bible, is another indicator of its divine origin.
Jewish Rabbis saw Jesus as a threat to their authority and lifestyle and wanted to get rid of Him and his followers, but they never said,

"He doesn't exist!"
I was struck by one example of a prophecy coming true: the nation of Israel, after 2,000 years of exile, was reformed on May 14, 1948, when Jewish people returned to the land. *(Aliyah)*

As surely as the Lord lives, who brought the Israelites up out of the land of the north and out of all the countries where he had banished them. For I will restore them to the land that I gave their ancestors. Jer. 16:15 ESV

The congregation truly cared about our spiritual and physical well-being. My continuous questioning and cynical attitude tested their patience, but they responded thoughtfully to my persistent probing. They even tolerated my scepticism, although Pastor Michael jokingly blamed me for his hair turning grey.

Kerry-Ann, now six, developed a warm connection with Hannah, a vibrant girl of similar age, who instantly felt like a kindred spirit. She was the youngest of five spirited siblings and the only daughter of Michael and his wife, Joan.

I was particularly grateful for their patience with my baby son, Adam, who delighted in the freedom to crawl across the church floor during the service. Despite my initial worries that his antics were bothersome and made me feel stressed, I constantly tried to keep him still, but I was relieved when they reassured me that it was perfectly fine.

Their understanding demeanour was a tremendous relief; it freed me to unwind, savour the content of the service, and immerse myself in the teachings of the Bible.

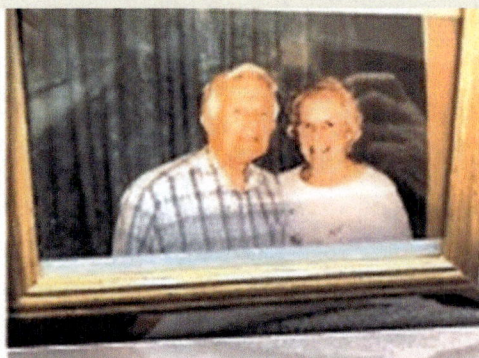

Pastor Michael & his wife Joan

We quickly became part of the church community and were invited to dinner at the Pastor's house or tea at the elders' homes. Having no family in London, I really appreciated this.

The church organised day trips to the beach using their minibus, as well as week-long vacations in Herne Bay, Kent. One particularly memorable trip was to Ostend, Belgium. It was not only fun and exciting but also provided a fantastic opportunity for deeper connections among the attendees.

A warm sense of belonging to this family of believers overcame me. They became a central part of our lives, and I grew fond of them all. Unbeknownst to me, they were praying fervently for my salvation in that little church.

"I in them and you in me, that they may become perfectly one, so that the world may know that you sent me and loved them even as you have loved me." John 17:23 ESV

Chapter Three

LONDON ~1982

When Kerry-Ann, now eleven, went on a youth camping trip organised by the church, Magid and I took Adam to Durham Castle for a long weekend, as a former colleague, now administrator of the castle, invited us to come for a visit. I experienced a memorable and life-changing encounter with God.

As soon as we got there, I sensed an icy atmosphere emanating from the staff and wondered what was behind it. Magid's friend and former colleague from Hammersmith Palais, where we both worked, Hughie, was the castle administrator.

I didn't know Hughie well, but I felt uneasy and uncomfortable in his company. At one time, he had tried to take his own life by jumping in front of a tube train.

Although he survived, he lost an arm as a permanent reminder of this incident. *How would he explain his missing arm whenever anyone asked, I wondered?*
He was outwardly pleasant and jovial, but there was something vaguely unsettling about him, something that made my skin crawl. He had spent time in jail, but I was unaware of the crime he had committed.

He asked if Adam, then four, would like to spend the night in his flat, as it would be more comfortable there with his own room rather than sharing with us. I felt uneasy about this suggestion, but I reluctantly agreed, as Adam seemed content to stay with him, and his dad raised no objections.

Adam seemed content at breakfast in the dining room. However, the tense atmosphere coming from the staff was almost palpable. They stared at us constantly, which I found unnerving. I desperately resisted the desire to approach them to find out what was wrong, but was constrained by Hughie's powerful position there. I remained silent. However, I remained on high alert.

Later that day, Hughie took Adam and me on a tour of the castle, leading us through the dungeons and the sights surrounding Bobby Shaftoe's Tower. He guided us up to the roof, and then, without warning, he grabbed Adam with his remaining arm and swung him around at a high and precarious spot. My heart was in my mouth. It was difficult for me to breathe. When he deposited my little son back on the ground, I lost control and told him never to touch him again.

I grabbed Adam by the hand and dashed down to find Magid, who was working in our room. He was on a long-distance business call, so I impatiently waited until he finished before imploring him to take us home.

A group of schoolchildren, mainly boys aged eight or nine, was on a sightseeing tour of the castle with their teacher. Hughie was rather too familiar with them; he joked and called the boys by name, but they seemed to recoil from him, and my suspicions were aroused, so I pressed Magid to tell me what his crime was.

He seemed reluctant to divulge this information, but I persisted and queried whether it had anything to do with the abuse of young boys.

(When there is a malevolent spirit present, I believe that's when God intervenes. I had a vague suspicion that this man could be a paedophile.)

His silence and guarded expression told me my suspicions were right, and I was horrified that he may have known this, and he still allowed our son to stay overnight with him in his flat. There was something radically amiss—this was beyond my comprehension.

Who was this person I was married to, and thought I knew as a kind and caring family man?

I was trying to understand his strange reaction to the incident, back of my neck stand up like those of a cornered cat. I mentally pushed the situation aside, unable to fully absorb or process it.

Thank you, Jesus, for your protection.

God's Angel Army was present that night, guarding us against the evil prevalent in that castle and preventing any harm from coming to Adam.

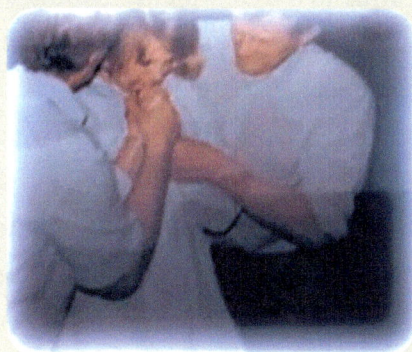

That's when God spoke to me**…telling me of seven things that would occur in my life** to refine me to the person He wanted me to be…

Ten months later, I was baptised by the pastor and elders, and they gave me this verse:

But seek ye first the kingdom of God, and his righteousness; and all these things shall be added unto you. Matt. 6:33 KJV

This was a holy and sacred experience. It was powerful and emotional to share a brief testimony of my fresh commitment to God and our church before Michael and Ralph baptised me.

I could have spoken for hours about God's goodness, faithfulness, steadfast nature, patience, and love. His fingerprints are all over my life! It was a joy to share how I have seen God work and how He has redeemed and restored a rebel like me.

There was a time when I wasn't fully aware of the subtle yet significant ways in which God's influence manifests in the world. However, I have since experienced a meaningful awakening to His presence.

Following my water baptism—a transformative event in my spiritual journey—we ascended the staircase to an upper room, where I was to receive the baptism in the Holy Spirit. As I made my way up the steps, someone kindly offered me a pack of tissues. While I was initially uncertain about the gesture, it became clear that they had a deeper understanding of the moment we were about to experience.

"Thanks, but I don't think I'll need them," I said.

Wow, how wrong I was!

In that room, I felt the presence of the Holy Spirit fill me and wept uncontrollably until my insides ached. It was a cathartic, releasing, purifying experience that left me emotionally drained. Eventually, a sense of peace settled in my spirit.

Jesus answered, "Very truly I tell you, no one can enter the kingdom of God unless they are born of water and the Spirit.

Flesh gives birth to flesh, but the Spirit gives birth to spirit. You should not be surprised at my saying,
"You must be born again."
The wind blows wherever it pleases. You hear its sound, but you cannot tell where it comes from or where it is going. So it is with everyone born of the Spirit." John 3:5 NIV

I was taught that in baptism, we die with Christ and rise again with Him as a new creation, with our old self dead and our sins forgiven. When we do anything for the Lord, it's because we are living that new life, not because we feel obligated to repay Him in any way. I began to embrace fully my new life in Christ and realised that until then, I'd been living half a life.

Suddenly, the air seemed purer, the flowers brighter, and I began to enjoy the company of people I'd previously shut out.

From then on, things were going to change…

Before my awakening to the more profound questions of life, I was on a vague quest for meaning, unaware that my yearnings were the pursuit of some form of spiritual purpose that could permeate my existence with significance.

My earlier explorations were driven by an interest in UFOs and the paranormal, immersing me in captivating mysteries about the universe.

I voraciously consumed a host of true stories documenting the experiences of individuals who claimed aliens had abducted them. Each narrative only served to fuel my imagination and suck me in deeper.

As my curiosity grew, I stumbled upon Spiritualism, a belief system that emphasises communication with the spirit world.

Immersed in a surfeit of literature, particularly books written by women, many of whom seemed to be called Doris. I was entirely captivated by these supernatural stories, which offered insights and perspectives I hadn't come across before. I was oblivious to the spiritual danger I was courting.

When I discovered that a renowned medium lived just a few streets away from home, my journey became more intriguing. I was told this while browsing at our local library when I borrowed various books on spiritualist encounters.

The librarian told me the author of one of them lived nearby, and she gave me her contact details. Eager to gain more insight into her abilities and work, I called her to arrange a visit.

When the day of the visit arrived, I stood at her front door filled with a mixture of excitement and apprehension. I knocked and waited. She took an incredibly long time to answer.

The door finally creaked open just as I was on the verge of giving up and walking away. However, my initial impression quickly soured when she greeted me with the claim that she could *'psychically'* discern that I had two children. This declaration was unimpressive and disingenuous, considering they were both clearly visible sitting in the back of my car, parked in front of her house.

This disenchantment caused me to question her claims, authenticity, abilities and effectiveness. I suspected, too, that her avid interest in my husband's line of work was to see if it was a trade that might be useful to her.

The first thing I noticed when she beckoned me in was that her house stank of stale urine, which repulsed me, causing me to leave quickly and never return. *Ugh!*

Spiritualist churches and psychic shows in nearby areas continued to draw me in. I even ventured to Central London to the Dominion Theatre on Tottenham Court Road with a few colleagues, to see Doris Stokes, a famous medium and prolific writer, several of whose books I had read. They are peppered with messages given to grieving families about their departed loved ones and stories of how she assisted them by alerting them to the location of important lost documents or missing objects left behind by them. This ability of hers intrigued me.

Despite the packed theatre, she singled me out, as I somehow knew she would.

Did I have a light above my head?
She gestured with her thumb to signal whether the person she was in touch with was alive or dead, signalling forward if they were alive and backwards if they were dead. And accurately indicated that Dad was still with us.

Mentioning my workplace, interestingly, she then declared there was someone in my life whose name she couldn't pronounce, but it began with an 'M,' adding that significant danger is linked to him. This alerted me, and I instantly made the connection with Magid, a name that was foreign to her, and I was unsettled and dubious about what she meant by this.
In a down-to-earth manner, she gave chillingly accurate information about my circumstances. It was unnerving, but my

burning desire for proof of the existence of a spiritual realm lured me down this path for a long time.

Demonic spirits are aware of what happens in people's lives and can lure them into this realm by offering information supernaturally.

I read later that when she was suffering from cancer and was approaching death, her agent asked her,

"Aren't you afraid to die?" She cryptically replied,
"Why would I be afraid to walk from one room to another?"

~

Even then, God's Hand guided me, preventing me from becoming too deeply involved in spiritualism and straying too far down that treacherous path.

While the information revealed by psychics and mediums may be accurate, its origin is from the wrong source, and it is demonic.

This scenario is illustrated and confirmed in the Bible in 1 Samuel 28:3-25, which recounts the story of the Witch of Endor who summoned the spirit of the prophet Samuel, only to be astonished when the real Samuel appeared instead of a demonic imitation.

Seven miles away in Uxbridge town, there was a Christian bookshop called ***'Maranatha'*** (Come Lord Jesus!). One day, as I walked past the window, I noticed a small, framed plaque with my name, *'Joann',* spelt without an *'e,'* a rare occurrence in the UK, though commonplace in Ireland and the US.

God Shall Prosper

"Delight yourself in the Lord, and He shall give you the desires of your heart." **Psalm 37:4**

God was speaking to me again.

That verse echoed the one that the elders gave me at my baptism. Of course, I went straight in and bought it. This little plaque still has pride of place in our hallway.

1985

At 14, Kerry-Ann announced that she no longer wanted to attend church. Dismayed, |I asked her why she felt that way. With a grimace, she explained that someone said something that upset her. When I pressed her for more details, she revealed that one of the elders made this passing comment: *"If you stop coming to church, you will end up as a bad lot."*
I found it perplexing that someone would make such an unkind remark to a young girl, given how profoundly it contradicted God's compassionate nature. The comment seemed entirely unwarranted, lacking any basis.

She was a well-behaved and kind-hearted child, always eager to help others and bring joy to those around her, so I was at a loss to know where this comment came from. I couldn't help but wonder if she would be able to move past this hurtful remark and muster the courage to reclaim her sense of worth and trust in people.

As humans, we often fall short of our expectations, leaving us grappling with regret, shame, disappointment and disillusionment. She, however, was still too young and innocent to fully comprehend this harsh reality, clinging to the belief that all Christians would conduct themselves with unwavering integrity, including myself. This misplaced assumption led her to the unfortunate error of measuring the essence of Christianity against the flawed actions of those claiming to embody its values.

In hindsight, that fleeting remark left a deeper imprint on her heart than I initially realised. Although she maintained friendships with the lively young people she had met at church, she has yet to rekindle her once-burning faith, a sorrow that echoes profoundly within me.

The pastor's wife, Joan, confided that Kerry-Ann had supernatural experiences with God at the youth camp. I hoped this would have a positive impact on her, but sadly, it wasn't to be.

My Prayer:

Dear Lord, please take care of her, keep her safe, surround her with your angels, protect her, and bring her back to You. I trust that You will complete the work You began in my daughter.

During this time, my mum, living in Lisburn, Northern Ireland, discovered that I was back in touch with Dad and quizzed me about his life and current circumstances.

She was still interested in him, hoping for reconciliation. When Dorothy, Dad's new lady friend whom he had met in Cardiff, suddenly died of heart failure, Dad was distraught and decided to leave Wales for his homeland, Northern Ireland.

He and my mother managed to resolve their differences. They happily reconciled and bought a house together in Lisburn, a small town half an hour from Belfast.

∞

EGYPT

Though I was already well-travelled, I was apprehensive when we first flew to Egypt to meet Magid's family, and I didn't know what to expect. I was anxious about whether they would accept a foreigner.

Disembarking from the plane at Cairo Airport, we were met by a wall of heat, as though we were walking into an oven, something I had to get used to very quickly.

Although the queue through security and passport checks was long, Magid walked past everyone and beckoned for us to follow.

Jumping the queue felt wrong and awkward. I was a little embarrassed. People were staring at us. They must have wondered if we were royalty or high-powered officials.

This was our first important lesson on how this country functions, primarily led by bribery for privileges at all levels.

Virtually any rule can be broken at the right price, and systems are constantly overridden due to the innate culture of bribery and corruption.

Magid had surreptitiously *greased the palm* of an airport staff member, enabling us to bypass passport checks and walk past the passenger queue. *I was astonished!* This was a whole new concept for me.

Amani, his younger sister, and Saida, their Sudanese surrogate mother, eagerly awaited us, visibly excited and bubbling over, standing behind a wire grill as we walked towards the reception area. They were thrilled, and we were met by beaming smiles and received an effusive Egyptian welcome.

The trip from the airport to our hotel was an eye-opener. I was amazed to see that drivers exchanged food and drinks with one another while stuck in traffic jams, cars just inches from one another, and whole families would ride on a single motorbike, often without any visible safety gear, sometimes carrying heavy items on their heads.

In this strange country, I couldn't detect any enforced rules or traffic systems.

The sun beat down relentlessly, transforming the asphalt into a shimmering mirage, while the air was thick with heat and swirling dust. Streets buzzed with an omnipresent cacophony of sounds, a symphony of blaring horns and shouted exclamations reverberating off the surrounding buildings.

At each intersection, the traffic lights flashed a cascade of reds and greens, yet it seemed to have little effect on the drivers. They manoeuvred through the chaotic crossroads with an air of nonchalance, as if they were participants in a high-stakes game governed by unspoken rules understood only by them.

The most intrepid drivers, emboldened by the chaos, often shouted colourful insults at each other, adding to the pandemonium as they jostled for position. The streets felt like a living entity, throbbing with a pulse of energy—aggressive, yet strangely exhilarating.

My initial immersion into Egyptian culture was a whirlwind of fascination and enlightenment, marked by moments of utter disarray that left an indelible impression on my mind. Each honk and shout reminded me of the vibrant life around me, a captivating clash of humanity that took my breath away.

The Ramses Hilton Hotel was completely different, enveloping our senses in an ambience of another world. Plush seating, air conditioning, and opulent surroundings featuring elegant marble and brass furnishings greeted our gaze.

Our rooms on the fourth floor were accessed by a magnificent circular glass elevator in the lobby; however, while using it, I noticed the doors clunked and didn't close properly, making it feel unsafe.

Towels were skilfully fashioned into artistic shapes of swans or flowers, adorning the beds, and a variety of lamps glowed, creating a welcoming atmosphere. Reading lights, vanity mirrors, and headboard panels blended seamlessly with the colour scheme. Although the room seemed a bit outdated, it offered a pleasant and fascinating view of the Nile, with boats sailing up and down this famous river.

To my astonishment and relief, Magid's extended family welcomed us warmly, their faces lighting up with genuine delight at our arrival. He introduced us to his circle of friends with pride, and although we faced a language barrier, a warm connection blossomed among us. Some family members spoke impeccable English, an unexpected gift that bridged our cultural gap and enhanced our interactions.

It was a true honour, it seemed, for them to have a foreigner join the family, and their warmth enveloped us, making us feel uniquely cherished and special.

Magid and his older brother, Hamdy, were brought up by their dark-skinned servant, Saida from Sudan, a surrogate mother to them who stepped in when their birth mother died of breast cancer while still in her forties. Saida was the exuberant lady with Amani when we arrived at the airport.

Magid told me he was just twelve years old when his mother tragically died in his arms. When reflecting on this, I realised this tragic event was bound to have had a far-reaching and damaging effect on his mental and emotional well-being and would inevitably have a long-term impact on his outlook on life, something I understood only in hindsight. I was also surprised to discover his real name was *Magdy,* a revelation to me, but he changed it to *Magid* after leaving Egypt. *(I preferred Magdy, but since I already knew him as Magid, I continued to call him by that name.)*

Cairo's high-level noise pollution comes from the crazy-busy, congested traffic. It is heavy and hectic, filled with honking horns and the constant noise of calls from the mosques, eerily intermittently echoing through the atmosphere. It was a culture shock, and I was dismayed at the poverty, noise, dirt, and overcrowding.

My new sister-in-law, Amani, lived in a tiny, dark flat with Saida and her brother Hamdy. There were no streets of houses that I could see, only towering blocks of flats.

They loved to come and see us at our hotel, sampling the food and luxurious surroundings.

Amani & Saida

The city was steeped in history, and some of the people resembled characters from the Old Testament in the Bible: men dressed in long, white, traditional robes complete with turbans and women gliding along with baskets of fruit and vegetables on their heads. It was so alien to us but strangely compelling.

Saida welcomed us into their home with open arms, radiating warmth and genuine joy in our company. As we spent time together, I earned the affectionate nickname *'Gigi'*.

One highlight of my visit was being introduced to ululating— a captivating, high-pitched rhythmic sound produced mainly by women in various African cultures. I was amazed to learn that this unique form of vocalisation serves as a celebration during joyous occasions and as a poignant expression of sorrow during times of mourning. The melodic waves of sound resonated deeply within me, illustrating the rich tapestry of emotion and tradition that this practice embodies.

Amani was very short and suffered from a spinal deformity, kyphosis *(marked hunched back)*. She had only half of one kidney that was functioning. In addition, she had various other challenging health issues. Consequently, she never married and led a restricted, insular life. Though diminutive compared to her brothers, there was no mistaking the family resemblance; her beautiful face, framed by striking, thick, attractively styled dark hair.

She was a devout Muslim who worked for the government and was a sweet, kind soul with integrity, devoid of the craftiness that some Egyptians I met possessed. She welcomed me warmly into the family, and they adored our children.

Me, Amani & Kerry-Ann

None of Magid's immediate family spoke English, except for a few basic words, so verbal communication was limited. As a result, numerous misunderstandings arose, and an abundance of hand gestures often led to comical situations.

One family we encountered, residing in the same block as Amani, had a young boy around seven or eight years old. Kerry-Ann enquired about his name, and they responded, *"Naim."* Kerry-Ann then repeated the question,

"Yes, name... what's his name?"

In the end, she grasped that his name was *'Naim,'* and we howled with laughter. Those were good times. We sailed along, having fun and partaking in daily life in this sprawling metropolis.

A persistent housing crisis loomed over the bustling city, home to a population exceeding twenty million inhabitants.

60

Faced with soaring rents and an acute shortage of affordable accommodation, some individuals found themselves with no choice but to seek shelter in the tombs, a circumstance that was both surreal and heartbreaking.

One such location, known as the *'City of the Dead,'* served as a striking reminder of this common issue. This sprawling necropolis, with its ancient mausoleums and intricately carved gravestones, came alive every Friday, the community's designated holy day.

Children, with hopeful eyes and warm smiles, stood at the entrance, expertly crafting and peddling delicate paper flowers, brightly coloured blooms designed to honour the ancestors and loved ones of visitors paying their respects.

Witnessing this poignant scene was truly heart-wrenching. The contrast between the vibrant life in the streets and the solemnity of the tombs sparked a deep appreciation for the comforts we take for granted, illuminating the profound human spirit that persists even in the face of such dire circumstances.

One poor family I met lived in a hovel, in the disused shaft of an elevator in one of the buildings on the main street in Saida Zainab, an old-established sub-district of Cairo.

The space they used as their living quarters was dirty, dark, and drab. They brought a crate of Coca-Cola in our honour. Coke distributed in Egypt seems to have twice as much sugar as in Western countries, and wasn't my favourite drink at the best of times, but was even more distasteful with all that extra sugar.

However, we couldn't refuse. To offend them, knowing that the outlay for this crate would have cost the equivalent of a week's wages, was unthinkable, so I gulped it down and smiled with feigned gratitude for their sake.

In the communal areas of the building, playful kittens darted about, bringing an air of liveliness. Despite the esteemed status of cats in ancient Egypt, they are seldom kept as pets today.

This trend is partly due to the belief that their saliva is deemed *'haram'* (forbidden in Islam), which contributes to their overall mistreatment. In some regions, packs of wild dogs roamed freely, and those who kept them often used them as guard dogs or status symbols.

As an animal lover, I experienced a profound sense of distress when I observed the conditions under which some unfortunate animals lived. They were unkempt and flea-ridden, some with open sores on their bodies.

Hamdy didn't resemble his siblings much. He was a gruff character, a heavy smoker with a neat moustache, a surly manner, and a habit of repeatedly asking if I was happy, which I understood and responded to as best I could in my limited Arabic.

He told us a fascinating story about a sheep that tumbled off the flat roof of their building, landing heavily on the roof of a car, rendering it a write-off. I don't think the sheep fared too well, either.

Ordinary conversations between Egyptians could seem alarming. They shouted and gesticulated so much that the uninitiated might think they were about to kill one another at any given moment.

The tone and phrasing in the Arabic language and culture can appear aggressive and can be easily misunderstood, for example, they would ask with an intense stare, eyes bulging,

"You are here, WHY?" rather than our milder,
"What are you doing here?"

We soon became accustomed to their mannerisms and language and realised it was ingrained in their culture, and we shouldn't be intimidated or take it personally.

Arabic is a language peppered with references to God.
A run-of-the-mill Islamic greeting is:
"As-salāmu ʿalaykum," which means 'Peace be upon you.'
Responses often include:
"Insha'Allah," meaning 'If God is willing,' and
"Alhamdulillah," meaning 'Thanks be to God,' when inquiring about someone's health.
If someone is going on a journey, you might say:
"Masha Allah," which means 'God go with you,' or
"Allah Khaleek," meaning 'God keep you.'

Crossing the roads around Tahrir Square can be quite dangerous, as the traffic is heavy, chaotic, and never stops. You must step into it, avoiding cars and motorcycles as they rush past, some at very high speeds. *It's nerve-racking!* I shadowed my new sister-in-law, Amani, who was skilled at weaving between cars, so I moved when she did. This strategy seemed to work well, but the potential for getting lost increased dramatically as we travelled around town; I didn't stray far from her side.

Navigating the city is exceedingly difficult unless you read Arabic, so I vowed to learn more. Having previously taken a course in the language at a school in Kensington, London, I had some basic knowledge. However, Classical Arabic was the version taught there, while Egyptian Arabic, which is quite different, was not. As a result, when I attempted to practise anything I had learnt, Magid and his friends fell about laughing, which didn't do much for my self-esteem.

An old Egyptian man in Saida Zainab, clad in striped pyjamas, gave me some cursory lessons.

Then I took formal lessons at a school in Cairo, but was disappointed to discover that they disregarded that I was a Christian, and their agenda included teachings about Islam. Such conversations led to petty arguments about whether Sunday or Monday is the first day of the week. None of that mattered. As far as I was concerned, it made no difference, but when I expressed this, the teacher insisted on making a big issue of it. We were taught common medical terms and the types of medication, as I was told Egyptians, as a rule, are hypochondriacs.

The health care available there is expensive, and the poor have basic care. Most locals don't speak or read English and seem to think that foreigners are walking cash dispensers with no brains *(some are),* which meant we were constantly fending off conniving touts and scammers. These tricksters speak

English well enough to beguile uninformed, trusting foreigners into their honey traps.

Each time we ventured out onto the streets, we were harried, and it meant we were on constant alert, knowing that nothing anyone who targeted us said was genuine and often a complete and utter lie.

Going out alone was always a risk, and we came to expect persistent hassle.

∞

Chapter Four

INTRODUCTION TO EGYPT

Khan el-Khalili served as Cairo's main tourist bazaar, offering a diverse range of items, including antiques, handcrafted goods, glassware, traditional costumes, such as the iconic tarboosh *(also known as the Tommy Cooper hat),* and silk and cotton galabayas in both plain and fancy styles.

Tantalising displays of Egyptian cotton towels in every conceivable size and colour were presented along with a variety of bed linen, perfumes, miscellaneous items, and an array of street foods and drinks. Stalls with dark green glazed pottery and others with coloured spices were piled high. The stallholders stopped us every few feet, offering bargain prices for their goods. The marketplace was littered with artisans selling a wide range of merchandise.

During our first visit, I felt overwhelmed by the novelty of it all. The heat, unfamiliar sounds, and scents of this lively, colourful, and bustling market left me lightheaded.

One of the stallholders kindly offered me a chair to help me recover when I almost fainted and reassured me that there was nothing to fear, as they cherished and respected all tourists. He spoke in his native Arabic, so Magid translated for me.

Sitting with these local men, serenely smoking shisha pipes, was an intriguing new experience for me. They were very friendly and accommodating, though they spoke little English.

The coffee they offered me in a tiny cup was so strong that I could hardly drink it. It smelled wonderful but tasted bitter. They meant well, and I didn't want to offend them, so I forced myself to drink it, leaving the black sludge at the bottom of the cup.

Flanked by Amani and Saida, or another local person, each time we visited the markets, we were inevitably overcharged, as it was quite dangerous to go to these vegetable markets alone. They protected us from the vultures that preyed on unsuspecting foreigners. Amani and Saida were adept at bartering and understood the actual value of most items well.

One day, unwittingly, I walked over a piece of cardboard on the pavement and was taken aback when an old Egyptian man spat at me and shouted, stating it was his prayer mat. Shaken and upset by his vitriolic outburst, I walked away, unsure of what I had done wrong, wondering if perhaps he just disliked foreigners, but it seemed he was outraged that I defiled his *'prayer mat.'* I still had much to learn. After that, I was certainly more circumspect about where I stepped.

The streamed call to prayer from the Imams at the mosques, five times a day, was foreign to us, but we soon became accustomed to it, although at 5 am, we certainly didn't appreciate it.

September evenings in Cairo were surprisingly chilly. Open braziers burned at the end of most main streets, and to my astonishment, I saw women in fur coats. Observing babies wrapped like mummies in layer upon layer of heavy knitted clothing at that time of year struck me as incongruous with my perception of Egypt.

Locals called out, *"Hello!"* or *"Welcome!"* These weren't touts trying to swindle us, but local workers at shops, cafes, restaurants and even uniformed police guards and the military who were just being friendly. Apart from these few greetings, they didn't speak any English.

Outdated phrases like *"Hello Dolly!"* or *"Lovely Jubbly!"* that they'd picked up from old songs or popular TV programs were bandied about. Curiously, they would ask us where we were from, always keen to know if we were Christian or Muslim. When we told them we were from England, the more inventive ones would pretend they had travelled to London and tell tall stories that they used to live behind Buckingham Palace, probably because that's the only place whose name they knew. It was amusing to hear these outlandish tales and to feign belief in them.

They were genuinely pleased to see foreigners visiting their city, but as we stuck out like a sore thumb, there was no peace for us when we ventured out on our own.

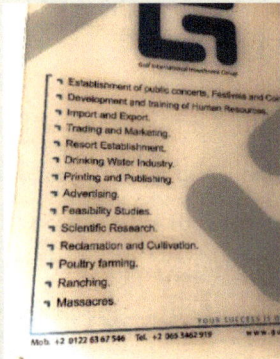

WE DO MASSACRES!

They were proud to say, *"Ahlan, Ahlan fil Masr!"* (Welcome to Egypt!)

My interest piqued when I spotted an advert for a pest control company with the attention-grabbing strapline,
I got their thought process… *it was hilarious*, but I didn't envisage using their services anytime soon.

Unlike other neighbouring Arab countries, Egypt is regarded as liberal, so alcohol is widely available.

Hamdy was very insular and drank excessively, mostly beer, occasionally supplemented with whiskey. Strangely, he liked his beer warm. Married with one son, Mohammed *(Hamada),* around the same age as our son, his cousin, Adam. He lived with his wife, Butheina, in a block of flats on a rundown street. When offered a drink in filthy glasses, we forced ourselves to swallow it. Butheina was an odd-looking woman with coarse features and spiky, dyed orange hair.

Unfortunately, she didn't enjoy good health and suffered from heart problems. Following heart surgery, she sadly passed away while still only in her late thirties.

Magid took me to visit one of his aunts, Tante Habiba, who is his late mother's sister. I was nervous about how she would react to her nephew marrying a foreigner.

When we arrived, a large lady dressed in traditional Arabic attire, with a white headscarf and thick glasses, greeted us warmly. However, I discovered that her adult son, Ahmed, was locked in a back room of her flat due to his antisocial behaviour. I thought that this approach was quite cruel and primitive, and it occurred to me that he might be struggling with mental illness.

Gradually, I began to understand that Egypt has no national health system to assess and provide the help and support they needed for conditions like this. Certainly, it was beyond their means, so they had little option. Psychiatric treatment was limited and expensive, as I was to discover years later.

Anyone who has visited Cairo will know that locals can be friendly and welcoming, and the city is blessed with a rich variety of museums and historic districts.

Ultimately, it is a place you either like or dislike. Carrying out simple tasks is exhausting, and nothing is straightforward; stress becomes a constant companion.

I immersed myself in learning basic Arabic phrases, which proved invaluable during our travels. Our driver and guide, Hag

Said, was a wonderful, humble, distinguished elderly gentleman whose dignified presence added warmth to our journeys.

Hag Said exemplified courtesy and respect, consistently exceeding our expectations. His comforting demeanour provided a sense of safety and reassurance amidst these unfamiliar surroundings. He stood out as one of the few genuinely kind souls we encountered, and his deep, insightful knowledge of the region and culture was a huge asset.

In Muslim tradition, pilgrims who make the sacred journey to Mecca are honoured with the title *'Hag'* or *'Hajj'*. The pronunciation of this title varies by region— in Saudi Arabia and many other Arab nations, it flows off the tongue with a soft *'J'* at the end, while in Egypt, it is pronounced with a hard *'G'*, creating a subtle yet distinct sound that reflects the rich tapestry of Arabic dialects.

Confidently communicating in Arabic is a gradual process requiring dedication, practice, and time to grasp and refine. In the meantime, the learning journey can feel daunting and arduous, as the letters are unfamiliar.

At some point, a breakthrough comes where everything suddenly clicks and becomes easier to understand. I had begun to engage in conversations in their language, even though my skills were still limited. I was starting to recognise the letters on shop signs and comprehend bus numbers, which filled me with pride over my progress. A new and fascinating world was unfolding before me.

One of the most striking signs I encountered was a Coca-Cola advertisement written in Semitic Arabic letters. The flowing letters swirled together beautifully, resembling an intricate dance formation. Coca-Cola is virtually the national soft drink and thus is prolifically advertised.

My new knowledge of this ancient language provided a deeper understanding of certain parts of the Bible, as Arabic, Hebrew, and Aramaic are closely related languages with many common words.

Significantly, the name of the town where Jesus was born is Bethlehem *(Bait Lechem)* *…Ping!!*

Bait (Beth) means house, Lehem means Bread (Heb.) *meat* (Arabic)

I realised that *'Bethlehem'* means *'House of Bread'* in Hebrew and *'House of Flesh'* in Arabic. This connection made me gasp. The bread and wine in Holy Communion help us remember Christ's sacrifice on the cross.

While they were eating, Jesus took the bread...and when he had given thanks, he broke it and gave it to his disciples, saying,
"Take and eat; this is my body."
Then he took a cup, and when he had given thanks, he gave it to them, saying,
"Drink from it, all of you. This is my blood of the covenant, which is poured out for many for the forgiveness of sins.

I tell you, I will not drink from this fruit of the vine from now on until that day when I drink it new with you in my Father's kingdom."
After they had sung a hymn, they went out to the Mount of Olives. Matt. 26: 26 -30 NIV

(I'd love to know what hymn they sang – possibly a Passover song like Ps. 118)

One of the things I admired about Egypt was the strong sense of community, which is sadly lacking in our country. Men sat outside in the street, smoking shisha pipes and playing backgammon on wooden tables.

Children played happily on the roads, some still clad in their pyjamas in the middle of the day, using rolled-up socks as makeshift footballs.

They jumped around, having innocent fun and interacting with one another. *Life for them was simple.*
They shouted, *"Agnabaya!"* (foreigner) at me, and I jokingly responded in my newly learnt Arabic,

"Ana mish Agnabaya, ana Masraya, meya fil meya!" (I'm not a foreigner; I'm 100% Egyptian.) It sounded punchy and rhymed, but given my European colouring, this claim was ridiculous and produced peals of laughter.

EGYPT – 1983

At the time of our next trip to Egypt, Adam was about six years old, and Kerry-Ann was twelve. Their blue eyes and blonde hair attracted attention, and local touts constantly badgered us to buy tatty and fake goods. Of course, we visited the pyramids and the usual tourist sites.

The local vendors tried to persuade us to pay for camel rides, but I declined their heavy persuasion. The idea of climbing onto one of those beasts looked uncomfortable and precarious.

Cunningly, the handler told me to sit on the camel for a photograph. The camel's name, interestingly, was *Michael Jackson. He* then instructed the beast to stand up as soon as I climbed onto its back. Off we went, whether I liked it or not.

Camel rides are extremely uncomfortable, as they sway from side to side on uneven terrain, and I agonised over whether I'd ever get off in one piece.

The sensation that you are going to tumble over the head of the beast, or that it will take off at speed, is paramount in your mind, with the added fear that the camel tied to the back of yours is going to bite your backside or spit at you *(it will!)*

Known for their remarkable memories, camels are creatures that bear grudges. Therefore, I was cautious not to provoke any of them unnecessarily.

However, the handlers at Giza often displayed cruelty, resorting to beating these animals with sticks, exploiting these magnificent ships of the desert to extract money from unsuspecting tourists.

Camels are deeply ingrained in Egyptian culture, featuring prominently in art, literature, and proverbs worldwide. They are intricately woven into the fabric of Egyptian life, so I presumed they would be treated with greater respect.

He made the camels kneel outside the city by the water well in the evening, when women went out to draw water.
Gen. 24:11 ESV

Me & Oscar, proudly wearing his new hat

I quickly discovered that recycling empty soft drink bottles, a precious commodity, is a valuable source of income. Collecting them and other items deposited in the rubbish to recycle was the job of young Egyptian children who hung around tourist areas. These children depended on finding and using anything they could to earn a few pence; nothing was wasted. They are highly resourceful and won my admiration for the amazing inventions they produced from this rubble.

By now, Muslim women were covering their heads, wearing the *hijab* (headscarf) and the *niqab* (face veil), as there had been an Islamic revival, but oddly, this did not impact the sale of alcohol in Egypt.

Later, they banned the niqab because of the increase in cheating, identity theft and other crimes. Sunni Muslims, who are the majority, derisively referred to women wearing niqabs as *'letterboxes'*, which I thought was strange as I've never seen a letterbox in Egypt.

We visited a Muslim family in the countryside who provided us with a vast and magnificent fish dinner. They were very hospitable. Everyone sat on the ground; no chairs were available.

A large cloth held colourful dips, traditionally made by the women there. Roasted eggplants, pounded and mixed by hand in a large copper bowl with tahini, garlic, yoghurt, olive oil, and hummus, were laid out for dipping into these dishes, accompanied by piles of warm, freshly baked flatbread.

Women in traditional dress baking in the streets were fascinating to watch. With their deft hand movements, they swiftly produced enormous piles of bread to sell.

Although we thoroughly enjoyed our time there, it was exhausting and extremely demanding. When our plane left the runway and took off into the sky from Cairo, a massive sense of relief swept over me.

Managing to escape this complex metropolis in one piece felt like a marvellous achievement. Life in Egypt was oppressive and draining, complicated, and, at times, intrusive.

I looked forward to getting home, appreciating that I no longer would need to gesticulate wildly to explain what I needed in shops. More significantly, I could trust the shop assistants to give me the correct change.

Magid's name was called out over the loudspeaker while we waited in the Departure Lounge, instructing him to report to security. I had foolishly bought into his tales about him being a pacifist, and he led me to believe this was why he didn't sign up to join the army. I assumed this was the reason for the security recall, as conscription was compulsory, and anger boiled inside me at my perceived injustice of it all.

After an hour of interrogation, they released him and permitted him to board the plane. Fortunately, we didn't miss our flight.

With the benefit of hindsight, it is more likely that he committed a crime to obtain the necessary funding and documents to leave Egypt.

Afterwards, I learned how difficult it is for Egyptians to leave the country. Unless someone from the host country sponsors them, they are not granted permission to go on a holiday abroad.

Consequently, we frequently received requests to compose invitation letters for individuals we barely knew. However, I was reluctant to take on that responsibility, so I graciously declined.

Five months later, we received the shocking news that Magid's older brother, Hamdy, had died suddenly under very mysterious circumstances.

This was a premature death as he was only in his early forties. Hamada was now an orphan, but as he was in his late teens, he could look after himself with the help of female relatives.

Early deaths are common in Egypt because of the poor standard of nutrition, lack of health care, abysmal living conditions and the absence of basic education.

Muslims bury their dead quickly, often within hours. The bodies are not embalmed or put in a coffin but merely wrapped in a muslin cloth and laid straight into the ground.

Cheap, efficient, and speedy!

The burial strictly prohibits women from attending.

~

Amani got engaged to Ahmed, a pleasant Egyptian man with curly ginger hair, freckles, and green eyes. When I remarked that he looked Irish with this colouring, he indignantly proclaimed he was 100% Egyptian. I mused that *the British occupation may have had something to do with his lineage*.

However, shortly before their wedding date, Magid took Ahmed to one side and told him that he wouldn't be able to have intimate relations with Amani, as she had an abnormality of her genitalia. As a result, Ahmed backed out of the marriage, and I found it unkind that Magid didn't think to mention this issue before.

Cynically, I wondered if his real concern was that she might not be as attentive to his needs if she had a husband to care for, but I kept my nagging doubts to myself.

Coincidentally, and much to my sorrow, shortly after that, Saida died of a brain haemorrhage. Amani would have to cope alone. This saddened me. I was concerned for her as she depended so much on Saida; I worried about how she'd manage, but surprisingly, she fared well.

Adjusting to Egyptian culture was quite challenging for me, as it felt very different from the culture I grew up in. I found that many people I interacted with were often untruthful about various matters, and even those in positions of power were not to be trusted.

There was widespread falsification of official documents, including death certificates. We were told that Hamdy died of vomit inhalation and alcohol poisoning, yet his death certificate stated that his cause of death was a brain tumour.

Almost anything could be bought at the right price. Baksheesh *(tipping)* was the main currency, and Magid was well-versed in this practice. I often watched him hand notes to people for menial tasks, such as opening a car door.

Theft was commonplace, and my rings, which I foolishly left in a box on the dressing table, disappeared from our hotel room. When I reported these incidents to the hotel security, I told them one was a valuable diamond set in gold, and the other was costume jewellery. Oddly *(or maybe not)*, the next day, the cheap ring was returned, but I never saw the diamond ring again. *(Interesting, that!)*

This attitude was ingrained in the culture and took some getting used to, although I was still caught off guard regularly when Baksheesh (tips) were expected, as I was unfamiliar with this custom.

~

Upon our return home, I fell back into our daily routine of school, work, and household duties, leaving me with little time or resources for socialising.

Despite this, we managed to host a few parties to which the Palais staff and other friends were invited.

We hired a magician and children's entertainer for Adam's fifth birthday party with his friends to celebrate the occasion. Kerry-Ann loved to pick Adam up after school and bring him home, which made her feel very grown-up, but the teachers often prevented her, thinking she was too young to take responsibility for him. She cared for him while they played outside with the other children on our street, giving me peace of mind to focus on the housework.

The First Of The Seven Trials

Shortly after visiting my parents and sister in Northern Ireland, I received a shocking call with the terrible news that my father had died suddenly. This news shook me to the core. I was distraught and struggled to comprehend it, as he was only sixty-four years old and in reasonably good health. I had just seen him in Ireland.

He and my mum had spent the previous evening at their local club, and I'm told he seemed in excellent spirits. However, she found him lying on the settee in the lounge the following morning; having suffered a massive heart attack, he had slipped away. He used to joke that he wanted to die young, so he'd be a good-looking corpse. Tragically, he got his wish.

We flew back to Belfast for his funeral. The Funeral Parlour had a Book of Remembrance and invited us to select a verse from Scripture to accompany Dad's entry, so I chose this verse from the Gospel of Matthew, as I knew Dad had endured a difficult life:

"Come to Me, all weary and heavy-laden, and I will give you rest. Take my yoke upon you and learn from Me, for I am gentle and humble in heart, and YOU WILL FIND REST FOR YOUR SOULS. For My yoke is easy and My burden is light." Matt. 11:28 NIV

I was beginning to comprehend the enormity of the message in my dream, and wondered what was in store for me, *but God is my rock and my comfort.*

EGYPT

Adam was still at school, so I arranged for my mother to come over from Belfast to London to take care of him when we next flew back to Egypt.

We stayed again at the Hilton Hotel near Tahrir Square. After a few weeks, things took a worrying turn when Magid ran out of money and clearly expected me to cover our hotel bill with my credit card. It was a large amount that I couldn't afford, and paying it would push me well beyond my credit limit. Yet, this didn't seem to bother him.

I quickly signed the payment slip, feeling stressed and under pressure, but the hotel clerk refused to accept my signature. She must have suspected that something was amiss. We were stranded because we couldn't check out of the hotel.

Meanwhile, my mum kept calling me, worried about Adam's behaviour; he was refusing to go to school. The stress of the situation at the hotel was overwhelming, and I felt trapped. However, I was too ashamed to confide in Mum about the real issue.

Finally, Magid found the funds to settle the bill, and we returned home. My mother flew back to Belfast, and Adam reluctantly readjusted to school, although he never truly enjoyed it.

Two years later, when the children were older, we returned to Egypt once more with a couple of Magid's business friends, Mike *(who bizarrely liked to call himself Mohammed)*, and his partner, Sue. We travelled to El Fayoum *(which is said to be the region where the patriarch, Jacob and his family settled after the famine in Egypt),* Alexandria, and Port Said.

By this time, Amani had moved into a much larger and more comfortable two-bedroom flat above a supermarket on the same street where she had previously lived. It was much more spacious, brighter and airier, so I was happy for her. She deserved better living conditions than the tiny, dark, poky flat she had lived in previously. Insisting we stay with her, she kindly gave up her bedroom for us and slept on the couch, something I felt uneasy about, but she seemed okay with it and assured us the sofa was comfortable.

Using her flat as a base, we visited the major cities and tourist sites in Egypt, hiring a driver and guide to ferry us about. Life was idyllic, floating on the sea in glass-bottomed boats, observing vast varieties of fish with a fantastic kaleidoscope of colours and patterns, swimming in formation below us.

We rode on horse-drawn carriages and generally lived it up. The food was significantly cheaper there than at home and was of surprisingly high quality.

In most places, we were well received, thanks to having a charismatic Egyptian in our company who carried a distinct air of authority, and this ensured we were treated like VIPs. Those were halcyon days indeed.

We often ate at one of the Gad restaurant chains, a favourite of the locals, as the food was typical Middle Eastern Egyptian. They didn't skimp on portions, and the quality and variety of their fare was incredible, considering they were fast-food outlets.

Gad was the name of one of the tribes of Israel, so I was intrigued that they named this restaurant chain after him. Cairo to Luxor was a fascinating journey in a rickety old light aircraft that had seen better days. There were broken seat belts and limited seating, forcing some passengers to stand in the aisle. Magid jested that this was a *'half-star plane'*; he wasn't far off the mark.

My luggage went on to Khartoum, and I was given a similar suitcase belonging to another man. When I opened it in the hotel room, my face fell as I scanned the sparse contents of men's dark clothing. In the end, it was sorted out after many phone calls and profuse shouting, at which Egyptians are particularly adept, and I made do with the clothes I stood up in until my baggage was returned a few days later. Consequently, if anyone asked me whether I had ever been to Sudan, I quipped,

"No, but I have a suitcase that's been there."

The tomb of Tutankhamun was found in the Valley of the Kings on Luxor's West Bank, roughly a forty-minute drive from downtown Luxor.

Stepping down into the burial chamber, you are surrounded by ancient images on all four sides.

On the north wall, directly across from the entrance, are illustrations of King Tutankhamun as a young boy. On the eastern wall, a depiction of a procession of mourners accompanying the king to his tomb is displayed. The opposite Western Wall is decorated with twelve baboons, symbolising the twelve hours of the night.

A young male tour guide joined us, speaking as if reciting from a memorised script. Whenever anyone asked him a question, he became flustered, lost his place, and often resumed his previous robotic narrative. This became tedious, sounding like a gramophone record, and we knew there was little point in distracting him with further questions.

Our life was soon set to change…

My flesh and heart may fail, but God is my heart's strength and portion forever. Ps. 76:26 NIV

Chapter Five

The Second Trial *~loss of security ~*

Our lives were turned upside down

LONDON 1989

A company curiously known as Mecca took over Hammersmith Palais, Magid's place of work, and it came as a huge shock when *Magid, along with all the Egyptian bar staff, was sacked in one fell swoop, with no plausible reason given.*

I pondered what was at the root of this and how it might have come about.

Momentous changes in our lifestyle and Magid's character were to follow.

We were a close-knit bunch, so the fallout from this dismissal had a major impact on us all, both socially and financially. Most of our friends were fellow bar staff, and their families were affected.

At this point, I didn't fully appreciate what a major life shift losing his job was for us, as I imagined that Magid could easily get another similar job in a hotel or elsewhere in the hospitality sector. That would have been right up his street, given his charm, magnetism and presence. He had charm and an easy way with people and was gifted at accommodating their needs and rapidly resolving conflicts, making him well-suited to the hotel industry.

More was going on than I reckoned; he didn't have a CV, references, or any of the necessary paperwork to present to a prospective employer, and he didn't seem inclined to rectify this. I was puzzled about how he secured the job at the Palais in the first place, where he had served as catering manager.

A story he shared with me came to my mind about one of the yellow plastic zip-up pouches used to hold the takings from each of the eight bar stations that went missing. This pouch was never recovered, and I wondered if this incident significantly influenced the decision to dismiss all the Egyptian staff.

Magid also mentioned that shortly before we met, he had won £12,000 at the Cromwell Mint, a casino he often visited after finishing work in the early morning hours.

However, there was no evidence of any major purchases he had made with this windfall. Doubts about his story began to creep into my mind.

London's West End beckoned him, and he began doing casual work, taxi-driving and accompanying wealthy Saudi Arabs to doctors' appointments to interpret for them. Most of them wanted to avail themselves of the medical services in London and took advantage of this while they were there. He was also involved in international commodity broking and had a growing army of dubious contacts in this field.

Bruce, a short, boxy business associate from Vancouver, with dark blonde hair, needed him to travel over there to negotiate an ongoing deal. However, Magid was hesitant to leave at this time because the company he planned to start up on Edgware Road in Central London was still in its infancy.

He suggested that I accompany Bruce back to Vancouver and represent him at the meetings. Given my long-standing desire to visit Toronto and Vancouver, I grabbed the opportunity and quickly agreed to stand in for Magid.

~

CANADA

We booked flights with Canada Air, and the journey took approximately ten hours. Seated by the window next to a large lady, getting in and out to use the facilities proved a drama, so I remained in my seat until she moved. Bruce was seated behind us.

It was early evening when we arrived at Pearson International Airport in Toronto.

Bruce booked us into the Royal York Hotel on Front Street, downtown Toronto, where his Aunt Verna was a permanent resident.

Sandra, one of Pastor Michael's nieces, and her son, Christopher, also happened to live in Toronto, so I contacted her and we arranged to meet. She wasn't a Christian despite Michael and Joan witnessing to her when she was in England, but she was delighted to see someone from home who knew her family there, and we arranged to go sightseeing together. She took me to fascinating Native American cultural centres and museums.

We stayed in Toronto for two more days while Bruce, an accomplished entrepreneur, met with his business contacts, and I enjoyed more sightseeing with Sandra.

The next leg of our journey involved a brief flight to Vancouver. *What a beautiful place!* It has a slight British flavour, complete with red double-decker buses reminiscent of those in London.

As we strolled past the office buildings, a glint of metal caught my eye—it was an elegantly crafted nameplate affixed to the door of a psychiatrist's office. A jolt of surprise shot through me as I recognised the name. Memories of a compelling book I read before flooded back, vividly portraying the evocative tale of a woman thought to be possessed by the devil. The true story in this book affected me profoundly when I read it, and the connection between the psychiatrist and that infamous case was startling, transforming the chilling narrative from mere fiction into a jarring reality. A wave of disquiet washed over me as I grappled with the weight of this unexpected association, my mind racing with the implications. I was astonished to discover that an actual Satanist temple is operating in Vancouver, openly promoting its activities to the public. I found the thought of people gathering to worship the devil deeply unsettling.

This temple not only has its own version of a Bible— *The Satanic Bible*, authored by Anton LaVey, also boasts a surprisingly large and dedicated following. The Church of Satan's acceptance within the community is evident through its presence in the local Yellow Pages. Despite my reluctance to acknowledge this belief system, I accept the necessity of properly capitalising its name.

Vancouver has a border crossing to the USA called Peace Arch Crossing, located approximately thirty miles away. On this visit, my cousin Bill and his wife, Judy, travelled up from Oregon to meet with me.

Their entrance into the restaurant was striking; they seemed to fill the doorway, their statuesque forms casting long shadows against the walls. Bill stood tall, easily over six feet seven inches, with broad shoulders and a solid frame that amplified his already imposing presence. Next to him, Judy, who almost matched his height, exuded a warmth and strength that complemented Bill's bulk. They appeared colossal compared to my petite stature, leaving me momentarily in awe of their sheer size. *(I began to wonder if they were descended from the Nephilim... giant fallen Angels in the Bible.)*

With a steaming cup of coffee in hand, Bill sauntered toward me, a playful smirk spreading across his face as he looked down at my much tinier frame. *"Ah,"* he said, his deep voice resonating with mirth, *"you must be Joann, one of the little people!"*

It was our first meeting in person, and a wave of laughter overcame me, blending humour with a welcoming embrace. The air was filled with the scent of fresh coffee and the promise of cherished memories yet to be created.

As we became better acquainted, I was impressed to learn that Judy was the Mayor of Salem, the capital city of Oregon. Their company was delightful; they had a wonderful sense of humour, and I was sad when it was time for them to leave, but not before taking me to a fresh fish market, where we were introduced to a vast variety of crustaceans and fish of every size and description, many with names I hadn't encountered before.

Another couple, Ruth and Eli, Messianic Jews who were friends of theirs from Israel, coincidentally also knew Michael and Joan from Emmanuel Assembly, joined us. We had a splendid time browsing the market's produce, as the smell of fresh fish filled the air.

Vibrant totem poles, once integral to Native Indian homes on their reservations, have become captivating attractions. I discovered that Christian missionaries viewed these totem poles as obstacles to their efforts to convert the American Indians to Christianity.

Meanwhile, Bruce went off to his pre-arranged business meetings and warned me that I needed to attend one of them as the representative of The Arab Trading Agency *(Magid's Company)*.

Bruce hailed a taxi to take us to the towering building where the meeting was scheduled. As I stepped into the expansive conference room, a palpable tension wrapped around me like an oppressive fog, while the whirr of the air conditioning unit purred in the background. The sharp sounds of raised voices erupted with harsh, aggressive tones, punctuated by profanities, reverberating off the walls.

Their rude demeanour on full display left me dumbfounded; each word cut through the atmosphere like a knife. It felt as though I had entered a battleground of ego. When their attention suddenly shifted to me, I was struck by the brusque, condescending, Godless and callous manner they adopted when addressing me. Their harsh words felt like blows, and I could sense my composure beginning to crack under the pressure.

During the meeting, realising I had reached my limit, I resolved to leave. A wave of relief, mingled with humiliation, washed over me as I stood up and turned to go. The chatter abruptly ceased, plunging the room into an unsettling silence.

Feeling lost and isolated in a hostile atmosphere, I longed to return to a world where kindness and respect prevailed. Bruce later explained that such language and attitude were considered standard in the business world in Canada and the USA, and that I'd need to adapt. However, I was adamant I would never adjust to this degrading culture.

When I spoke to Magid about the incident, I was relieved that he wasn't concerned that the deal wasn't completed, making me wonder if it would have been questionable anyway.

LONDON/N. IRELAND

Shortly after my return, we set off on an eagerly anticipated journey to Belfast to visit my family. The air was fresh and crisp upon our arrival.

My brother-in-law, Eddie, kindly picked us up from the airport and drove us to my mother's house. During the conversation, Magid promised my mother he'd take her with us on holiday to Cairo the next time we visited.

Typically, Magid made off-hand promises with no intention of following through, so I didn't take much notice.
However, my mother was not one to let such a promise slip by; she started asking about the details of any upcoming trips, often reminding Magid of his commitment.

This piqued her interest, and she persistently brought it up. It was then that I realised that her determination was unwavering, and she fully intended to make him fulfil that flippant promise. She was like a dog with a bone.

EGYPT 1990 ~ *A New World opens up...*

My mother duly accompanied us on our next trip, delighting in the luxury of lounging by the Hilton Hotel pool, ordering snacks and drinks, and being waited on hand and foot.

During one of our trips to Cairo, we met Amr and Hassan, two very polite Egyptian lads. Amr was a relative of Magid's and Hassan, his best friend.

They were inseparable and full of life, captivating the attention of our children who adored them. Hassan, robust and distinguished with his moustache and spectacles, possessed a sharp intellect, and I often caught a glimmer of mischief in his eyes. He would sometimes mimic a French accent, speaking utter gibberish as though it were fluent French. *It was very comical!*

They wormed their way into our hearts and morphed into my lovable, adopted little brothers, and the kids adored them. Their presence brought abundant joy, presenting a wonderfully hilarious double act.

As staunch Muslims, I appreciated that they didn't mind taking us to look around Coptic churches, quite different from those we were used to.

Amr & me

Amr & Adam

The combination of history and culture makes Alexandria a compelling destination. There are fewer pharaonic sites compared to those in cities such as Aswan, Luxor, and Cairo.

Alexandria's historic places offer a unique glimpse into what Egypt was like during the Greco-Roman period. Additionally, Alexandria boasts an unparalleled wealth of modern buildings found nowhere else in Egypt.

Coptic Christians comprise approximately ten per cent of Egypt's population. They claim to be direct descendants of Egypt's ancient Pharaonic people, who were first converted to Christianity with the arrival of St Mark in Egypt. It is important to note that they are not Arabs, which is a source of enormous pride among them.

In the ninth century, a significant difference existed between the Copts and Arabs. Copts were an Egyptian-speaking Christian population with a culture which was influenced by Greek and native Egyptian elements.

On the other hand, the Arabs who had recently conquered Egypt were a Semitic-speaking group with a nomadic Bedouin/Arabian culture and Islam as their main religion. Coptic Christians believe St Mark arrived in Alexandria around AD 42 and remained there for seven years.

This saint converted many people to Christianity during this period and performed numerous miracles. Regarded as the founder of the church in Alexandria, he went on to become its first bishop.

St Mark's Orthodox Cathedral is a Coptic church, serving as the historical seat of the Pope of Alexandria, the head of the

Coptic Orthodox Church. We strolled around inside, admiring this beautiful, serene and peaceful building.

A poignant display marks the life of St Mark, including his tortured death. His body was buried in the chamber below, but it was stolen, and relics of it are still present at St Mark's Cathedral in Venice.

A relic of the saint's body from below the neck remains buried in this church. We wanted to visit the crypt, but we couldn't go down into the chamber as a service was in progress.

Back in Cairo, in the Coptic churches we visited in the district of Old Cairo, women sat on one side of the church wearing black, while men sat on the other. There is no charge to enter the church, but a priest sits near the exit with a collection box, expecting visitors to drop in some change.

We discovered that Egypt has a rich and enduring Christian heritage, and the Christians there show a genuine hunger for God's Word.

Bible distribution takes place at an incredible Christian hub, the Cave Church, which was next on our agenda.

There are actually three churches in the area. The walls display beautiful artistic Arabic writing, with various dots and dashes. Meetings take place on Thursday evenings, drawing vast throngs of people, and a distinct acrid smell permeates the atmosphere, as it's located near the rubbish dumps.

Next, we visited the renowned Hanging Church, named for its construction atop a Roman fortress. Its nave is suspended above the original ground level, a unique architectural feature that serves practical purposes, such as protecting the church from flooding, while also giving the building a stunning and imposing appearance.

Our knowledgeable guide shared the rich history of Old Cairo, tracing its origins back to ancient times when it was known as Babylon in Egypt. Founded by Pharaoh Ramses II around 1250 BC, the city has thrived as a vital trading centre for centuries, adorned with temples dedicated to numerous deities.

In AD 641, Old Cairo became part of the Islamic Empire when Amr ibn al-As conquered it in the name of Islam, leading to the construction of a mosque considered to be one of the oldest in Africa. During that period, the mosque was a principal place for Muslims to gather and worship.

Overall, Old Cairo boasts a mesmerising tapestry of history and deep religious significance, making it an extraordinary destination for anyone eager to delve into Egypt's ancient past. As we ventured into one of the venerable church buildings still inhabited by devoted nuns, we were greeted by an air of tranquillity and reverence.

The entrance, a modest door encased within imposing wooden gates, is affectionately referred to as the *'eye of the needle,'* hinting at both its small size and the profound interior that lies beyond it.
Exploring Egypt's culture and ancient history was an educational experience.

When Magid had money, he was generous and flamboyant, and often gave us expensive gifts. We stayed in a suite at the Hilton Hotel in Cairo's infamous Tahrir Square for extended periods.

It was a hectic, bizarre, luxurious, artificial lifestyle!
He hosted lavish dinner parties for his extended family, typically consisting of more than thirty people. It was a surreal existence. As a result, he was highly esteemed by his family and treated like a king.

On my birthday, they hosted a surprise party for me in a large room at the hotel, and guests gifted me with traditional gold jewellery.

Some pieces were inappropriate, such as the gold Islamic evil eye, which is used to protect the wearer and ward off envy, and the Islamic symbol of a crescent that my sister-in-law gave me. Someone also gifted me a gold letter *'G'*, mistakenly believing that *'Joann'* began with a *'G'* instead of a *'J'*.

It was a tricky situation, and I didn't want to upset anyone or seem ungrateful, so I accepted them graciously and later had them melted down and made into a cross.
I don't think they were any the wiser.

Reading coffee grounds in a cup, popular among superstitious individuals, was a familiar occurrence after enjoying their favourite brew. Fortune tellers interpreted the swirling patterns left by the dregs at the bottom of the cup. These divinations, steeped in mystique, were sought after to gain insight into pivotal life events, such as marriage, childbirth, death, travel, and future employment.

Magid, along with several acquaintances and family members, often engaged in this arcane art, drawn to its promises of foresight into their future. Conversely, the darker side of their tradition involved the nefarious practice of cursing their adversaries. In hushed whispers, they gathered clandestine tokens—nail clippings and a lock of the victim's hair—each item steeped in urine. They then buried this morbid concoction in the earth, encased in a plastic bag and accompanied by secretive chants brimming with harmful intent and superstition.

Amidst this, Amani stood resolutely apart, her convictions unwavering. She disdainfully rejected these practices, steadfast in her belief that they were both misguided and perilous.

Dear Lord, open their blind eyes.

Commenting on someone's clothing or giving compliments is generally discouraged because it often implies that you desire the item being commented on.

This can lead to awkward situations, as the person may feel compelled to offer you the item, regardless of the context, for example, shoes that are four sizes too big for you; therefore, it can be embarrassing. I resolved to be mindful about this, although I have fallen into this trap a few times.

Egyptians can appear rude to us because they freely make personal remarks, bluntly pointing out when they think someone is old, bald, short, or overweight, which can be disconcerting if you are not used to it. They are also generous with compliments, which are generally not about clothing or jewellery. We also learned that expressing hunger or thirst could be viewed as impolite.

Life became much easier when we began to understand the culture in Egypt. We made fewer *faux pas* and became better acquainted with Magid's family and friends.

A deeper understanding of the language and culture enabled us to integrate more effectively, helping us feel more relaxed and accepted.

∞

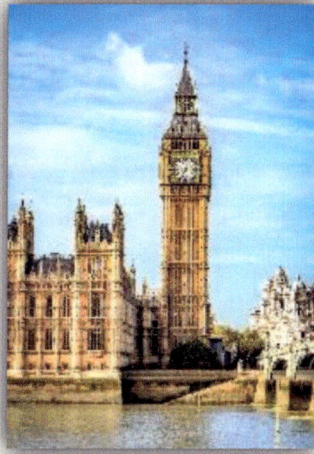

Chapter Six

LONDON

When Amr and Hassan visited us in London for a holiday, we were delighted to have the opportunity to return their kindness by showing them around London.

Since we conveniently lived near a tube station, they enjoyed staying at our home, and they were delighted to discover that it took only twenty minutes by tube to reach the centre of London from our house.

One evening during their stay, I sent Kerry-Ann to the corner shop, just twenty yards away, to get a few items for tea.

"Kerry-Ann's been knocked down by a car!" yelled one of my neighbour's children. I rushed down the street and found her lying in the middle of the road with one of her legs splayed at an awkward angle. While we waited for the ambulance, I held her hand and tried to calm and reassure her. When they arrived at the scene, she was taken to our local hospital, where, following an X-ray, they confirmed that her right leg was broken. A greenstick fracture of her right arm was also identified, caused by the impact of instinctively putting her hand out to break her fall.

Poor Kerry-Ann, my heart went out to her, but she was stoic and didn't complain much. I watched her drag her heavy, plastered leg up and down the narrow staircase of our little house without complaint, and I was proud of her endurance and resilience.

The car driver didn't switch his lights on, a significant contributing factor to this collision, especially since his car was black and the darkness was falling. Consequently, she didn't see him coming.

During her recovery, I began the process of claiming compensation for her accident, and approximately six months later, she was awarded £9,000.

She was still a minor, so I deposited this money into our bank on her behalf for safekeeping until she was old enough to use it sensibly.

~

Late one afternoon, Magid arrived home and stunned me by triumphantly dumping £20,000 in cash out of a bag onto the table, exclaiming that it was money he received for gold bars he had sold as a commodity broker.

"Go and pay it into the bank!" he demanded.

Walking through the streets with this money in a simple plastic carrier bag felt surreal yet oddly bold. I wasn't afraid of being robbed.

Who would have thought this unremarkable plastic carrier bag contained so much cash?

I found it interesting that I felt safer carrying cash this way than if it were in an expensive handbag. It was a strange experience.

Looking back, I can hardly believe how blind and compliant I was. *What was I thinking?*

As it was late in the day and the bank was about to close, I quickly walked to the counter and emptied the bag of cash into the well in front of the cashier. His mouth dropped open in disbelief. *"I wasn't expecting that!"* he exclaimed. This cashier would, of course, have informed the police as soon as I left, as it was most irregular and suspicious.

Shortly afterwards, I spotted an unmarked police car parked opposite our house, with two men watching us, though they didn't come to our home or approach us.

Naïvely, I assumed they were verifying if Magid was legitimately in the country or if he had entered into a marriage of convenience to remain in the UK.

How naïve I was! Naïveté and desperation often go hand in hand, they say. When I look back now, I can't believe how compliant I was. I wanted to believe everything he told me, no matter how bizarre, and closed my mind to the truth.

The base for Magid's activities was a suite of offices on Edgware Road near Marble Arch. His company's primary function was catering for all aspects of life for Saudi men while they were in London.
These men faced severe restrictions in Saudi Arabia and sought opportunities to take advantage of their freedom when they were away.

Magid owned two Mercedes stretch limousines as well as his own private Mercedes saloon. The company ticked over for a while, and as most of the Saudi Arabs were hypochondriacs, they typically had medical appointments at private hospitals or with Harley Street consultants, where Magid accompanied them to provide interpreting services.

Drinking alcohol is strictly forbidden in Saudi Arabia, so some Arabs craftily drank neat whiskey from a teacup and saucer to fool anyone who might be watching them.

Abdullah, whose surname was difficult to pronounce, was an associate who owned two tower blocks of flats in Riyadh.

Despite his significant wealth, he appeared quite out of place. A large safety pin held the zipper on his trousers together, and his light-coloured jacket was splattered with food stains. No one would have guessed he was a billionaire; his face was grey and lined with worry. He looked unwell, much older than his forty-five years.

The sleep of a labourer is sweet whether they eat little or much, but as for the rich, their abundance permits them no sleep. Ecc. 5:12 NIV

He often ranted at me in his native Arabic, as I suspect Magid told him that I handled the accounts, making everything my responsibility. I believe the fact that I had not converted to Islam when Magid and I married was another factor in his displeasure.

When things didn't go to plan, I was to blame. Shouting at me had a negligible effect, as I had no idea what he was saying, so I ignored him; it washed over me, although his tone effectively conveyed his annoyance.

As was their custom, he brought me strange, inappropriate, and outlandish gifts each time he visited us in London, such as an expensive home incense set with joss sticks and matching reed diffusers. I still have a monogrammed leather briefcase and a fancy bottle of sweet, sickly perfume with real gold flakes in a maroon-coloured velvet pouch.

I appreciated the thought behind these extravagant gifts; the briefcase was useful, but as for the perfume.
'What's the point of that? I thought, I'd never wear it.'
Cast but a glance at riches and they are gone, for they will surely sprout wings and fly off to the sky like an eagle.
Prov. 23:5 NIV

Two and a half years later, Magid's company went bankrupt due to mismanagement and lack of regular income, forcing him to relinquish his office suite. As he had a penchant for the finer things in life, he took several casual jobs to afford his Fleur de Lys cigars and Royal Salute whisky.

While his shirts were elegant and made of *pure silk*, I was content in my denim jeans and T-shirts. Our elderly neighbour often remarked on how distinguished he looked compared to me in my casual attire.

"People judge you by your appearance" was one of his pet mantras.

Magid frequently travelled to various European countries for his work as an *international commodity broker*, often leaving me to care for the children for extended periods.

I had a well-paid and responsible position at Hammersmith Hospital, which enabled me to provide a stable income for our household. Later, I discovered that Magid had accumulated debts by using my credit cards for travel and accommodation. Additionally, he had relied on a bank overdraft, of which I was unaware.

Our home was a modest house, which I had purchased before marrying him; therefore, it was in my name only. Although small and simple, it met our needs. I remember feeling slightly uneasy when Magid approached me one day and asked to have his name added to the property deeds.

He claimed that he felt like a lodger since the house wasn't in joint names and reasoned that shared ownership would foster a deeper sense of unity between us. Despite my reservations about this arrangement, I agreed to his request, believing it was an acceptable step, given that we were married.

At the time, I wasn't particularly focused on financial issues and aimed to maintain harmony in our relationship. However, looking back, I realise I should have pointed out that he hadn't contributed anything toward the purchase or maintenance of the house and rarely contributed to paying the bills. This oversight on my part left me with lingering questions and nagging doubts about the fairness of his suggestion.

In time, I duly co-signed the necessary documents, thereby making him a joint owner of the property. At that moment, I believed it was the right decision. In retrospect, I wish I'd been more assertive, but I blindly ignored the many red flags. Immature, inexperienced, and vulnerable, I buried my head in the sand and was easily led astray.

He occasionally arrived home with large sums of money with no plausible explanation I could grasp about its source. At other times, we scrimped and scraped to make ends meet, but I learned not to ask too many questions and let him handle his business affairs.

Evading reality, I accepted his grand tales and ambitions regardless of how implausible they seemed, solely because I was fooling myself and wanted to believe they were true.

As the sole breadwinner with a regular income, I settled into a new pattern of living. During the day, I worked in the hospital pharmacy and for three evenings a week, in the hospital Casualty Department, to make ends meet.

"Be not anxious about tomorrow," the Lord said. I will not be anxious; I will take things one day at a time.
Matt. 6:34

At the hospital, I co-produced a medical secretary's magazine, and one of my tasks was to write the horoscope page. Habitually, I read my horoscope most days, but producing these fake horoscope readings every month cured me of this nefarious habit.

The other secretarial staff often told me how accurate the predictions were in line with their current circumstances. These conversations made me smile inwardly because I knew I made up all sorts of nonsense to entertain and titillate their imaginations. To me, it was just a bit of fun.

My understanding of what it meant to be a true Christian still needed close attention. I started to realise that we all have an inherent need for validation and are often captivated by any prophecies regarding our lives, making us vulnerable to deception.

As I moved through various hospital departments, I gained a wealth of experience and enjoyed learning new things in the medical field.

The Rheumatology Unit was my next step, and I worked there for three years, transcribing letters about patients' musculoskeletal problems and treatment options, as well as organising their medical consultations. During my time there, an accident at home threatened my career in medical administration. Blue, a gorgeous Persian cat I bought from a local breeder, followed me everywhere around the house.

One morning, while getting the kids ready for school, multitasking as usual, like many young Mums, with an armful of school shirts, I tripped over the cat on the stairs, landing with an almighty thud at the bottom. The middle finger of my right hand was knocked out at right angles from the rest of my fingers, and *looked alarming!*

A host of hospital staff routinely walked past our house en route to work at the hospital, as we lived just around the corner from the tube station. Spotting a young doctor I knew, I called out to him. He rushed over, and after I showed him my finger, he took my arm and walked me quickly to the Casualty Department.

The A&E nurse cunningly distracted me by remarking that we had the same name, *Joanne*, but hers had an *'e'* at the end. Deftly pushing my finger back into place when I least expected it, she reassured me as I yelped in pain, and she then strapped it up.

The Head of the Rheumatology Department, where I worked as a Medical Secretary, was less than encouraging when he heard about my hand injury and ominously declared, *"You'll never type again!"* However, I'm happy to report he was proved wrong. Six weeks later, I was back at work, albeit typing more slowly. Mercifully, my finger healed, and my typing speed gradually returned to normal.

After a state-of-the-art Cancer Centre was built on site, I transferred there, working under the guidance of the remarkable

Dr Pat Price, who has since risen to prominence as a distinguished oncology professor, and I also worked for the renowned Professor Karol Sikora.

At twelve, Adam was dedicated to the Lord at Emmanuel Assembly Church, and his dad joined us to witness the ceremony. Pastor Michael's words struck a chord: *"You know what this means, don't you?"* I nodded confidently, assuming he meant that Adam could be used in God's service and sent out as a missionary to China or another far-off country.

If he were doing the Lord's will, I would have readily accepted this.

God sometimes gives us hints about the future, but we can misinterpret them.

If only I had known then what was in store, but perhaps it's a good thing I didn't.

Magid came to our church only once for Adam's Dedication, aside from attending the wedding of our friends Eric and Sonia.

When Magid was unemployed, I walked home from the hospital where I worked during my lunch break to find him either still in bed or sitting in our lounge, smoking a cigar with one of his dubious associates, their feet propped up on our coffee table.

On one occasion, I saw red and ordered his friend to get out—*Enough was enough! Resentment boiled inside me!*

VIENNA

Magid once took me on an unforgettable trip to Austria, even though my British passport was with his solicitor to support his application to become a British citizen.

Surprisingly, at the airport security in Vienna, they allowed me to go through security checks with only my prepaid bus pass as identification after Magid called an influential politician acquaintance.

Vienna was a captivating and picturesque place. I enjoyed strolling around its historic churches, where talented singers often rehearsed their opera recitals, and onlookers could come in and watch these deeply moving performances.

Magid once returned from a business trip with a streetwise Egyptian lady named Seham, one of his distant cousins who could secure discounts at all the major hotels in Cairo through IBM, the company she worked for, making her a useful person to know. Seham often visited us in London, and we spent time with her in Cairo, so we knew her quite well.

A few months later, a young, dark-haired, attractive Austrian woman in her twenties accompanied Magid and Rafaat, an Egyptian bar staff member who worked with us at the Palais and was a close friend of Magid, who accompanied him to Austria.

She was a stranger to us, and I wondered what she was doing with them. Tall and quite pretty, with a perfect figure, accentuated by skin-tight, pink-patterned leggings and a tight black low-cut top, she was over familiar with them both.

Rafaat approached me with a conspiratorial look and said he had something important to share. I motioned for him to come into the kitchen and asked what was on his mind. What he revealed next shook me to my core, making it feel as if the ground had been pulled out from under me.

"Magid slept with this girl while they were in Austria."
I was astonished, struggling to fully absorb what Rafaat had told me.

When Magid came home, I confronted him about this, but he predictably denied everything. Nevertheless, my suspicions were raised; Rafaat had no reason to lie, and I didn't see him as someone who would intentionally cause trouble.

At that time, Kerry-Ann, a teenager, noticed that I was upset and asked me what was wrong. I explained what Rafaat had told me, but she quickly refuted it, declaring... *"No, he would never do that."* Still, doubts set in…

The following evening, while strolling through the West End of London with Magid, I was taken aback to spot Rafaat ahead of us, walking hand in hand with this Austrian girl.

Given that Rafaat's partner, Debbie, was one of our close friends, and we had known them as a couple for seven years, this moment felt surreal. It was evident that Rafaat was having a fling with this girl behind Debbie's back. None of this made sense; it was far from normal. I felt a surge of outrage on Debbie's behalf, as I had presumed they were a happy couple.

A baffling chain of events was unfolding around me, and I felt like I had banged my head on a lamppost and entered the *Twilight Zone*. I had no idea what was happening and desperately wanted to acknowledge them, to gauge Rafaat's reaction since we were only yards behind them and clarify the relationship dynamics. Oddly, Magid insisted we should ignore them, so, against my better judgment, I didn't acknowledge them.

Things were becoming very muddled. Immediately, rightly or wrongly, I suspected that this girl, Andrea, was taking advantage of both my husband and his colleague, Rafaat, enjoying a free trip to London for services rendered.

Whoever commits adultery with a woman lacks understanding. He who does so destroys his soul.
Prov. 6:32 AMP

Fortunately, she didn't linger long, and when we took her back to Heathrow, Magid asked her in front of me to confirm that what Rafaat told me was false. She confirmed this, but the whole scene felt contrived. I was so furious that when I later saw her in the Ladies' Toilet, I slapped her hard across the face.

She stepped back in shock, grasping her now bright red cheek, and ran outside. She returned to Vienna that day, and we never heard from her again.

In our now-strained marriage, one issue seemed to spark a dozen others. His cigar smoking and lavish lifestyle became unbearable for me, prompting me to ask him to change or leave. He moved out, but we stayed in regular contact. A bedsit in the popular area of Hammersmith, four miles away, became his new home.

While Magid lived apart from us, Kerry-Ann was curious about her biological father, Peter, so she made a brief trip to Jersey, where her natural father, Peter, lived and arranged to meet him.

Because he tended to be constantly stuck in a pub with his drinking buddies, she was disappointed, inferring that he had no genuine interest in getting to know her. Unsurprisingly, she wanted to close the book on him and had no interest in maintaining any further contact.

One day, out of the blue, Magid called me, urging me to come quickly over to his bedsit. His behaviour was unusual, and the urgency in his voice worried me.
Jumping into my car, I drove to Hammersmith and found him looking pale and distressed. He beckoned me inside, and he sat on the edge of the bed while I perched on the settee.

"What's wrong? "I asked, by now deeply concerned… His brow furrowed, *"Look at the bottom of that chest of drawers. "* His eyes were wide, and he had an incredulous expression on his face. *"Those are the same numbers the fortune teller in Egypt gave me!"*

Written on the lower panel was a series of numbers in black crayon that eerily matched those he received many years previously. They held such significance for him that he had them engraved on the inside of his ring. She told him *they were his life numbers*, whatever that meant… He removed the bottom panel where these numbers were written and turned it around, so he wouldn't have to look at them. I didn't know what to make of this *Very creepy!*

Magid arrived at our home on Valentine's Day laden with flowers, chocolates, and an elaborate cake. We managed to talk things through, agreed to try to mend our relationship and agreeing to give our marriage another try.

He moved back in, but everything changed when he found out that Kerry-Ann had visited Jersey to meet her biological father, Peter, while he was away. His rage was explosive, and he blamed me for allowing her to go, perceiving it as the ultimate betrayal. I have never seen him so furious.

Even though Kerry-Ann hadn't connected with Peter and had no plans to see him again, Magid still perceived him as a threat.

The intensity of his anger was alarming; his face pale and twisted, and the tension in the room felt overwhelming.

Guilt from letting Kerry-Ann go to Jersey to meet Peter weighed heavily on my shoulders for years afterwards, as Magid was the only father figure she had known, and I now recognise how hurtful this was for him. I desperately wished I could turn the clock back and stop her from going; no good came from it.

At that moment, it seemed as though a dark spirit took hold of him, a stark reminder of the lurking demons in our lives. Warnings about our adversary came to my mind, recalling that he is perpetually vigilant, like a lion, eager to exploit our weaknesses and lead us to ruin. In my moment of vulnerability, I unwittingly opened the door for chaos to creep in.

Be alert and of sober mind. Your enemy, the devil, prowls around like a roaring lion looking for someone to devour. Resist him, standing firm in the faith because the family of believers worldwide suffers the same suffering.
1 Pet. 5:8 NIV

However, I now acknowledge that our values were very different. Magid's god was money and the high life it could provide *(he was a nominal, cultural Muslim)*, and had never shown any inclination to know the true God; despite many conversations about Him, he remained indifferent.

Following this incident, he underwent a significant transformation. He became callous and uncaring, even with the children, which was totally out of character.

Our home life was miserable and incredibly stressful; the atmosphere was dreadful. The kind, loving man we once knew was replaced by a cold, uncaring, self-centred individual who became increasingly distant from me and was frequently offhand with the children.

Regular phone calls became a significant source of stress, primarily because people were pursuing him for outstanding payments or because he had failed to fulfil other commitments he had made to them. Blatantly refusing to answer the phone, not wanting to speak to those who sought him out, I had to deal with the resulting onslaught of verbal abuse! I was forced to lie repetitively, pretending he wasn't there.

Being kept in the dark about his dealings was dreadful. Without knowing who they were or what I was hiding from him, I was being used as a buffer against these people.

The Third Trial ~ *My husband never returned*

On a chilly, misty Monday morning in October 1991, Magid set off on a business trip to Portugal.

> *He never returned—*
> *Three years of angst would pass before I set eyes on him again—*

An Unwelcome Early Morning Visit

Oblivious to the impending danger, I carried on as usual, accustomed to coping alone with daily tasks and household duties, as well as working full-time at the hospital.

Two days after Magid left, while alone in the house with the children, we endured a devastating turn of events that had an impact that reverberated long after the initial shock.
My racing mind was beginning to settle after another sleepless night of tossing and turning.

It was 6 am, and I was starting to drift off, aware that it was almost time to get up, when the doorbell rang insistently. I jumped up, wondering if I'd imagined it, *'Was that the front doorbell?'* It rang again! *'Who could it be at this hour?'*

The person outside wasn't planning to leave, and I harboured a sinking feeling that they weren't bringing good news. A feeling of grave apprehension overtook me. My heart raced as I peered out the window to see who was there.

A strange middle-aged man in a beige trench coat lingered outside, looking up at me. A knot formed in my stomach when he crooked his finger, beckoning me to come downstairs and open the front door.

I quickly slipped on my dressing gown, the cool fabric a stark contrast to the rising tension in my chest. As I wrapped it around me protectively and opened the front door, my heart raced at the sight of two stern-faced men standing on my porch.

They introduced themselves as detectives from the Criminal Investigation Department (CID), displaying a neatly folded warrant card and a badge glinting in the morning light.

With an air of authority, they informed me that they had come to arrest my husband, raising a shocking allegation involving a massive fraud scheme linked to a Spanish bank, amounting to a staggering $2.7 million.

The sheer magnitude of this accusation sent a chill down my spine. Before I could fully process their words, they informed me they were authorised to search our home for any evidence relating to this case.

My mind was whirling with questions and confusion as they stepped inside, their heavy footsteps echoing through our quiet house. Mystified, I stared at them, stunned and bewildered by what he said, and thought, *'This must be a mistake.'* It felt surreal! I raised my hand to my mouth, wild thoughts spinning round my head.

Magid was in Portugal on business, I told them this, but it was blatantly obvious they didn't believe me and began to search the house.

"Please don't go into the children's room, as it will scare them half to death if a stranger barges into their bedroom at this time of the morning." I pleaded.

Mercifully, they heeded my request and left them alone. They rummaged through the house, yanking open drawers, and they even peered inside the fridge and oven, leaving a trail of chaos behind them.

I couldn't help but notice the imposing stature of one of them—over six feet tall and heavily built.

"Why are you searching in these unlikely places? What are you looking for?" I asked.

Their frantic search came to an abrupt halt when I contacted Magid at the hotel in Portugal. The staff relayed more disturbing news. *'The doctor was currently attending to Magid, who was supposedly dealing with the sudden onset of alarming heart problems.'*

This revelation struck me like a bolt of lightning; I had never seen any hint of a heart issue before. A wave of disbelief washed over me, making me feel as though I was suddenly thrust into a surreal world. Two or three minutes later, Magid came to the phone and, upon learning of the charges against him, he assured me he was innocent, vehemently denying the allegations.

When the lead detective took the phone and spoke to him, he foolishly told him,

"As soon as you set foot on British soil at Heathrow, you will be arrested on the spot."

He must have thought, *'Thanks for the heads up!'*

After engaging in an intense conversation with Magid, they finally took their leave, abandoning me to process this unexpected turn of events.

As I stood there, grappling with the implications of what had just happened, I felt the weight of more responsibility settle on my shoulders.

The sounds of the bustling household brought me back to reality; I quickly got the children ready and could hear their laughter and chatter echoing through the house, oblivious to the turmoil swirling around in my mind.

Feeling an increasing sense of urgency, I prepared breakfast for them and packed Adam's lunch box. Once they were dressed and ready, I glanced at the clock and reminded myself I still had to get to work on time.

The morning was a whirlwind of activity as I fed the cat and juggled my responsibilities, all the while wondering how this dire situation would impact our lives.

When I spoke to him next, Magid claimed that the doctor the hotel called advised him not to travel for a while. Bottling my anxiety and trying to stay calm for the children's sake, I tried to remain in control.

Still, I was worried sick at this new turn of events and concerned about this new alleged health problem, along with the unexpected police intrusion and accusations.

I was still attending Emmanuel Assembly, which was a lifeline to me. They were so supportive, though I didn't give them the whole picture as I wasn't sure what was happening myself. I was putting my trust in God.

Weeks rolled into months, and Magid kept making excuses about why he couldn't come home. He had racked up several bills on my credit card, on which he'd persuaded me to add him as a joint holder. By then, I was struggling financially, unable to keep up with two jobs and looking after the children.

Bills were piling up daily; yet trustingly *(or foolishly),* I still held onto the false hope that he would return with a plausible explanation. Things would return to normal… *(on what planet?)* Our world was turned upside down…

He never returned. We had been married for 14 years.

Hear my cry for mercy as I call to you for help and as I lift my hands toward your Most Holy Place. Ps. 28:2 NIV

Chapter Seven

Divine provision ~ *the next few years were hell!!*

Final demands mounted, and I reached a point where I even felt anxious about opening the front door. Brown envelopes landing on the doormat made me feel jumpy and reluctant to read their contents. Debt collectors called under various pretexts, prompting me to stop answering the phone.

Telegrams arrived demanding immediate payment. I stopped answering the phone. Consequently, they resorted to phoning my elderly neighbour to ask her to persuade me to come to her house and speak with them, which she kindly did.
I complied and spoke to them on her phone, as I didn't want to cause any further intrusion into her life, and told them to call me on my number.

I apologised to her for the inconvenience and invasion of her privacy. She didn't seem to mind; as I guessed, she was lonely and welcomed the distraction and drama. After that, I answered all the calls to prevent them from bothering any of my neighbours again. Their pursuit of his debts was ruthless and relentless.

When their intentions were apparent, I felt vulnerable, stressed and fearful. They even came to the hospital where I worked to harass me for payment, but thankfully, my boss gave them short shrift and ordered them out.

More debts that Magid had incurred came to light. My credit cards were maxed out, and he had amassed an overdraft of £8,000 on our joint bank account. *When was this going to end?*

He had callously left me up to my eyeballs in debt! When I went to the bank and found out he had also taken Kerry-Ann's £9,000 compensation, I couldn't believe it, my heart missed a beat, and I felt sick.

This escalated things; *how could anyone be so callous?* His moral compass was unlike anyone I had ever known. This was far beyond my comprehension. My husband's true identity and the full scope of his financial offences remained a mystery to me.

Over the next few months, my stress levels mounted; he phoned occasionally, always careful to keep his whereabouts secret. Feeling irate and exasperated, I yelled down the phone at him, berating him about his decision to take Kerry-Ann's compensation money. His response was cool:

"It's only money!"

I didn't tell Kerry-Ann at the time about this as I knew she would be devastated, and I didn't want to damage her relationship with Magid. I knew this would shock her to the core and turn her against him, so I kept it to myself, vainly hoping somehow that he would pay it back for her.

After that, he didn't call again for more than a year. I was distraught over the whole situation and tried desperately to hold things together for the sake of the kids.

I didn't know what to tell people at the church when they asked where Magid was.

Former business associates believed I was complicit in his fraudulent dealings and pursued me to pay his debts.

However, I was unaware of Magid's business dealings and had no means to repay them, nor did I know his whereabouts.

What a nightmare!

My salary barely covered the mortgage, utility bills, school uniforms, council tax, and credit card payments. The list was endless.

In my despair, I could see no way out…and cried out to God.

I confided in my pastor and his wife, Joan, as well as Ralph, one of his brothers, and they prayed constantly about my predicament. They were an incredible support at this low point in my life.

Credit Suisse Bank contacted me to add to my burden, informing me that Magid owed them £17,000. This bank had mistakenly credited him twice for a deal he had made, and, of course, he had not returned the overpayment.

Things began to fall into place as I recalled the time when this incident occurred, while on holiday in Egypt, he suddenly began to splash money about and had the means to afford luxuries that were previously out of reach. Whispering and collusion between him and Mike, his partner in crime, were going on, so I knew they were hiding something.

I remained in ignorance of this banking error that had provided an unexpected windfall. They knew I would have insisted they return the overpayment.

Suddenly, expenditure wasn't an issue — we lived it up, stayed in posh hotels and had expensive restaurant meals. Little did I know then the ramifications, and that ultimately, I would be the one to pay for all this.

Debts continued to spiral, now totalling over £120,000. It was clear that we would lose our home; now that Magid's name was on the deeds, the future seemed bleak.

I was distraught, but took comfort that God was still with me, yet I struggled to put complete trust in Him.

Our little house in East Acton was the only home Adam had ever known, and Kerry-Ann had spent her middle childhood and early teenage years there.

However, by this time, she had moved a few miles away to Acton to share a flat with her former school friends.

How could I explain the ins and outs to Adam and Kerry-Ann
without turning them against their dad? These were very
dark times. My entire world had imploded.

Overwhelmed by anxiety about the future, I prayed and felt God
telling me to trust Him. He prompted me to stop paying the
mortgage, as continuing would be pointless.

It suddenly occurred to me that I should explain my situation
to the Building Society and request a mortgage holiday. I had no
idea that such things were even possible before this.

They were surprisingly sympathetic and granted me a few
months' reprieve. I saved whatever I could, acknowledging that
there was little I could do to control the bureaucratic downward
spiral, and that the bank and other creditors would ultimately
demand their pound of flesh, most likely leading to the
repossession of our modest home due to the mounting debts.

How I wish I had never been so trusting as to put his name on
the deeds of my house. (but God was on the case as I was later to
discover, all this was in His plan!)

When I approached the council to apply for council housing,
they informed me that they couldn't assist me unless I gave up
my job because I was earning too much to be granted social
housing. *What a joke!*

I was furious…There was no way I could give up my job and
live off the welfare state at the expense of others without
making any personal contribution. It was morally wrong and
went against everything I was brought up to believe.

Besides, I was well-regarded at the hospital, enjoyed my job,
and was reluctant to leave. *'Why on earth should I?'*

God closed that door and opened new ones for me.

"I know your deeds. See I have placed before you an open door that no one can shut. I know you have little strength, yet you have kept my word and have not denied my name."
Rev. 3:8 NIV

~

Norrie, an elderly Irish lady who lived across the street from us, was someone whom I checked on periodically. One evening, after work, I went across the road as usual to ensure she was okay.

When I returned home, I found bags of groceries propped against the wall outside my front door. Surprised and overjoyed, I carried them inside to examine the contents. These luxury food items were left by Pastor Michael, who collected food past their sell-by date, and discarded by supermarkets. He then distributed this to those in need.

We had been getting by with just bread and soup, so this food felt like manna from heaven. That evening, we enjoyed an exquisite meal, courtesy of Marks & Spencer, and we were truly spoiled for choice.

Thank you, God; thank you, Pastor Michael; and thank you, Marks & Spencer.

In their hunger you gave them bread from heaven, and in their thirst you brought forth water from a rock; you told them to go in and take possession of the land you had sworn with uplifted hand to give them. Neh. 9:15 NIV

The knock-on effect of this situation on Adam was devastating. He began to get into fights and conflicts with other kids at school, which led to further pressure on me and frequent calls from the school to come in to discuss the situation.

By nature, Adam wasn't an aggressive child; he idolised his dad and couldn't understand what had happened. He was clearly in turmoil and expressed his anger in this way, irrationally blaming me for his father's disappearance.

In comforting him, I didn't want to turn him against his dad, so I didn't tell him the actual situation or any details about what his father had done, as I felt he was still too young to comprehend the dire and complex circumstances.

Then to compound matters, one of Adam's teachers rang to inform me that *he hadn't been to school for three weeks,* adding another layer of shock on top of everything else. He had been leaving home in the mornings, wearing his uniform, and returning in the afternoons at the usual time, so I was completely fooled.

Why had they left it so long before informing me?

I confronted Adam, and he became upset, saying he hated school and didn't want to be there. He told me gangs were bullying him, and groups of boys were engaging in *witchcraft and Satanism*. As a result, I went to the school and demanded that they investigate this matter and resolve it.

A counsellor I engaged to support Adam had several sessions with him over six months, but she didn't involve me or disclose what they discussed during those sessions.

Finally, she declared, *"He's fine, there's nothing wrong with him,"* and promptly discharged him.

Following the consultations, she often appeared grinning while I waited outside. She clearly found either something Adam said or the whole of our circumstances amusing.

Guilt overwhelmed me; I was so focused on keeping a roof over our heads and fending off the debt collectors as well as the fallout from Magid's disappearance that I wasn't emotionally available to Adam. He was coping with his dad's sudden disappearance from his life and missed his big sister, so he was dealing with this all by himself.

Hindsight is a wonderful thing!

~

A new and welcome addition to the household was a cute little tortoiseshell kitten that I named Casey. I had seen an advert and navigated through the busy London traffic to Streatham and crossed over Tower Bridge to pick her up from two friendly guys who I discovered had taught her to *kiss* on request, which I thought was sweet. Adam has a symbiotic rapport with animals, so she was a welcome distraction for him. He adored her, and she slept on his bed most nights. It was a good decision.

The Fourth Trial ~ *Mum's death*

During my last phone conversation with my mother, she complained of a prickly sensation in her breast and mentioned various aches and pains.

Still, I wasn't unduly concerned, as she often grumbled about her health, so I attributed it to her advancing age.
How wrong I was; she later received a diagnosis of breast cancer.

Coincidentally, I was working in the Cancer Centre at Hammersmith Hospital. Dr Randall Harrison, an oncologist there, who originally hailed from Belfast, resolved to move back home to Northern Ireland.

He eventually climbed the ranks to become the lead oncologist treating my mother at Belfast's Royal Hospital, so I obtained inside information *(another God-incident?)*. Randall helpfully kept me updated on Mum's treatment and progress and assured me she was doing well.

Despite that, one morning when I was at work, my sister's husband, Eddie, rang to say that Mum had been given a prognosis of three months. Randall didn't give me any indication that her cancer had progressed this far, so I was shaken at this news.

Frustrated that I couldn't see her and help with her care, I worried about how she was coping.
However, I couldn't afford to take any time off work because of my obligation to pay all the debts left by Magid, and I had no

one to look after the children, so it just wasn't feasible for me to go to Ireland for an extended period.

My sister Violet had her husband and six children to care for, so she wouldn't have the time or energy to also look after Mum into the bargain.

I consoled myself that these prognoses were dodgy at times. Randall didn't seem concerned when I last spoke with him, and I knew from experience that patients who had cancer frequently lived years longer than their doctors predicted. Sadly, that wasn't the case with Mum.

On 22nd November 1994, six months later, *I was given the shock news of her death.* Though Mum and I weren't particularly close, she was always there, and this news left me dazed and rudderless.

NORTHERN IRELAND/*Lisburn*

Kerry-Ann and I flew over to Ireland for the funeral. My sister, Violet, was very offhand with us and refused to let us use Mum's empty home, citing that she had left instructions that no one was to enter her house, which was now empty, so we had nowhere to stay. I couldn't even afford a B&B.

Embarrassingly, I found myself in the awkward position of having to approach the neighbours on her road and ask if we could use their bathroom. This request felt humiliating, and though they were friendly and accommodating, I could sense the sting of vulnerability at that moment, though I understood my sister's anger and resentment towards me; throughout our mum's illness, she had been carrying the weight of everything on her own.

The long nights spent at the hospital, the countless phone calls to doctors, and the frustrations and burdens I perhaps hadn't fully grasped at the time. To her, it likely seemed like another sign that I did not genuinely care about what she was experiencing. If the roles were reversed, I probably would have felt just as hurt and abandoned.

On entering the church for Mum's funeral, I noticed the coffin was closed, so I couldn't see her. Violet explained that her face was sunken, and she looked terrible. Therefore, she thought it was best to have the coffin lid nailed down.

We had no choice but to fly back to Heathrow on the same day due to the constraints of my tight budget. Embarrassed by our predicament, my brother-in-law Eddie offered to take us to Aldergrove Airport.

Startled, I turned to see the man at the check-in desk who approached me, exclaiming, *"Excuse me, are you Twinkle?"*

"It's a long time since anyone called me that," I responded.

Twinkle was my nickname in our old biker gang from my teenage years, and then I recognised him as Davy Gray (*Spinney),* one of the gang I used to hang out with. He looked much older, and his distinctive red curly hair was now streaked with white. It was wonderful to see him again.

Flattered that he recognised me and remembered my nickname after so many years, I explained the reason for our visit. He kindly offered his condolences on the loss of my mother, remarking how much alike Kerry-Ann and I looked. We had a quick chat, exchanging information about our lives now, and he proudly told me that he was married and had two teenage sons and twin girls, aged ten, *a mental picture of two identical little girls with flame-red hair and freckles flashed across my mind.*

He animatedly updated me on developments in the lives of our former mutual friends.

ENGLAND

Kerry-Ann has always possessed a strong work ethic. She worked for a local, popular fast food outlet to support herself. Huddersfield University was where she chose to pursue a degree in media studies. I drove her up there, the car heavily loaded with her belongings.

For her first year, she stayed in the University Halls, a situation she found quite suffocating and stressful. She elected to relocate to a shared house with several other girls for the second year. Fortunately, this new living arrangement provided a more conducive atmosphere that suited her much better.

DIVORCE

I was legally married, but alone, so I began divorce proceedings because I could see no way our marriage could survive, but I didn't want to go against God's standards. This verse from the

Bible gave me the peace I needed that my actions were biblically acceptable under the circumstances.

> *But if the husband or wife who isn't a believer insists on leaving, let them go. In such cases the believing husband or wife is no longer bound to the other for God has called you to live in peace.* 1 Cor. 7:15 NLT

For three years, we heard nothing about Magid's whereabouts and were uncertain whether he was alive or dead. Because the solicitor didn't have an address to send the divorce papers, they were unable to serve them, resulting in a lengthy legal process.

Eventually, after extensive legal manoeuvring, the judge agreed to waive the service requirement, allowing the proceedings to accelerate, declaring *Dispensation of Service,* three words that were music to my ears.

The decree nisi was granted in his absence, finalising our divorce six weeks later in 1995.

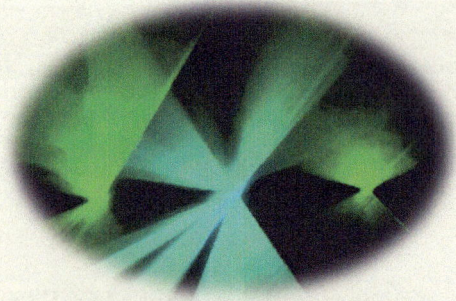

Chapter Eight

The Fifth Trial ~ *Eviction ~ We lost our home*

In some instances, when someone in your family goes missing, it's worse than coping with a death, as there is no closure, and those left behind are in a perpetual state of limbo. Imagination works overtime, and all kinds of scenarios go through your mind.

Credit Suisse Bank had put a charge on the house to reclaim the money Magid owed them, so a repossession order was submitted.

The date of the repossession was looming. By that time, I had managed to squirrel away enough money to put a deposit on a cheap flat for Adam and me in Northolt, a suburb of West

London. It was further out than our current home in an area where property was much more affordable.

My friend Sonia's husband, Eric, from our church, kindly came over to assist us with packing, take a final reading of the electric meter and to ensure everything was in order.

We moved our belongings out just moments before the dreaded council workers arrived in their van to evict us, potentially carting us off to a squalid halfway house.

Thankfully, the humiliation of being ferried away in a council van was thwarted, denying the nosy neighbours on our street the pleasure of gawping at us as we were driven away.

They knew about our impending eviction because the council *discreetly* posted an *Eviction Notice* on our front door.

I longed to look back as we drove away at the little house that held so many memories, and was our home for over seventeen years, but I kept my eyes firmly focused on the road ahead.

The paperwork for the new flat wasn't yet complete, and it would take another week or so to get the keys, so we had nowhere to go.

Ralph, Michael's younger brother, an elder of the church and his wife, Vera, offered to have Adam at their home in South Ealing. I pretended I was okay and had organised somewhere to stay, as I didn't want to trouble anyone; however, the truth was that I didn't have anywhere to go.

Eric and Sonia put me up for one night in their small home, but with them and their three boys, it was a bit of a squeeze.

Trishia, a close friend of mine, worked for a travel agency in Earls Court, a vibrant neighbourhood known for its multicultural atmosphere and bustling streets. When she learned about my predicament, she graciously offered me temporary refuge. For three nights, I slept on the comfortable settee tucked away in the back room of their office, a cosy space filled with travel brochures and maps that hinted at adventures waiting to be explored. The office also had a clean washroom, making it a surprisingly accommodating spot for my unexpected stay.

However, after three nights, I found myself without any options once again as Trish's boss was coming down from Birmingham so I had to leave.

With a heavy heart, I decided to relocate to Heathrow Airport, which became my makeshift home for the remainder of the week. The airport, typically bustling with travellers eager to reach their destinations, now served as my final refuge. My personal belongings were safely stowed in another friend's garage, providing a small comfort amidst the chaos of my circumstances.

It's impossible to overstate the relief I felt when the completion of my flat eventually came through. It was on the ground floor of a small block in a reasonably priced area, and it was spacious, featuring three good-sized bedrooms and a decent-sized lounge. As a bonus, a garage also came with the flat, which meant I didn't have to worry about parking, and it also allowed me to store some of our belongings there until we sorted out suitable storage within the flat—*a blessing!*

Kind people from our church, Michael's older sister Doreen, and James, one of Michael's sons, came over to help us clean the flat and settle in.

We continued attending Emmanuel on Sundays for as long as was feasible. Adam had endured enough changes in his short life, and I knew he was feeling adrift having moved to a new and unfamiliar place, so I wanted to maintain some stability for his sake and mine.

One Sunday morning, I dropped him off at Emmanuel church, but didn't go in myself, as he, at that time, was directing all his anger at me, treating me like something from the bottom of his shoe. He moved his chair away if I sat next to him.

I was hurt, humiliated, and crushed, it was soul-destroying to be treated that way. I accepted that he was using me as a scapegoat to vent his anger, but the emotional pain his behaviour caused was deep, adding to the already heavy burden I carried.

In my emotionally fragile state, a fierce battle was raging in my mind. It was all getting on top of me. Doreen, Michael's older sister, declared in her sing-song high-pitched voice,

"You've got to get the victory, dear!"

At the time, I had no idea what she was talking about, and anger rose in me. The last thing I needed was a lecture, and I felt that Christian jargon was being employed to dismiss me and the gravity of my situation, causing me to feel rejected and belittled.

Pastor Michael pleaded with me to enter the church, but I couldn't bring myself to go inside. Instead, I drove to Kensington Temple, a large and vibrant church nearby. The building was designed in the shape of a cross. I found a seat in a pew in the right wing of the church, and feeling alone and free from accountability was exactly what I needed. I was anonymous and inconspicuous.

Charles and Paula Slagle, an American couple, were prophesying in KT that morning. Wrapped up in my thoughts and misery and never having heard of them before, I didn't pay much attention until Charles Slagle said,

"Someone here is not using their own name," gesturing in the direction of where I sat.

He went on to describe what I was wearing, and the hair on the back of my neck stood up. I began to squirm in my seat as I perhaps irrationally thought everyone in the church must know he's talking about me.

I had changed my surname by Deed Poll, because I didn't want to be associated with Magid's debts any longer, and I didn't want to use my birth name to protect my family from being traced and bothered about Magid's debts. It seemed wiser to remain completely anonymous.

Charles went on to say,

"Those who should be supporting you are not doing so. They are not treating you right. The Holy Spirit understands what you are going through and does not condemn you."

My mouth fell open in amazement, and I felt uplifted and cheerful, brighter somehow. God was aware of my situation, and that truth was now right in my face. I felt as though a weight had been lifted off my shoulders, and my mood elevated as the oppressive weight of *religious remarks,* condemnation, and

143

judgment from others fell away like a set of chains that bound me. I took that message away with me and pondered on it, treasuring his words of comfort.

The Holy Spirit was with me and filled my thoughts, but it was difficult to fully grasp this validating truth.
Feelings of unworthiness still reared their ugly head now and then, and compared to others in the church, I continued to feel unworthy and a bit like an outsider.

The Lord who gathers the outcasts of Israel declares, "I will gather yet others to him besides those already gathered."
Isa. 56:8 ESV

My Perspective Changed Completely ~

(from one of anxiety to one of euphoria ~
God was on my case and was still getting my attention in
various ways…)

Soon after this prophecy, on my way home from work one
evening, a car pulled out in front of me from a side road on
Western Avenue, and I was drawn to a sticker on the rear
window that read:

> **THEREFORE THERE SHALL NOW BE NO
> CONDEMNATION FOR THOSE WHO ARE
> IN CHRIST JESUS …**

Well, that certainly grabbed my attention. My heart leapt!
…Why hadn't I heard anyone mention this before?

(Jesus does not condemn, the Holy Spirit
convicts…. condemnation comes from Satan).

That car remained on the carriageway long enough for me to
read this message before turning back onto the next side road.
Who does that? My heart was pounding.
These actions didn't make sense, God was speaking to me again.
I was ecstatic, driving the rest of the way home on a high.

That evening, the enemy did his best to burst my bubble by whispering in my ear, *"God's not talking to you. Why would he speak to the likes of you?"*

The Wang Word Processor I used at the hospital had a version of the Bible uploaded on it, so I went into work early the next

morning, determined to find this verse.
My knowledge of the Bible at that time was limited.

The Old Testament seemed to me like a large, dark, gloomy house I was disinclined to enter, and my understanding of the New Testament remained superficial.

I searched from Genesis to Revelation, but couldn't trace this verse. Just as I was about to quit in defeat, my mouth fell open when, incredibly, it flashed up before me on the screen:

Therefore there shall now be no condemnation for those who are in Christ Jesus...Rom. 8:1 NIV

I could hardly believe what I was seeing!
(This has also happened while I was writing this book...)
Wow!

Then I heard Jesus' voice saying with a chuckle,
"Yes, I am talking to you!"

No one could get any sense out of me for the rest of the day; I was on cloud nine, walking six feet in the air.

This uplifting message removed the barrier that was blocking the truth from my troubled heart.

This became my life verse from that time forward. When I need to make a weighty decision, such as attending a specific church or meeting, God's will becomes apparent to me if the speaker mentions this pivotal verse, Rom. 8:1, especially when it's spoken out of context.

I know that's where God wants me at that time, just as Gideon used a fleece to determine God's will in the Book of Judges.

Gideon said to God "If you will save Israel by my hand as you have promised— look, I will place a wool fleece on the threshing floor. If there is dew only on the fleece and all the ground is dry, then I will know that you will save Israel by my hand as you said."
And that is what happened. Gideon rose early the next day, squeezed the fleece, wrung out the dew, and filled a bowl with water.
Then Gideon said to God, "Do not be angry with me. Let me make just one more request. Allow me one more test with the fleece, but this time make the fleece dry and let the ground be covered with dew."
That night God did so. Only the fleece was dry; all the ground was covered with dew. Judges 6: 36 – 40 NIV

Back in Ireland, when we were children, the church we attended was cold and dull. The Apostles' Creed was drummed into us, though I had no idea what it meant, and I just spouted it parrot fashion, knowing some of what I recited was gobbledygook.

I was confirmed at the age of thirteen in the very formal and dour Church of Ireland, but it had no spiritual significance and was a ritual that children of that age in Ulster were expected to perform.

The girls got to wear pretty white dresses with matching gloves and were given a little white prayer book—

Who could resist…

~

LONDON

Meanwhile, life settled into some semblance of normality, and I was managing to cope. I had now left Hammersmith Hospital as the journey was no longer feasible and had secured a new post at Northwick Park Hospital, as it was closer to where we now lived. I was the Team Leader in the Cardiothoracic Unit there, which was quite a stressful job.

For fifteen years, we had faithfully attended Emmanuel Assembly, a vibrant community that became a cornerstone in our lives. The memories of that cherished time remain vivid and deeply etched in my heart, filled with warmth and nostalgia.

~

We hadn't given up looking for Magid or trying to obtain information on his whereabouts.
Late one evening, about eighteen months later, I had a phone call from Egypt; one of Magid's friends and business associates, Hany, informed me that Magid was in Cairo.

This revelation gave us hope that we might get the long-awaited answers we sought, so I immediately headed to the bank and took out a loan to fly there with the kids as soon as possible. After three years of uncertainty, this new revelation presented an opportunity for closure that I couldn't afford to miss.

The bank clerk was an angel and was extremely helpful. It was almost as though she understood our circumstances and sensed the vital importance of this trip for us. Without further ado, she efficiently transferred a loan of £800 to my account. She didn't ask any more questions. It was a huge relief to secure

149

the funding I needed to travel so easily, so I booked a week's leave from work and arranged to fly to Cairo with the children.

EGYPT ~ *More than I am able…*

Hany collected us from Cairo airport and drove us straight to his holiday home near Alexandria. We were upset and frustrated because we weren't there for a holiday and were eager to catch up with Magid again instead of being diverted in this way.

Azza, Hany's wife, seemed on edge throughout the time we were there, and the atmosphere was tense. I began to suspect that this was an elaborate setup to keep us out of the way, which was odd because he was the one who let us know where Magid was. Although it was a beautiful place on the beach, we didn't enjoy our time there because we couldn't relax, as we were anxious to return to Cairo to resume our quest to see Magid.

Hany's response to any questions about Magid's circumstances was unfathomable, which frustrated and angered me. *Something dubious was going on.*

Eventually, they drove us back to Cairo, and Hany dropped us off at the building on the main street where Amani's flat was in Saida Zainab.

She was delighted to see us, offering a warm and enthusiastic welcome. She confirmed that he was in town and was staying at the Hilton Hotel.

Leaving the kids with Amani, I took a taxi there, but the receptionist was under instructions not to give out guest room numbers or contact guests when they had visitors, unless they were expected. I was all too familiar with this hotel's regulations from previous stays, and I was sorely tempted to linger near the entrance in case he showed up. I pictured the shock on his face if he were to catch me suddenly. Though it was tempting, I decided against it. Amani would have told him we were in Cairo, and he would have deliberately stayed out of the way.

Frustrated by the endless games he was playing, I wandered through the familiar shopping arcade across the street from the hotel. The vibrant storefronts and the mingled sweet scents of coffee and pastries were nostalgic and provided some small comfort, yet my mind wandered elsewhere.

Suddenly, I felt a tap on my shoulder, breaking my contemplation. It was one of the hotel doormen. He greeted me warmly, using my married name, his face lighting up with recognition from our past stays at the Hilton. Despite his friendly demeanour, I sensed a guardedness in him, as though he were concealing some unspoken truth. A subtle tension hung in the air, piquing my curiosity.

We settled at a small table in a quaint café within the shopping arcade, where the sounds of clinking cups and hushed conversations faded into the background. As we sipped our coffee, chatting about life in general, his stories were lively, yet he revealed nothing of substance.

It felt as if we were each acutely aware of the elephant in the room, and I couldn't shake the feeling that something deeper lurked beneath the surface.

Time was marching on, and later in the week, I began to fear that we wouldn't see Magid, who was still evading us. Our return flight was imminent…

Feeling deflated as it was beginning to seem like our trip would be fruitless, I was worried about the knock-on effect this could have on the children, who were desperate to see their estranged father again after such a long time.

My new job as office manager at Northwick Park Hospital, in the Kennedy Galton Centre, a separate diagnostic genetic unit, established to help people assess the risk of inheriting genetic diseases and syndromes, was too important to lose, and I didn't want to jeopardise it by overstaying the leave I was granted.

Two days before we were to fly back to London, we took a taxi to Amani's flat to say goodbye, feeling disillusioned and let down after three years of mystery and confusion about Magid's whereabouts.

That was when she surprised me by saying he had contacted her, and wanted to see us, and was on his way to her flat. I cancelled our previous flight booking so we could have a few more days to sort things out.

Poor Adam was so distressed, his face pale and tense, he had diarrhoea and kept running to the bathroom. Kerry-Ann and I felt anxious, too, but being more mature, we managed to maintain a strong front and kept our feelings in check.

When Magid eventually arrived at Amani's flat, it was such a shock to see him after so long. This man, who was such a huge part of our lives, whom we loved, but who had caused much pain and disruption. He had lost weight and aged somewhat with grey streaks running through his black curly hair. Though he appeared pleased to see us, his demeanour was defensive; he was guarded, subdued, and rather sheepish.

He had booked a room for us at the Hilton Hotel and initially made polite small talk, taking us for a meal at the hotel and spending time with us, but the conversation was light and superficial. I was eager to speak to him alone to uncover the truth about where he had been for the past three years and what had been happening. I was grateful when Kerry-Ann tactfully took Adam up to our hotel room, giving me a much-needed opportunity to have a private conversation with him.

Windows on the World is a phenomenon: a prestigious, revolving restaurant and nightclub at the top of the hotel, providing a breathtaking view of the city lights, and it was the setting for our subsequent confrontation. He remained aloof and elusive.

My Irish temper got the better of me, causing me to snap. A fist of anger and outrage lodged in my gut; the red mist descended. I told him in no uncertain terms about the nightmare he caused us with his selfish, irresponsible behaviour. I called him *'a coward, and spineless jelly of a man,'* among other things.

He ended up in tears and, surprisingly, pleaded with me for another chance. He tried to persuade me to spend the night with him, explaining that he couldn't go back to London because of the charges against him. He mentioned that he was staying in Portugal before eventually returning to Egypt.

He could have phoned.

What was his responsibility to his family? How did he think we could move forward from this? Questions clouded my mind.

Little did I know that he was already in a relationship with a German woman named Heike, who had just flown back to Munich to visit her family for a week, so he was betraying her, as well.

Quite the charmer, wasn't he?

He had been biding his time, patiently waiting for her to leave Cairo, meticulously planning his treachery. With her safely out of the country, he felt at liberty to see us behind her back, as if our lives were merely a game of chess. The pieces were moving into place, and each decision he made tightened the web of deceit.

That night, I tucked the children into bed in the hotel room and stayed with them, finding solace in their presence, before returning to London the next day. Leaving the kids with him for another week was a wrench, but it felt like a necessary sacrifice; they needed this time to reconnect emotionally with their dad, to bridge the widening gap his choices created. It was painful, but I hoped it might ease the wounds that were beginning to fester.

Since my booking was last-minute, there were no available seats on the flight, and they sensed the urgency, so the crew did their best to accommodate me by providing a staff member's seat.

As the plane levelled out, the attendant walked past with the drinks trolley, so I ordered a glass of wine to settle my stomach. Feeling utterly alone, I felt my shoulders tightening as tears flowed during the long, lonely journey back home. Packed into a crowded plane, I felt emotionally drained by all that had transpired.

Watching other passengers chat and interact with their children in the adjacent seats, I felt detached and thought,

'This should be my family.'

It felt as though another phase of my life was closing, yet I had no excitement for the new one. The thought that this forthcoming episode could bring more heartache lingered in the back of my mind.

God does not intend for us to be lonely and isolated. How quickly things can change…

LONDON

Some weeks later, I received a surprise sum of £200 from Heike, his new partner, through the Western Union Money Transfer service.

Kerry-Ann and I blew it all at Whiteley's Shopping Centre in Bayswater. We recklessly indulged in expensive haircuts and treated ourselves to a lavish lunch. Even though we needed that money for more essential expenses, it felt good and empowering to spend it freely instead of being responsible.

When he called again, I asked him to thank Heike for sending this. I appreciated that she had a conscience, even if he didn't. His new relationship didn't upset me as much as I thought it might. He began to connect regularly by phone afterwards to get updates on the children.

I didn't want Magid to know that our divorce had been finalised because, perhaps unkindly, I didn't want him to benefit from the freedom I had initiated and had struggled financially to achieve.

However, to my dismay, Adam inadvertently revealed this information during a telephone conversation with him. Adam relished sharing all my business, including unnecessary details; nothing was off-limits. He had little understanding of what led to our situation and consequently placed all the blame on my shoulders.

Four months later, one of my colleagues invited me to a birthday party for her husband, where I was introduced to Paul, an upholsterer. He was a slim, wiry, capable-looking guy with closely cropped light brown hair, a trim, neat beard, a moustache, and a disarming smile that instantly drew me to him. We first became friends and eventually began dating.

My friends at Emmanuel supported me as best they could. Even when I began seeing someone else, they were not judgmental. Paul was tall and quite attractive. Recently divorced, Paul had just lost a stepson to the evils of anorexia, which I encountered many times during my years in the Health Service. I sensed he harboured misplaced guilt and shame from this tragic experience.

He took a fatherly interest in Adam, almost as if he wished to compensate for his perceived lack of parenting towards his stepson, Dale, before his passing. He lived and worked in Denham, several miles away, and had another son, Paul, named after him, who resided with his mum in Maidenhead, so I didn't see much of him.

Over time, it became evident that we needed to find another church closer to our new home, as continuing the long commute to Emmanuel was unsustainable.

For Adam's sake, and to maintain some stability, we continued making the journey for a time, as his behaviour was becoming erratic and unpredictable. He was in a new environment and missed his dad and sister. The house in East Acton was the only home Adam had ever known.

The enforced changes on him were a cause for concern, and I struggled with his open defiance when he stood in front of me, eyeballing me if I didn't let him have his way. He began saying strange things like, *"The cat is crying because she doesn't like the flat."* I sensed he was projecting his feelings onto our cat, Casey.

Occasionally, he became aggressive, but I stood my ground, never allowing him to intimidate me, much to Paul's surprise and, I suspect, a modicum of admiration.

Chapter Nine

The Sixth Trial ~ *Adam went missing...*

When I returned home with Paul one evening, I noticed the light on my answering machine flashing. It was a message from Pastor Michael, his familiar melodic Welsh accent relaying troubling news about Adam's unusual behaviour at the church hall.

He disturbingly described how Adam sang loudly in an uncharacteristically deep voice, jumped over chairs, and ranted at people at the meeting about watching TV, threatening to smash the television in the back room of the church with a hammer before abruptly striding out of the meeting.

I was taken aback when I went into this room to find that he had covered his TV with brown paper, secured haphazardly with parcel tape. At that moment, my concern deepened.

Alarm bells began ringing!

For the first time, Adam didn't come home that night. Frantically, I searched the local area and the main road for any sign of him, but there was no trace. He wasn't the type of boy to mix with street gangs, so I contacted the police; however, they offered little help.

When they arrived around midnight, I showed them a photo of Adam in colour. The younger officer, whose name was Keith *(though oddly he spelt it 'Kieth' on his badge),* held the colour photo in his hands and asked me what colour Adam's eyes were. It was evident that his eyes were blue, and I began to wonder about his competency.

The officers contacted all nearby police stations through a central number and requested that local hospitals report any sightings of Adam. Nothing had been reported.

During the night, unable to sleep, I paced the floor of my bedroom.

I Yelled at God!

---experiencing a mixture of frustration, desperation, and hopelessness, telling Him,

"If He didn't sort this out, He and I were finished!"
(like a dog barking at the moon!)

The day before, I had bought a little booklet called **'My Fivepenny Fortune'** at a local jumble sale for the princely sum of 10p.

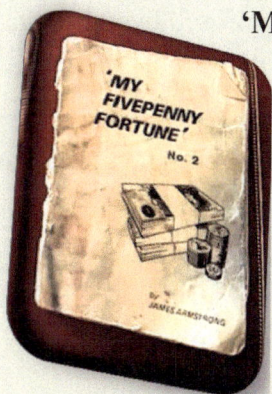

A beam of light shone on it as it lay on my bedside table. I picked it up and read:

"For I have seen you through six troubles, I will not forsake you in the seventh."

Goosebumps prickled all over my body......Then God spoke,

"When you wake in the morning, your God will be with you."

A comforting warmth surrounded me, as if warm oil flowed from my head to my toes, and unexpectedly, exhaustion took over, prompting me to lie down and let sleep wash over me.

The sound of the phone ringing jolted me awake the next morning. A woman from University College Hospital in Central London informed me that my son, Adam, was taken there by the police after having been rescued from the Serpentine River, where he spent five hours struggling in the deep water and was suffering from hypothermia. She went on to ask if there was any history of mental illness in our family, which was bewildering.

While I was relieved to hear that he'd been found and was safe, I couldn't help but feel uneasy and confused by her inquiry about mental health and candidly replied that I wasn't aware of anything like that in our family's background.

When I called him, Paul came over, and I brought him up to speed on what had happened to Adam. He took me to the hospital in Central London before returning to work.
The receptionist guided me to the department where Adam had been taken for assessment and monitoring.

A strange sight met my eyes; he lay on a bed wearing peculiar green trousers, too short for him and a shirt I didn't recognise. His feet were bare, and his watch was missing. He was pleased to see me but relayed an alarming tale involving *a gang of youths chasing him with knives.*

His account sounded dramatic and far-fetched, and I was perturbed, not knowing what to make of it.

This, I learned later, was his first psychotic episode, and I was convinced that the stress of his father's disappearance, coupled with losing his home and familiar lifestyle, was the trigger for his mental health breakdown.

"Don't look at my eyes!" he implored me.

Naturally, my gaze was drawn directly to them. His bulging, blood-red eyes`appeared to be spinning in his head, which caused me to faint in shock, and I was then laid on the bed next to him.

What a fiasco!

Eventually, an ambulance took us to St Bernard's, the Mental Health Unit at Ealing Hospital, where they admitted him and assigned him a room. Throughout the journey, Adam chatted with the paramedic on board as if nothing had happened, discussing the intricacies of various first aid procedures.

It was surreal!

Sitting in the rear passenger seat of the ambulance, in a daze from the shock of the last twenty-four hours, I felt like a spectator watching a film, detached from the situation, as though it were happening to someone else.

The staff carefully guided us through the routine admission procedure, and their reassuring demeanour instilled confidence in their expertise.

They suggested that I return home for the night and come back the next day after they had conducted a thorough assessment of Adam's mental state.

However, as I stood in the waiting area, a wave of uncertainty washed over me. Leaving him there, alone and vulnerable, didn't feel right. I longed to stay, to hold his hand

and reassure him that he wasn't alone. Yet, I had no choice but to trust the professionals' expertise, knowing they preferred that I remain out of the way.

Sitting quietly in the waiting room, grappling with a sense of helplessness as time passed, I called Paul, who came to pick me up and take me back home.

When Magid, who was in regular contact with Adam, heard the painful details of this latest incident, I detected the distress in his voice as he reacted; his concern was palpable. He believed the story of the gang of youths, but when it came to the possibility of a mental illness diagnosis, he refused to acknowledge it due to the stigma it carried.

I understood that he was reluctant to accept this diagnosis, as no one wants their child to be associated with such a label. Still, my thoughts drifted to his cousin Ahmed, who was locked away in a back room, and I couldn't help but wonder if there was a hereditary factor involved here.

A deep sense of anxiety about what might lie ahead engulfed me, though I sensed the presence of God in this; the pain and uncertainty felt profound, and I wished we could find a way through this turmoil and provide Adam with the specialised support he desperately needed.

Paranoid schizophrenia was the eventual initial diagnosis, marking the beginning of a long, arduous journey. After reading everything I could find on this condition, I needed to understand what was happening in my son's mind and what the future held. It wasn't straightforward and the diagnosis kept changing.

I learned that research shows that a considerable number of people who are diagnosed with schizophrenia aren't even aware of it until it progresses into the later stages.

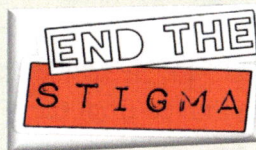

Imagine going about life as you usually do and suddenly experiencing an illusory manifestation or an auditory hallucination without a single warning...*very scary!*

For we do not wrestle against flesh and blood, but against principalities, against powers, against the rulers of the darkness of this age, against spiritual wickedness in the heavenly places Eph. 6:12 NKJV

Feeling guilty and in a quandary, I had booked a two-week holiday on the Greek island of Kos months earlier. The date was fast approaching, and I timidly mentioned the booking to the psychiatrist who was treating Adam, expecting him to recommend that I cancel it.

Instead, he surprised me by saying *(using the vernacular)* to go ahead on my own, as it could benefit us both to have a short break from each other.

Paul drove me to the airport, and Kerry-Ann joined us as she was on a week's break from her university course in Huddersfield. Roadworks delayed our journey, increasing the likelihood of missing my flight. However, in the light of recent traumas, this experience felt trivial. I felt numb inside and detached from reality.

Paul noticed my composure under the circumstances, commenting that his ex-wife would have been going *'up the wall'* if she had been in my position. Flatly, I responded that *it was hardly a matter of life and death;* I felt removed from the situation.

As it turned out, I did miss my flight. Paul had to leave us at the airport to return to work, and I spent the day with Kerry-Ann at the airport, which afforded us valuable and rare mum-and-daughter time together.

Wishing she could join me for this holiday was uppermost in my mind, but I understood she had to return to Huddersfield to continue her studies.

∞

Kos, Patmos—*The Island of the Revelation*

At a quarter past seven that evening, I managed to board another flight that arrived in Kos early the next morning, which was quite unsettling due to the darkness and unfamiliar surroundings.

I was unsure how to find the holiday accommodation I had booked on the island, so I searched for transportation options and chose a taxi to take me to the address provided.

Unfortunately, I was grossly overcharged for the ride; I later learned that the correct fare was less than half of what I paid. Since I wasn't familiar with the local currency and rates, there was little I could do about it.

The room I booked was sparse but sufficient. Feeling lonely with my thoughts and emotionally exhausted, I spent the entire first week confined to my small room, immersing myself in the Gospel of John. Equipped with a neat little booklet containing only this gospel, I read through the entirety of John, my favourite of the four gospels, which stands out from the other three synoptic gospels and is written in a distinctive style.

It possesses warmth and directness that speak directly to my heart. John 14, warm and reassuring, is littered with promises from Jesus. I could recite this passage of scripture by heart, having learnt it parrot fashion as a child. However, now it was such a blessing, as I recognised its full significance.

*"Let not your heart be troubled; you believe in
God believe also in me.
In my Father's house are many mansions; if it
were not so I would have told you. I go to
prepare a place for you.
And if I go and prepare a place for you, I will
come again and receive you to myself; where I
am, there you may be also.
And where I go you know and the way you
know."*

Thomas said to Him,
*"Lord, we do not know where You are going
and how can we know the way?"*
Jesus said to him,
*"I am the way the truth and the life. No one comes to the
Father except through me."* John 14: 1 6 KJV

I spent the first week alone in my room, pondering on all that
had transpired.

When I eventually emerged, I was a different person, one
who depended solely on God, not myself.

John is one of Jesus's beloved disciples whom I resonate with
most; his gospel is deep and highly personal, providing unique
insights into Jesus's identity as the Son of God, His divine
mission, and the limitless love He shows to believers. It has a
captivating appeal, lacking in the other three, as it is a gospel of

signs, recounting the first miracle Jesus performed—turning water into wine at the wedding in Cana.

As I later understood, it all began with a wedding and will finish with *the Wedding of the Lamb* to His people at the end of time.

When the wine ran out at this wedding in Cana, Jesus instructed the servants to bring Him six large water jars, used for ritual ceremonial washing, each holding about twenty-five gallons (95 litres). To everyone's amazement, He turned the water into wine. Furthermore, it was the finest wine, usually served first at a wedding rather than later.

> *Your children will commit themselves to you O Jerusalem just as a young man commits himself to his bride. Then God will rejoice over you as a bridegroom rejoices over his bride.*
> Isa. 62:5 NLT

This reminded me of man's wedding vows, but this is a different kind of marriage, where vows are unnecessary because they have already been made through God's covenant with His people.

We are invited to the Wedding Feast with a seat at:

His Banqueting Table

The Apostle John was one of Jesus's three main disciples, along with his brother James. Peter, John, and James were the sons of

Zebedee and were known for their passionate nature, which led Jesus to nickname them: *'Sons of Thunder.'*

Unlike his brother, James, who was killed by a sword, and his fellow apostles, who also met violent deaths, John lived to a ripe old age. Legend has it that he miraculously survived being boiled in oil in Rome before being exiled to the island of Patmos. On this remote island, he received the divine Revelation of Jesus Christ.

After his exile, John, now elderly, returned to his home in Ephesus, where he documented his writings for posterity in the Book of Revelation, the final book of the Bible.

~

After a week of isolation to assimilate recent events and gather myself together, I called Adam to see how he was doing.

He was upset and complained that I hadn't contacted him for a week. Typically, he attempted to guilt-trip me, but I refused to take it on board. Other than that, he seemed relatively stable and told me, reassuringly, that Paul visited him daily. I was incredibly grateful to him for stepping in.

Suzie, another guest staying in the next room, invited me to join her and her friends to explore the local shops and have a few drinks later in one of the local bars. It was a relief to be with new people who were there to enjoy a break and who knew nothing of my situation, so I didn't have to explain my circumstances.

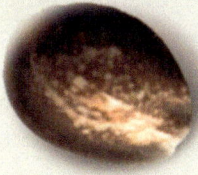

One bright, crisp morning, while strolling alone by the harbour and perched on a low stone wall to enjoy the view, I watched as an old, weather-beaten Greek fisherman approached me, opened his hand, and offered me a beautiful, closed, shiny brown shell with a speckled pattern. It was beautiful! Gratefully accepting his thoughtful gift, I treasured it, later discovering its name, a *'Snakehead Cowrie'*.

With deep, rheumy brown eyes that shimmered beneath the weight of countless life experiences and reflected a rare and profound wisdom, this stranger's unexpected kind gesture—cradled in his gnarled hand—stirred something deep within me.

The moment felt almost sacred; I sensed an immediate connection with this elderly fisherman, as if unseen threads of understanding bound us. Words were unnecessary in the face of such a profound exchange. With its intricate patterns and smooth curves, the small shell became a treasured token. This precious gift symbolised our fleeting yet strong bond, igniting a spiritual connection that went beyond the ordinary.

Later in the day, I went on a day trip by boat to Nisyros, an intriguing volcanic island renowned for its production of sea sponges. There were also boat trips to Patmos, and Suzie and I embarked on one of these trips the next day.

After reading the Gospel of St John, I became eager to visit the distant island of Patmos, which I eventually had the opportunity to explore. This small, rocky Greek island in the Aegean Sea is aptly nicknamed "The Island of the Revelation."

The sacred cave where St John was imprisoned was high on my agenda to visit. This is where he received the visions found in the Book of Revelation at the *Cave of the Apocalypse.* Several notices pinned to wooden posts outside provided historical information surrounding this event, although the details I read were unfamiliar, and I'm unsure of its origins or accuracy.

Three distinctive cracks, caused by lightning strikes, were visible at the top of the cave entrance. Our local guide told us they represented the Trinity, the Father, Son, and Holy Ghost. *Awesome!*

Inside the cave were metal rings attached to the walls, along with a notice stating that they were similar to those used to incarcerate St John.

There was a spiritual presence that I could not deny in that cave, a nostalgic experience that transported me back to ancient days, instilling a hunger to learn all I could about the story of this dear saint's life.

The timing of our trip was fortuitous, as the locals in Patmos were celebrating a special day with traditional dance in the streets. The other passengers and I were treated to a glorious kaleidoscope of colour from the swirling local costumes, which highlighted traditional Greek dancing routines.

It was a remarkable and heartening sight, and I consider myself extremely privileged to have witnessed this elaborate display.

Sailing back to Kos, our faces flushed from the sun, our skin stinging and peeling from the splashes of salty seawater, we combed our hair with our fingers as it was stiff and tangled from the salty air.

The next day marked the final day of the holiday. Feeling spiritually refreshed and rejuvenated, I was ready to face any challenges. I boarded the flight back to London.

That holiday was God-led.

At this point, I was confused by the number of trials I had faced, so I prayed, asking the Holy Spirit to reveal what number I had reached.

"Count the things that are beyond your control; the rest is your own making," was His sagely reply.

Though it wasn't easy to understand, I knew it was fair.

Who was I to question the Holy Spirit? I knew what God had told me, and that He was with me unconditionally. I held this in my heart.

Reflecting on the events since my life-changing dream.
I identified six significant traumas I had experienced.
The final trial was yet to come.

God was bolstering me throughout this grim time and had not abandoned me.

Harrow International Christian Centre (HICC) became our new church home. It was much closer to us, and after visiting there a few times, I decided to join this church.

The deal was sealed when the pastor, another Michael from Solihull, suddenly said:

"Therefore there shall now be no condemnation for those in Christ Jesus."

My heart skipped a beat when I heard this, and I knew it was where God wanted us to be; that was my confirmation.

It was a much bigger church than we were accustomed to, and the services were held in a plain hall with a few side rooms and a café upstairs. The congregation were friendly, and we were invited to join their small study groups, where we made new friends.

~

Adam was granted a placement in an Assessment Centre in Harrow alongside others who had experienced similar mental health crises, and I was thankful to God for this breakthrough.

There, he learned crucial life skills, like budgeting and cooking. The environment was bright and welcoming, staffed by competent individuals and inhabited by fellow residents on similar journeys. I was optimistic that he could build a solid foundation for managing his life there. Even though it was operated by a secular organisation.

Fortuitously, the local council assigned him a council flat after his discharge. However, a few weeks after moving in, he went missing again. Using the spare key to his flat, I entered and found two empty mugs on the table in the lounge. The bed appeared untouched, which was alarming and made me feel very concerned.

Two days later, he was found in Stevenage, around twenty-three miles away. He had walked there, sleeping in fields and was eventually picked up by the police while wandering on the motorway.

When Adam disappeared for the second time, I was distraught and called every believer I knew to ask them to pray for his safe return, as I was too burdened to pray myself, but God prompted me to do so.

Literally within seconds of my prayer, the phone rang; one of the CID officers shared the good news that they had found him, bringing me incredible relief.

Derek, one of the church leaders, kindly collected me and drove me to the police station in Stevenage to pick him up, as I was in no fit state to drive myself. Adam looked dishevelled and mumbled something like, *"The deer in the fields were talking to me."*

The strange things he said compelled me to try to comprehend his muddled mindset, but this was far outside my knowledge and experience.

HARROW

One afternoon, while browsing through the property ads in the local gazette, something suddenly jumped out at me. It was an advert for a terraced house in South Harrow for sale at £50,000. Surprised by this low price, I thought it must be a misprint; Harrow properties at the time usually sold for at least twice that amount.

When I called the estate agents to enquire about it, they told me the price was correct. It was a run-down house which had been unoccupied for ten years, the agent exclaimed in a rather snooty tone,

"Oh, you mean the derelict one, I wouldn't touch it with a barge pole!" adding disdainfully that I'd need another £25,000 to make it habitable. Scoffing inwardly, I knew deep down that this was the one God had planned for me.

I drove up to Harrow to view it and enlisted Jim, a burly, pleasant, grey-haired, middle-aged Irish builder we had gotten to know from HICC. After his initial inspection, he declared it to be *"Sound!"*

That was good enough for me. Jim was an experienced builder who knew his stuff. The location was very convenient, just a few yards from a mainline tube station. At the end of the road was a huge Waitrose, which I laughingly called my corner shop. It was a short drive from Northwick Park Hospital, where I worked and not far from the church, so I made an offer. Everything went smoothly.

My flat sold quickly, so I moved to South Harrow. After all I had gone through, I loved it and couldn't believe I owned a three-bedroom terraced house yards from the shops and tube station. August 1995 saw me settled into my new home.

You have not given me into the hands of the enemy but have set my feet in a spacious place. Psalm 31:8 NIV

Work began on the house, and my new friends Jim and his wife, Peggy, truly went the extra mile.

I was happy there, putting my stamp on the house, which I christened *'Bethany,'* after the town in the Bible where Jesus' friends Mary and Martha lived, and I fastened a little wooden nameplate to the outside wall next to the front door.

Shortly after moving in, I received a timely check from my parents' estate for a modest amount. I decided to send my sister a portion of it since she was the one who took care of our mother during her illness. It didn't seem fair for us to receive equal amounts when she was the one who did all the work.

This left me with enough to cover the necessary improvements and bring the house up to scratch by installing central heating. I paid Kerry-Ann's compensation back to her and was immensely grateful for this timely windfall. It felt good to right some past mistakes.

In hindsight, I realised that God was at work to restore my finances as only He could. To help cover the mortgage and utility bills, I advertised one of the spare bedrooms for rent, and a petite black lady from Zimbabwe named Delores came to my door enquiring about the room. She seemed very keen, was pleasant, and had excellent references.

A district nurse and devout Christian, who was a member of Kensington Temple, the large church near Emmanuel Assembly. She moved in shortly afterwards and lodged with me for several years. Delores was noticeably quiet and had a limited social life, typically only going out to work or church.

HICC differed from Emmanuel Assembly in several ways: it was much larger, less personal, and more polished. We made many new friends there and joined an evening Bible Study Group.

One evening, a video entitled *'Testimony of the Jellyfish Man'* by Ian McCormack from New Zealand was shown. His story made a lasting impression on me. He was saved from certain death after being stung by a box jellyfish, and I pondered his experiences, particularly the emphasis on the importance of forgiveness.

The main message was that God does not tolerate bitterness or unforgiveness, regardless of how justified it may be. It holds people prisoner and stunts their spiritual growth, erecting a barrier between them and God. Thus, I resolved to release and forgive anyone who had wounded me or my loved ones, realising that forgiveness is not about fairness but grace.

It was liberating!

Sheep

People often say that sheep are unintelligent. This perception of their limited smartness explains why they frequently wander away from the herd and become lost.

The Bible often uses sheep as a metaphor for God's people. We are compared to sheep due to our tendency to follow others blindly. We lack a sense of direction and can't defend ourselves in times of trouble.

All we like sheep have gone astray; we have turned—every one—to his own way; and the LORD has laid on him the iniquity of us all. Isaiah 53:6 ESV

I wasn't sure I liked being compared to a sheep, as they're such dumb animals, but after some thought, I accepted that in a lot of ways, we are like them. We share many of their stubborn, blinkered and mindless ways.

You have anointed my head with oil, Ps. 23:5b NASB

Pastor Michael Carr stood outside the church entrance after each service to shake hands with everyone as they left the building.

One Sunday, as I was about to shake his hand, a wasp stung me on the thumb. Instinctively, I yelped and let out a mild expletive, exclaiming, *"S**t!"*

Feeling acutely embarrassed and ashamed of my spontaneous outburst, I carried on walking, nursing my injured thumb. Pastor Michael seemed unfazed.

Compared to Emmanuel, HICC had a stronger and more international flavour. Speakers from America and Canada, such as Marc Du Pont, a very accomplished speaker with a magnetic personality, contributed to this. He always dressed like a cowboy and frequently preached there.

The era of the Toronto Blessing was upon us, characterised by a heightened awareness of God's love and power. There were outward displays of ecstatic worship, falling over in the Spirit, laughing euphorically, healing, animal noises and speaking in tongues. It was a sight to behold.

Unfamiliar with this strange behaviour, I was unsure how to interpret it. This unusual phenomenon was compelling, but criticism arose regarding whether this movement aligned with biblical teachings.

Initially, many people perceived it as a new wave of the Holy Spirit, but over time, the excitement waned, and regular church activities resumed.

Three years later, I received a strong impression from God that the single members of the church were feeling marginalised and isolated.

Harmony, a Christian singles group, was born, and I had tremendous fun designing eye-catching flyers for this group. Every fortnight, we enjoyed dinner together in a chosen restaurant, providing an opportunity for the group to interact.

Michael Carr, the pastor, asked me to give a talk about the Christian single life in the church. The night before my talk, I couldn't sleep because I was so nervous and excited about my assignment.

The Lord God said, "It is not good for the man to be alone. I will make a helper suitable for him." Gen. 2:18 NIV

In the early hours of the morning, I switched on the radio by my bedside and for the first time, heard Sinead O'Connor's song, *'This is to Mother You'*.

   Wow! .... The words were powerful and appropriate!

It was an emotional experience, a sign from God that reassured me He was with me, bolstering the confidence I needed to deliver my talk the following day. This song, though not overtly Christian, feels as if it takes on the persona of Jesus, conveying a mother's unconditional love like a warm, comforting hug, infusing tenderness and life into every single word.
The lyrics are sung to a haunting, soothing lullaby..

This is to mother you,
To comfort you and get you through
Through when your nights are lonely
Through when your dreams are only blue
This is to mother you.

   ~

This is to be with you.
To hold you and to kiss you too,
For when you need me I will do
What your own mother didn't do
Which is to mother you.

~

For when you need me I will do
What your own mother didn't do
Which is to mother you.

~

All the pain that you have known
All the violence in your soul
All the *'wrong'* things you have done
I will take from you when I come
All mistakes made in distress
All your unhappiness
I will take away with my kiss yes.
I will give you tenderness.

~

For child I am so glad I've found you,
Although my arms have always been around you
Sweet bird although you did not see me
I saw you.   *Sinead O'Connor*

Listening to the words, I felt deeply moved. The singer's
emotive delivery and the raw, honest intensity of the lyrics
brought tears to my eyes.

It identified in me the emotional absence of my own mother during my childhood. My father didn't know how to be a proper dad to my sister and me; he did try his best, and though he was very strict, I knew he loved us. He was always there for me at times when I was heading down a destructive path.

Can a mother forget the baby at her breast and have no compassion on the child she has borne? Though she may forget, I will not forget you! Isa. 49:15 NIV

The next day, the church was full, and my talk was well-received, but I sensed something was still lacking. Pockets of unmet spiritual needs remained among the singles within the church.

My Harmony group was purely social and didn't address the intellectual or emotional needs of single people. As a result, I felt the Lord prompting me to create Quest, a supplementary group that facilitated weekly discussions on pertinent issues affecting singles. We debated the pros and cons of singlehood and explored various related topics, such as the dangers of being in a relationship with someone who does not share our beliefs. Hearing different perspectives was a revelation; I learned a lot from the experiences of others and looked forward to these sessions.

Everyone was welcome, and our group included a diverse range of individuals, such as divorcees, widows, widowers, ex-prisoners, people with special needs, hesitant singles, and a few who chose to stay unmarried. Among us, some bitter divorcees looked for a way to vent their frustrations. These meetings often revealed profound insights into the diverse emotional states of the participants.

Over time, I became attuned to the emotional responses that these deep discussions evoked and learned how to offer comfort and support to those who are distressed and undergoing psychological pain. Emotional overload, I discovered, often arises from conflicting feelings, a flood of emotions happening simultaneously, or an inability to act according to gut instincts.

We have feelings for a reason – they're there to tell us something. Ignoring those feelings doesn't make them disappear.

Our group provided a space for members to connect with others experiencing similar issues and support one another. One marriage that resulted from introductions made in the group gave me a sense of satisfaction, and I was delighted for the couple involved, who have since moved away; sadly, we have now lost touch.

Two intriguing lads, bikers from West London, heard about our group and travelled to join us. They became welcome regulars on our social outings, and their presence enhanced the group's ambience.

Wills, tallish with frizzy light blonde hair that stuck out all over the place, giving him the appearance of an absent-minded professor, while Glenn is the smooth, good-looking, capable one who captured the ladies' interest. He is a fun-loving guy with a dry sense of humour and a quirky appreciation for the slightly bizarre. They were true believers and great fun to be around, and we thoroughly enjoyed their company.

This was the beginning of a long-lasting and valued friendship.

Chapter Ten

EGYPT ~ INTO THE DESERT

LONDON

In 2003, a magazine I picked up from my dentist's waiting area featured a paragraph appealing to people with intriguing life stories to get in touch.

I called them to share my experiences. They showed interest in taking things further, and two weeks later, Alison, their lead journalist, came to my home with a photographer to take photos to accompany my story, which they said they would publish in their next edition.

A copy of the magazine with the article was sent to me… sporting the hook line:

'The Day that Changed My Life' on the front page.

Inside, it relayed the entire story I told them about what had transpired in my marriage, with a few inaccuracies and embellishments regarding the circumstances and additions to what I had said.
Now I know firsthand to question anything I read in magazines and newspapers, as they are seeking sensationalism over truth.
Preferring to keep my past life private from close friends and colleagues, I didn't share my experiences with my colleagues at work.

(I know. I know... (it was counterintuitive to put it in a magazine, but I foolishly thought they'd never read it.)

While working at my desk a week later, Debbie, one of my favourite doctors, came into the office and whispered,

"You're a dark horse," as she passed my desk.

I was at a loss as to what she meant, until she explained that, while at the hairdresser's, she flicked through a magazine and my picture and story in it grabbed her attention — *Busted!*

News spread like wildfire around the office, and the Practice Manager thought it was a clever idea to pin the article on the noticeboard as news about my magazine story rapidly spread throughout the office. I took it down at once, knowing the entire place would be abuzz with gossip about my past life.

Having permitted it to be published in a popular women's magazine, I should have anticipated repercussions. Still, I was naively relying on the fact that none of them read this magazine. It was a hot topic for a week or so, but the attention waned when they found something else to gossip about.

One afternoon in the upstairs office lounge stands out in my mind: while a few of us were having lunch with the TV on in the background, the news of the *9/11 Twin Towers World Trade Centre* disaster in Manhattan, New York, was broadcast.

We stopped eating, our attention focussed on the unfolding of this momentous terrorist attack on the TV screen. As we watched the buildings fall and the ensuing chaos, it felt like we were watching a movie rather than a real-life event. Terrorists claimed the lives of 3,000 people and injured more than 6,000 others in the most devastating attack on America in the nation's history. Profoundly, I remarked that *the world would never be the same again.*

My lodger, Delores, moved with me into the bungalow and transformed the spare bedroom at the front into her own cosy refuge. The bungalow was about a mile from the nearest tube station, making it an ideal location for her to execute her role as a district nurse. She often went out into the community to care for patients throughout the day, so I took comfort in knowing that someone was present in the evenings whenever I was away.

∞

EGYPT 1997 ~ *Deception* ~ *Adam had a Relapse…*

Adam kept in regular contact while in Egypt and mentioned that he didn't see much of his dad because he was always busy, which is exactly what I feared would happen; so this was no surprise.

Magid called one evening in February to inform me that Adam was in the hospital with stomach problems. This set alarm bells ringing and greatly disturbed my peace of mind. I prayed he'd be alright.

Kerry-Ann and I flew out to see him, and we were horrified to learn that he was in a catatonic stupor at a private psychiatric hospital in Maadi, a modern sub-district of Cairo. Magid had thoroughly misled us about his condition.

The hospital room was comfortable and spacious, featuring a peephole in the door for staff to check on him.

Various elaborate flower arrangements adorned the room, which I later discovered were from Ahmed Al Fayad, one of Magid's wealthy business friends.

Lying on a bed connected to copious drips, his eyes were open yet unseeing, and he repeated: *"God is Love,"* in a flat, expressionless voice. He was emaciated, clad in a pale blue galabaya that seemed to accentuate the pallor of his skin beneath his suntan.

Adam had been found in the street in his underwear, having been missing for three days before his admission and was brought to the hospital by the police. Bruises and scratches were evident on his feet, legs, and arms, and he was severely dehydrated. He told me later he had been watching a horror film, which disturbed him at one of Magid's relatives' homes.

Routinely, he was tested for drugs, and the results came back negative, which was no surprise, as Adam wouldn't even take aspirin for a headache. I was furious and frustrated to discover that he underwent electric shock treatment without my consent.

Once again, we were deceived and assured that this was not the case. I was unaccustomed to this culture of deceit and felt vulnerable and out of my depth.

One afternoon, while walking through the yard, a nurse, whom I later learnt was the lead psychiatrist's wife, cornered me and revealed that Adam had indeed received electroconvulsive therapy, authorised and paid for by his father. Incensed, I realised these treatments could potentially cause permanent brain damage.

However, Adam's private treatment was a blessing, as public healthcare in Egypt is, at best, gruesome and rudimentary. Hygiene in some medical facilities is seriously lacking.

The consultant psychiatrist spoke with me and denied administering any such treatment, despite Adam maintaining that he did experience this and reported sharp pain and wires being attached to his skull and legs.

It was eye-opening to discover that even senior officials in this country would lie at the slightest prompting. Documentation I reviewed later confirmed that he had received six of these treatments. Indignant and appalled at being deceived once more, I feared this experience might have long-term negative impacts.

Kerry-Ann and I visited him daily for the remainder of his time in the hospital. Once he was well enough, we insisted that he come home with us because the environment he was living in was too stressful and contributed to his mental decline.

He couldn't handle it. In his apartment, we noticed a Bible on one side of his bed, a Koran on the other, and a large picture of angels on the wall above, indicating his confused mental state.

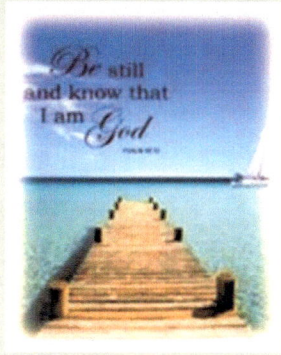

EGYPT

During our next visit to Egypt, Magid suggested Amani, Adam, and me take a break in Sharm el-Sheikh.

We undertook a 500km-long, arduous journey by road in a battered taxi across the desert. It was barren, hot, and uncomfortable, especially when we stopped halfway at a shabby and less-than-clean rest house in the middle of nowhere.

I was transported to the Biblical story of the Israelites' journey through the desert, which has a strange, mesmerising, uncluttered beauty, and I envisioned their lives and struggles. With no Mothercare, McDonald's, bathrooms, toilets, or any other everyday comforts and facilities which we take for granted, only that which nature provided, yet their clothes lasted throughout the forty years. God miraculously provided for their every need.

God was with them as a pillar of cloud by day and a pillar of fire by night, guiding them on their journey.

Absorbing the vastness of the desert is an inspirational and deeply moving experience.

The timeless tranquillity feeds the soul in a way nothing else can, free from worldly distractions. In the stillness, one's spirit is exposed to the breath of God and hears His gentle whisper. *There is an inherent sense of the presence of a higher realm.* Picturing the Israelites feeding their animals from the sparse bushes and tufts of grass, lapping from the wadies, I pondered that finding water would have been tough.

I imagined the noise and smells that permeated the atmosphere. Their sandals never wore out during their forty years of wandering.

I have led you forty years in the wilderness, and your sandals have not worn off your feet. Deut. 29:5 ESV

Unrelenting rays of the sun scorched the land. Yet, there was an indescribable peace and otherworldliness in the stillness of that vast space that remains in my soul — a palpable connection with these ancient wanderers that truly melted my heart, transporting me back to ancient days.

My imagination took hold, and I pictured them in their tents, tending their animals and small children. The High Priest would have blown the shofar *(goat's horn)* to gather them to prayer in the Tabernacle.

These people experienced God's tangible presence under the leadership of the prophet Moses, yet they still rebelled. *Like us*, they were quite stubborn.

When we arrived at the hotel in Sharm el-Sheikh seven hours later, Adam immediately placed his mobile phone and trainers in the fridge as they were boiling, which greatly amused Amani and me.

Two days later, while in a taxi en route to St Catherine's Monastery, my heart was in my mouth when we were stopped at an army checkpoint. Soldiers carrying rifles were overly aggressive with our driver, goading and intimidating him, demanding to know how much we were paying, what he was doing with us, and if he was selling us cannabis.

My heart raced, but I played dumb, pretending I didn't understand what they were saying. Beads of sweat poured down my back; I held my breath as they began to interrogate Adam about his identity documents. His mental health was still unstable, and I was nervous about how he would respond to them. Fortunately, he had a gold Hilton card, which I took from his shirt pocket and showed them. This did the trick, and to my immense relief, they waved us on... *Phew! We could breathe again!*

St Catherine's is a fascinating Greek Orthodox monastery on Mount Sinai, sacred to all three monotheistic religions: Islam, Judaism, and Christianity. Each sees it from their own spiritual viewpoint. Its location, reputed to be the very place where God appeared to Moses in the Burning Bush, is around eight miles south of Eilat.

The relics of St Catherine of Alexandria are enshrined there, hence its name. In the ninth century, these relics were discovered on Mt Sinai and are now stored in the monastery.

According to the legend of St Catherine, this young woman converted to Christianity after receiving a vision. At the age of eighteen, she debated with fifty pagan philosophers. Amazed at her wisdom and debating skills, they embraced Christianity—as did about two hundred soldiers and members of the emperor's family. Many of the monks are Greek, and they gave us a guided tour.

We were reliably informed that it is the oldest continuously inhabited Christian monastery, with a history that can be traced back over seventeen centuries.

Now Moses was tending the flock of Jethro, his father-in-law, the priest of Midian, and he led the flock to the far side of the wilderness, where he came to Horeb, the mountain of God.
2. There the angel of the Lord appeared to him in flames of fire from within a bush. Moses saw that though the bush was on fire it did not burn up.
3. So Moses thought, "I will go over and see this strange sight—why the bush does not burn up." Exo. 3: 1 - 3 NIV

The earliest description refers to God's revelation at the Burning Bush, and a chapel of that name now stands on this site.

Gobby Americans mocked the guide and made irreverent and dismissive comments about his description of the surroundings. sneering at those who respected this holy site, making us wonder why they had come to such a sacred site in the first place if they felt that way.

The monastery, dedicated to Moses, is purported to be where God spoke to him and where he received the two stone tablets of the Law, also known as *the Ten Commandments*.

Located in a remote region, it boasts a captivating history and serves as a pilgrimage site. It has been maintained in its original state. A small chapel dedicated to the Virgin Mary sits atop the mountain behind the monastery. Although we were curious about what lay ahead at the peak, we opted against climbing to the top in the sweltering heat. The ascent appeared daunting, so we remained at ground level.

The sleeveless dress I wore that day was a poor choice for that environment, as one of the monks kept gently rubbing his finger up and down my arm, which was somewhat unsettling, and a wake-up call for me to cover up. They explained that when monks sin, they must remain in the outer sanctuary and are not allowed to enter the inner part of the monastery until they have completed their penance. I felt a little sorry for this monk, and I hoped he wouldn't be penalised for this minor indiscretion.

As the oldest continually operating library, with its unique, rare works, it is home to the Codex Sinaiticus, a manuscript dating back to the 4th century. It is the most well-known of these manuscripts as the earliest and most complete surviving copy of the Greek version of the Scriptures (the Septuagint).

It also features icons depicting Jesus as Christ Pantocrator with two contrasting facial expressions on each side, emphasising His dual nature: God and man.

Visiting the monastery was an incredible experience. In the outer area, there was an icon of St Paul with short hair. He didn't look as I had imagined him at all. Another icon of St Peter, with short grey hair, was displayed, and one of St Catherine.

Many legends and miracles are attributed to this amazing lady, who was brutally beheaded.

A tribe of Bedouin Arabs lived around the monastery's perimeter and practised a unique hybrid religion, combining elements of Islam and Christianity. Eager to capture this experience, I took photos of these primitive tribespeople. I poised my camera, but they resisted this idea.

Their reluctance to have their picture taken stems from the belief that it is considered *'haram'* (a sin) to create images of themselves, whether they are three-dimensional, drawn, painted, or photographed. To my shame, my desire for a memento of our time there overcame my consideration for their feelings. The few photos I sneakily managed to take didn't develop, which was extremely disappointing. It did occur to me that supernatural intervention was involved, chastising me for not being respectful and for disregarding their religion and culture.

It was well worth the visit. However, Adam didn't absorb much of what the guide said due to his mental state, and Amani struggled to comprehend his talk. He spoke only in English, but it was too complex for me to interpret. Still, I did my best to translate what little I could for her.

I was touched when she surprised me with a small gold pendant she bought, fashioned into the shape of a map of Egypt.

∞

LONDON – 1996 ~ *Adam left for Cairo*

Six months after we returned home, Adam, now nineteen, opted to return to Egypt to be with his father. He packed his belongings and caught a flight to Cairo. I felt uneasy about this and worried that Magid would not allow him enough time.

However, I was confident that Amani, Amr, and Hassan, along with other relatives, would do their utmost to support him and ensure his well-being, though I appreciated they had their own lives and obligations to consider.

Magid phoned to tell me that he arrived safely. He commented that he was horrified when Adam came off the plane wearing a gigantic cross around his neck in a mainly Muslim country, revealing his total innocence and lack of understanding of the culture he was entering; I smiled inwardly and thought,

'Good on you!'

He attended the American University in Cairo to study film, art and music, excelling for three years. During this time, he

201

participated in theatre programs and discovered a passion for filmmaking.

This experience benefited him when he returned home, where he showcased his artistic talents through notable drawings, including a self-portrait, as well as poetry, writing, music composition, acting, and directing plays. He starred in a show called

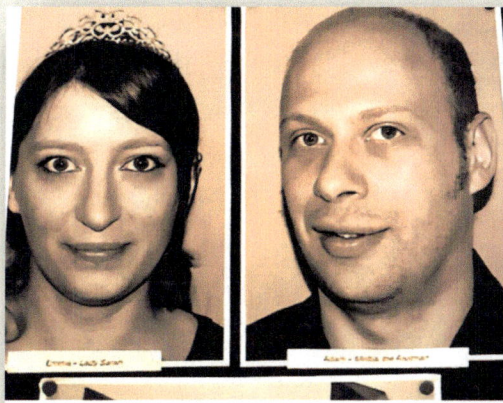

'Putting on the Blitz' when he got back home. He was also featured in a TV advert for a soda syphon soft drink, so he was kept busy.

    Kerry-Ann came to stay with me for a week and was intrigued when Casey, my cat, wrapped herself around my neck like a scarf. She was such a quirky little character, and dropped socks, underwear, and babies' mittens she had stolen from neighbours' washing lines onto each step of the stairs.

On one occasion, when a plumber came to fix a leak in the bathroom, he appeared puzzled by the items on the staircase, although I don't think he believed my explanation. He gave me a funny look.

Collecting them in a basket, I took them round to the neighbours to see if anyone might claim them, but, surprisingly, no one did.

Much to everyone's amusement, Casey meandered up our street with a carrier bag in her mouth, as if she were going shopping. Her habit of sneaking into my bedroom and jumping down from a high shelf on top of me in the middle of the night drove me crazy. She would bring me a flower in her mouth and drop it next to me when I was ill, which was sweet and touching, so I could never stay cross with her for long.

In this little terraced house in Harrow, we had frequent social gatherings in my cosy front room. Our group was close-knit, filled with lively conversations and laughter.

David, whose mother was Jewish, taught me about Jesus' Hebrew name '*Yeshua*'.

Although a Christian, he wore a *kippah* (skullcap) and took immense pride in his Jewish heritage. Jewish heritage is only valid if your mother is Jewish. (*I was amused when I thought, Jesus was alright then, as His mother was Jewish).*

What he shared was vital to my understanding of Jesus' ethnic origins and a blessing and encouragement to my devotion to the Lord. The Jewish aspects and interpretation of Scripture are enormously enriching, revealing new insights and precious truths. I'm grateful for God's Word and appreciate David's enthusiasm and patience in explaining things clearly and thoroughly.

Alice became a special friend, part of a small Saturday morning ladies' group with me and others of a similar age at the church. The group, known as *'The Broken Circle'*, consisted of six or seven of us who met regularly to discuss our struggles and experiences of God at work and to pray about one another's problems.

Not long after, I changed jobs and began working in a GP Practice. Working there was fascinating because I learned about conditions I had never encountered before; the general practice encompassed every aspect of medicine.

Laura, a medical secretary, shared an office with me. Jewish, and quite loud, with a penchant for drama, when I told her I was a Christian, she responded,

"Not a fundamentalist, I hope?"

Her question made me think, and I concluded that I am, indeed, a fundamentalist, since I uphold beliefs in Biblical infallibility and inerrancy in keeping with traditional Christian doctrines concerning the interpretation, the role of Jesus in the Bible, and the role of the Church in society.

However, I am neither legalistic nor do I feel superior to those with alternative beliefs. Our culture and faith are an accident of birth, and I accept that we are conditioned by the things we're taught when growing up.

Life carried on with its ups and downs, and after five more years, I decided to sell my house and relocate to a bungalow a few miles away.

LONDON

Adam returned home with us when he was well enough to travel.

Since he had given up his accommodation in Harrow to move to Egypt, he now had nowhere to stay. He stayed with me in the meantime while waiting for new accommodation to become available, but was annoyed that he had to sleep in the box room as I had let out the bedroom he had previously used.

Fortunately, he didn't have to wait long and was temporarily moved into a lovely ground-floor flat with a glass door leading to a small, tidy patio garden in Central Harrow. Six months later, a third-floor flat in a block in Northolt, just a mile from me, became his new home.

Although this permanent accommodation wasn't in as good a location and was of a lower standard than the temporary one, I was grateful that he was offered this new place, given his circumstances.

Ben, a gentle giant, a builder, a talented musician, and a friend from (HICC), known for his impressive musical talent *(he was a celebrated tuba player)*, invited Adam and me to join him, his girlfriend Julie, and a few other friends at Christ Church, located a few miles away at Harrow-on-the-Hill, the following Sunday.

Upon our arrival, we found ourselves enthusiastically recruited to join the church choir and practised singing *Handel's*

Messiah, scheduled to be performed in the local shopping centre over Christmas.

The other members of the choir and the conductor were inspirational, so I opted to join them. Dressed in a striking red and gold uniform, I felt exhilarated as I sang this stirring chorus with the choir, catching the shoppers by surprise and grabbing their attention. It was uplifting and inspiring.

FLORIDA

In early May 2001, I travelled to Florida once again. My former pastor's wife, Joan, provided me with the contact details of a Christian friend, Phyllis, a New Yorker who was living in Fort Lauderdale, and asked me to visit her.

Hearing that she was looking forward to my visit was comforting when I rang her. Despite being in her mid-sixties, she was attractive, a lookalike of Elizabeth Taylor.
She was a one-of-a-kind, unlike anyone I had ever met before, a fascinating, loud, straight-talking, committed Christian lady. I was astounded when, despite never having met me, she told me she'd be out when I arrived at her home, so,

"Just walk in and make yourself at home till I get back," she announced in her New York drawl. She had left her front door unlocked, so I pushed it open and entered a beautifully furnished split-level home. She invited me to stay with her. We got along well, and she introduced me to her friends, one of whom was also named 'Joann'.

"Would you like to come to my church with me?" she asked. I was delighted to join her.

Phyllis wouldn't tolerate anything she considered unbiblical or duplicitous and had no qualms about expressing her views if something didn't align with her Biblical beliefs. Several churches asked her to leave due to her outspoken nature.

The most recent church service she attended was held in the community room of a local bank, and some people strolled in dressed casually, with some carrying kayaks over their shoulders. This was a strange sight for me.

As a visitor, the leader asked me to speak at the front and share a bit about myself, so I summarised my background and Christian walk.

Phyllis's friend, the other Joann, took great delight in calling me in the mornings to say *"Hi Joann, ... it's Joann!"* in her distinctive Florida accent. She had a reputation for being a hypochondriac, so most people dismissed her constant health complaints as trivial.

Sadly, they were all put to shame when her lifeless body was discovered on her bathroom floor one morning, after suffering heart failure. Her friends and family, including us, were in a state of shock, as she was only in her late forties. There was a deep sense of shame for not taking her seriously and failing to give her the support she needed. Phyllis and I talked late into the night, comparing our experiences.

She had two daughters, Re and Vicky, and Scott, her rebellious son. Phyllis had been married five times. She married two more times while I knew her, making her even more like the legend Elizabeth Taylor. We became close friends, and I admired her very much. She made me smile when she remarked, waving at her clothes,

"If it isn't permanent press, it's goin' to the Thrift Shop!"
Her abrasive tongue concealed a kind heart. One day, she gifted me a beautiful wine-coloured, leather-bound American Standard Bible with my name embossed in gold on the front cover. It was such a thoughtful gift that I treasured it, and it remains my constant companion.

Phyllis was a force to be reckoned with, a devout if unconventional Christian, and nobody dared cross her. Any unbeliever who came to her home wouldn't escape without saying the *Sinner's Prayer* before leaving. She would make them sit on a chair and recite :

"HEAVENLY FATHER, I come to you in the name of JESUS. I acknowledge to YOU that I am a sinner, and I am sorry for my sins and the life that I have lived, and I recognise that I need YOUR forgiveness."

Her devil-may-care attitude regarding what others thought was both refreshing and amusing at times. Her eldest daughter, Re *(short for Marie),* was just as glamorous, but not as brash as her mother.

Occasionally babysitting for her, I enjoyed minding her two young sons, Alex and Davy. We had a marvellous time, playing games and chasing raccoons from Phyllis's backyard.

One day, on the boardwalk of the back porch, Davy looked at me and yelled, *"Get inside now!"*

I glanced down, and there was a snake, a water moccasin, slithering along the boards. *Yikes!* White-faced and stricken, he yelled anxiously,

"One bite from that, and you're dead!"

We sprinted inside as fast as we could, having had a narrow escape!

Phyllis then moved further up the coast to a town called Stuart, where I stayed with her two or three times after that.

Another friend, Barbara, living at Daytona Beach, and a cousin near Jacksonville, were on my list for a visit while I was there. Daytona Beach is 250 miles from Stuart, so I planned to travel by Greyhound bus.

However, Phyllis insisted on driving me there herself, which meant a 500-mile round trip for her, but I knew better than to argue with her about it.

Throughout the journey on the freeway to Daytona Beach, she declared all *'soul ties'* broken in my life. Phyllis believed that these are real effects that come from past relationships.

Significant bonding occurs in most relationships. That's a good thing, and how God planned it to work. It's normal and healthy to be emotionally connected to someone you're in a relationship with. Whether it's from past relationships, family issues, or cultural expectations, that baggage will come up.

However, that doesn't mean you can't work through it or that people with emotional baggage *(everyone)* are *'damaged goods'*. This was an emotionally draining experience.

After spending such a long time together, we bonded, and I was choked when she left me at Barbara's, suddenly missing her intense company. As it happened, that was the last time I saw Phyllis.

Barbara was a lovely, charming, well-groomed lady with many bracelets jangling on her wrists. In contrast, she was more self-conscious and introverted than Phyllis.
In her elegant house for the afternoon, we had coffee and chatted until my cousin Betty and her husband, Ronnie, arrived. They drove from Florahome, an hour's journey from Jacksonville, to collect me from Barbara's house.

Betty is an attractive lady and looks a lot like a younger version of my mother; she bears such a striking resemblance to Mum that she looks more like her than I do. It gave me quite a shock when I first saw her. Her father, William, was one of my mother's five brothers.

Their secluded home, nestled in Florahome, a beautiful countryside area, was designed in a style reminiscent of American Indian architecture and entirely crafted from warm, inviting wood. The guest room I stayed in was a delightful space filled with character, featuring a massive bow and arrow mounted on the wall, in homage to the rugged spirit of the location. I was enchanted by the surroundings; everything was different, new, and thrilling. There was a strong smell of sulphur, and the scent of pine and fresh earth wafted throughout the atmosphere. The sounds of nature created a symphony all around.

In the backyard, a hot tub bubbled invitingly, surrounded by lush greenery and twinkling fairy lights, making it a perfect spot for us to relax and revel in the warmth of this tub, revelling in each other's company.

As we soaked in the bubbling water, laughter echoed through the yard, interrupted only by the deep croaks of an army of bullfrogs serenading us from the nearby pond. The entire experience felt like a dream, rich with new adventures within the comforting presence of family. *What a Blessing!*

Ronnie is a mature, handsome, jovial, chatty ex-Navy man and a true gentleman. They are strong Christians and took me to their little church, where Betty serenaded us with a well-known hymn.

With a quirky sense of humour, Ronnie had cleverly positioned a real iron bedhead at the front of their house, creating a playful pun with the term *'flower bed.'*

Betty has a spacious studio where she makes elegant table lights shaped like angels. She kindly gave me one of her beautiful creations as I was leaving.

Regretting that I had booked a return flight home the following day, I felt sad to leave Florida, as my time there had been special, and I thoroughly enjoyed it.

Chapter Eleven

EGYPT ~ THE LION

By this time, I had lost my parents, my marriage, my financial security, my home, and each of my children in different ways. God had stripped me of everything I relied on.

These were the seven things God had warned me about in my dream.

I had to come to terms with this new chapter of my life,
leaning solely on God with no other support of any kind,
though I still made mistakes in my distress.
Trusting God completely takes time, and I still try to sort
things out myself before consulting the Ruler of the Universe.

He alone is my *Rock* and my *Salvation*. my *Fortress* where I will not be shaken.
Psalm 62:6

Back home in July of that year, my colleague Laura and I grew close, and we often enjoyed having lunch together either at her home or mine, as we both lived near our place of work at the GP practice.

Her only son, Shalev, had just turned thirteen, a significant milestone in Jewish tradition. He had some mental health condition, perhaps somewhere on the autistic spectrum, but I'm not sure exactly what his diagnosis was; however, he was now considered responsible for his actions.

She invited me to attend his bar mitzvah ceremony at a synagogue in North Finchley. I was excited to be a part of it, as I had no prior experience with a bar mitzvah and was eager to learn more about this ceremony.

Traditional rituals, such as reading the Torah and the symbolic act of breaking a glass, are integral to various aspects of the ceremonies. These ancient customs, rich in cultural significance, remind individuals of their Jewish heritage and roots. Although the meanings behind some of them may not always be immediately apparent, they often embody profound historical and spiritual values, passed down through the generations.

~

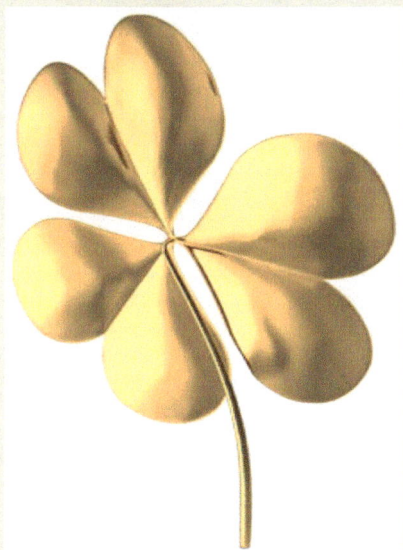

IRELAND

In November 2001, I was informed that my Aunt Sadie, Mum's younger sister, had sadly passed away, and I arranged to fly to Ireland with the children for her funeral.

Since I was in regular contact with the staff at her Nursing Home, I was the first to be notified of her death, and it was then that I gained access to her medical notes. Shock filled me when I read that she had received a diagnosis of schizophrenia, which resonated because of Adam's diagnosis. This was the hereditary connection, as well as the strong possibility that this illness was also in his dad's lineage. Adam had a predisposition to this condition on both sides.

My sister Violet, her husband Eddie, and their six, now adult, children were there. It was lovely to see them all again, despite the sad circumstances.

Aunt Sadie had lived in Londonderry all her life. As we were also born and spent our early childhood there, we had many other relatives whom we hadn't seen for some time to catch up with.

EGYPT

Magid called again and this time asked me to come to Cairo, promising to help me renew my Egyptian passport, which had expired about five years earlier.

I rarely used it, except to obtain reduced rates at tourist sites in Egypt, but he knew I enjoyed having it. I wondered why he was so concerned about my expired passport now. However, the thought of seeing Amani and their extended family again drew me there.

Once again, he booked me into the Hilton. I confided in Amani that Magid's passport must have been revoked, given that he hadn't travelled in a long time, which was most unusual. I wondered if this enforced stay had any connection with his request.

He was a frequent globetrotter, but when she confronted him about this, he responded with characteristic arrogance, declaring,

"I can travel anywhere I like, whenever I like." However, significantly, he couldn't act upon it.

Pride will delude you into thinking you have almost God-like qualities that demand the respect and reverence of others.
(see 1 Kings 1:5)

The three of us had dinner in an Indian restaurant the evening after my arrival, and I noticed the atmosphere was tense. Even Amani, who was usually incredibly happy to see me, seemed cold and distant. Amani's attitude led me to suspect that Magid had created a story portraying me negatively, to turn her against me.

I desperately wanted to leave, but didn't know how to get back to the hotel by myself. I was relying on them for directions, so I reluctantly decided to stay.

When I got back to the hotel, a surge of anger and frustration welled up inside me at their dismissive attitude. I had done nothing to deserve this, so I stormed off to my room, needing space to process my emotions. The atmosphere in the restaurant had been thick with unresolved tension, and I felt my heart racing as I replayed his degrading attitude and cutting words. About an hour later, as I began to calm down and settle for the night, I flinched when the phone's shrill ring broke the silence. Glancing at the caller ID, I saw it was an outside call, and suspected it was Magid. Hesitating momentarily, I didn't really want to talk to him, but I was curious about the reason for his call, so I picked up the phone. His tone was markedly different from earlier; backpedalling, he was trying to smooth things over.

"Hey, what are you up to?" he asked in a casual and friendly manner, as if nothing had happened. He quickly shifted the conversation to our plans for the next day, wanting to make sure that I would still accompany him to the Government Building *to renew my passport*. As he spoke, I still wondered why he was so concerned about the status of my Egyptian passport.

Why did it matter to him?

I briefly considered his motives, but in my agitated state, I dismissed the thought, concluding that it wasn't worth pursuing. However, I smelled *a rat* and knew he must have had some ulterior motive.

The building he took me to was old and imposing. At the formidable entrance stood a young girl who whispered,

"Enti gameela!" (You are beautiful.)

I whispered, *"Shoukran"* (Thank you).

Her impromptu, childlike compliment made me smile and lifted my spirits.

A warren of corridors stretched throughout the dismal interior of this building. We walked through, and I was led to one of their dark, musty offices, where an official-looking document in Arabic was presented to me for my signature. I signed it without question, but I noticed the clerk giving me an odd look.

Why didn't I ask for a translation?

What was I thinking?

Oh, how gullible I was! Like a lamb to the slaughter!

It was a divorce petition. I later learned he was desperate to acquire this because Heike, his new German partner, was pregnant, and they wanted to get married. It all began to make sense.

I was annoyed with myself because I had spent so much time and resources finalising our divorce in the UK and expected him to contribute towards the cost; instead, once again, he pulled the wool over my eyes and got off scot-free, making me feel frustrated and humiliated that I had been taken advantage of yet again.

He pulled it off and must have been laughing up his sleeve, but I resolved to move on, let it go, and just let everyone get on with their lives.

Isaiah 41:10

"Fear not, for I am with you; be not dismayed, for I am your God; I will strengthen you, I will help you, I will uphold you with my righteous right hand."

Cairo Zoo was on my list to visit on my last day, as traffic was too congested to go anywhere on a Sunday *(I didn't want to stress about being late for the airport),* and it was within easy walking distance from the hotel.

A revelation, though for all the wrong reasons, was that this zoo kept animals in poor conditions, as highlighted in negative reviews. They appeared skinny, many were caged alone, and their enclosures were visibly dirty and reeked of urine. The care for these unfortunate creatures was of a low standard. Hopefully, they will make improvements in their welfare and environment.

Since it was a Saturday, the zoo was packed with families and kids enjoying picnics on the grass or benches. Some young couples were clearly on a date; their eyes fixed on each other. The animals seemed curious about the visitors but not overtly friendly.

Life is far from easy in Egypt, and its values differ from ours in the Western world. However, this brief visit to the zoo gave me a glimpse into their daily lives that was both insightful and revealing.

Amr called me after I returned home, and I was bewildered when he declared, *"Joann, you are my hero!"*

Bewildered, I asked him why, and he explained that he had seen a photo of me holding a lion. I'd forgotten that I posted snaps of my Cairo Zoo exploits on social media.

They had allowed me to lift a young lion when Baksheesh changed hands. It felt heavy, but I wasn't frightened; it was docile and like lifting a large dog.

∞

The Seventh Trial ~ *Kerry-Ann emigrated to New Zealand in 2000*

On returning from a three-week holiday in New Zealand, Kerry-Ann told me she had decided to emigrate there and a few months later, at the age of 29, she left.

She had met Julian, a former colleague from a large accounting firm in London, in Auckland. They began a relationship that lasted seven years and ultimately led them to rent a place together. *(She had still not regained her faith.)*

While it was a huge wrench to see her go, I respected her choice and hoped they'd decide to settle back in England eventually, but sadly, it wasn't to be.

Julian and Kerry-Ann eventually moved to Melbourne, Australia, where they married and now have three wonderful children: their eldest son, Oliver, followed by twins Elsa and Charles, born two years later.

We flew over for their wedding.

AUSTRALIA

In March 2007, Kerry-Ann and Julian arranged their wedding at a picturesque winery near Melbourne, promising a beautiful and memorable setting.

Tony was determined to make the most of our trip, so he enthusiastically organised a hire car and kicked off our adventure in vibrant Sydney.

I wondered how Kerry-Ann was getting on with the wedding arrangements and was glad she had her friends there to help, so I gave her a call to let her know we had arrived in Sydney.

After our meal, we embarked on our long road trip adventure to Melbourne, excitement bubbling within me as we began the journey, with stunning coastal views on one side and sprawling landscapes on the other.

This journey also gave me the chance to reconnect with an old friend, Daphne, a devout Christian lady from HICC, our former church in Harrow. She had emigrated to Australia four years earlier and settled in Narra, a charming small town on the coast.

Along the way, we were captivated by the sight of kangaroos and wallabies roaming freely in their natural habitat. We bravely ventured close to a few of them. They looked threatening, especially the large, muscular bucks, so we quickly backed off behind a wall to safety.

Kangaroo males can reach 7. 5' *(over 2.2 metres)* from the tip of the nose to the end of the tail, and a large male can weigh up to 180 lbs. *(81 kgs).*

Females can reach 5. 5'*(1.6 metres)* in total length and weigh about 70lbs *(32 kgs)*.

We were filled with anticipation for the festivities ahead. Kerry-Ann and Julian's wedding was just around the corner.

As a special treat and a memento, we ordered personalised chocolate bars with Kerry-Ann and Julian's names printed on the wrappers and carefully kept them in a cool box to ensure they remained pristine for their special occasion.

The wedding itself was a joyous affair attended by many, and in the absence of Kerry-Ann's dad, I was honoured to deliver a heartfelt speech and read this well-known Irish blessing over them:

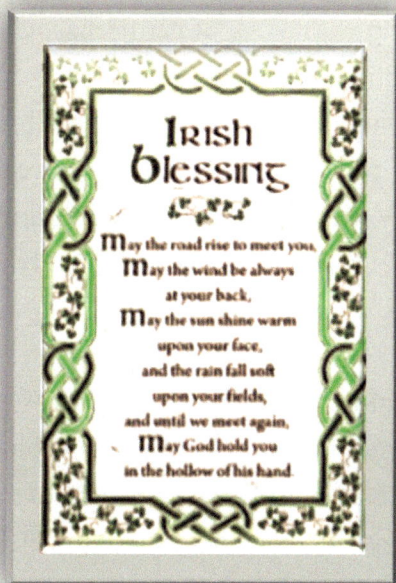

Irish
blessing

May the road rise to meet you,
May the wind be always
at your back,
May the sun shine warm
upon your face,
and the rain fall soft
upon your fields,
and until we meet again,
May God hold you
in the hollow of his hand.

Kerry-Ann looked stunning in her elegant white dress, yet I couldn't help but feel a tinge of sadness that they hadn't chosen to exchange vows in a church.

However, the entire experience was truly unforgettable. It was nice to catch up with a few of her friends who had made the journey from the UK.

The following October, they flew back to England to have their wedding blessed in a church in Gloucestershire with Julian's family and to give friends and relatives who were unable to travel to Australia the opportunity to join them for the blessing event.

~

Julian hails from Gloucestershire and returned to the UK with Kerry-Ann mainly to have their marriage blessed. This way, friends and family who hadn't been able to travel to Australia for their wedding would have the chance to celebrate their union.

During a later visit, they also planned to have their children christened, which they believed would improve their chances for better school admissions. Unfortunately, neither Julian nor Kerry-Ann had a strong Christian faith, and their motivations for these ceremonies were purely secular.

The joy of being reunited with them and spending precious moments with my grandchildren made their visits something we always looked forward to with excitement.

In the early years of their relationship, Julian and Kerry-Ann embarked on adventurous journeys, exploring distant lands and immersing themselves in diverse cultures.

Upon their return, they planned a stopover in the dazzling city of Dubai, where Kerry-Ann had arranged to reconnect with Magid, who had established a new life there.

A palpable anticipation must have filled the air as they waited to meet him. However, when Magid failed to appear, the atmosphere must have quickly shifted.

Knowing Kerry-Ann, she would probably have wrestled with a surge of emotions—hurt, bitter disappointment, and a nagging worry about his well-being. She rang to tell me about this and sounded very worried. Their attempts to reach him through his office and personal mobile deepened the mystery, leaving her restless and anxious.

The enigma surrounding Magid's disappearance was ultimately unravelled when Amr contacted me with shocking news:

Magid had been arrested and deported to Egypt.

He was confined in a notorious prison near Alexandria, Borg El-Arab, a detention centre known for its harsh conditions.

Filled with uncertainty about the specific charges levelled against him, I suspected they involved the misappropriation of funds; his non-violent demeanour sharply contrasted with his dubious business practices. Driven by a relentless hunger for wealth and an unscrupulous attitude toward money, fraud and embezzlement were unquestionably high on the list of potential crimes.

While he was confined to prison, he called and painted a vivid picture of the grim conditions he was enduring. It struck me that the harsh realities of his unfamiliar environment would be particularly jarring for someone so accustomed to a life of ease, indulging in the comforts and luxuries he had acquired at the expense of others.

This drastic shift from opulence to squalor and confinement would be a harsh and rude awakening for him, though it was hard to feel pity.

A year later, he was transferred to *Al-Aqrab Prison* in Cairo, in an industrial area south of the city. This facility primarily houses individuals convicted of political and white-collar crimes. Details about his detention and upcoming trial remained vague.

Obtaining information on such matters from government agents in Egypt can be extremely challenging. Government workers are very tight-lipped, especially when interacting with foreigners.

When he was able to, he reached out to me.

Kerry-Ann, Adam, and I flew to Cairo to gather more information about the situation. We were concerned about how this would affect Amani, who was unaware of our visit, and we surprised her by arriving unexpectedly outside her apartment.

Knocking on her door, I called out, *"Open!"* in a very authoritative tone. When she opened the door and saw the three of us standing there, her face was a picture of surprise. She was overjoyed to see us, hugged each of us in turn and urged us inside. She wanted us to stay there with her in her flat, but we preferred to keep our independence rather than inconvenience her.

Instead, we opted to stay in an Anglican Diocesan Guest House, located in Zamalek—a popular area in central Cairo—recommended to us by a friend from our church.

This guesthouse was situated on a narrow street opposite All Saints' Cathedral, and although it was quite basic, it had a homely atmosphere that suited us well.

Outside my room was a small balcony, and in the mornings, I was serenaded by sweet singing emanating from the large, opulent cathedral across the road.

Glorious! — This angelic sound seemed to echo off the walls, instantly transporting me to a higher realm. The guests, most of whom were visiting missionaries of various nationalities, used the dining area, and numerous engaging conversations ensued around the large breakfast and dinner table. The dining style was mostly a help-yourself buffet, featuring plain and simple dishes without any fancy options. We had a rota for dishwashing duties, and we prepared our own drinks and other necessities. The guesthouse didn't offer any services, and we enjoyed taking care of things for ourselves.

The manager was a young, efficient woman in her late twenties from Upper Egypt. Her name was Helbees, which I found intriguing, as it was a name I had never encountered before. We got to know her well and we became good friends. She is a strong Christian and has kept in touch with us for many years afterwards.

The Marriott Hotel became our unexpected sanctuary, conveniently located at the top of the street where we were staying. By sheer good fortune *(or God's blessing),* an Egyptian friend of mine, who worked for the General Electric Company of Egypt, provided us with a valuable lifeline; a room number for their permanent guest accommodations at the hotel.

Such a simple act of kindness opened the door to a world of comfort and luxury we eagerly embraced. We took advantage of the hotel's inviting amenities, basking in the sun by the glistening swimming pool and relishing the pristine bathroom facilities, with a sauna, steam room and jacuzzi—an oasis compared to our guesthouse's cramped quarters, where we often found ourselves waiting in line to navigate the unreliable, leaky showers.

All Saints' Cathedral was a fascinating place to visit. We often attended services there and prayer meetings and strolled around the vast courtyard, where the on-site shop sold papyrus, icons, and other tourist items. Groups from Sudan, Eritrea, and Upper Egypt often gathered, and it was interesting to chat with them and the clergy.

Whenever they were available, they prayed with us for Magid and his situation after we explained the circumstances to them. Appropriately, this was the inscription on a stone on the grounds of the cathedral:

And out of Egypt I called my Son. Hosea 11:1

The Christian Guesthouse was closed to Muslims for security reasons and was constantly monitored by a guard carrying an intimidating machine gun, ready for any eventuality.

Amr didn't take offence as he understood the culture and was accustomed to these measures. He was supportive and an invaluable friend, always obliging and compliant with these rules. We met at the café in the Marriott Hotel, and he took us to see Magid at the prison, although he declined to enter.

On our arrival, Adam inoffensively told the Prison Officer in charge, *"I want to see my dad."*
He replied in a mocking tone, *"Oh, your dad; has he got a name?"*
Rigorous security measures were in place during each visit. We were frisked and our bags thoroughly checked before being allowed to enter the prison interior.

Though it was an unsettling and invasive experience, we eventually became accustomed to and resigned to this degrading procedure. After being herded into another room and photographed, we were escorted to the visiting area, where we endured a long wait before Magid appeared to see us.

He looked well, considering the circumstances, and we tried to find out what had happened, but he was reticent to elaborate and kept changing the subject. It was evident he wasn't prepared to give us any details, so we stopped asking.

By now, Amani had retired from her lengthy government career and had received a substantial pension. Many Egyptians either avoid using banks or distrust them, often concealing large sums of money in their homes. Amani was no exception, hiding her pension payout in large bundles at the back of her bedroom wardrobe.

Knowing that she had this cash payment, he constantly implored her to provide him with funds for his cigarettes and to bribe the guards for special privileges. As a loyal, kind, and sensitive soul, she obliged and brought him her money. Each time she visited him, she brought him cash and food in plastic containers wrapped in foil, as he often complained about the quality of the food.

As an innocent and compassionate person, she typically sacrificed her needs to support her remaining brother.

We returned to Cairo when Magid's case went to court. I hired a young, athletic guide and driver, interestingly named Caesar. Of medium height with eyes that looked black, he was serious and formal. When he relaxed and let his guard down and began to trust us, we discovered he had a dry sense of humour and an incredible talent for doing impressively accurate and hilarious impersonations of the people we encountered.

When he did his impressions, it helped lighten the mood, making me laugh, easing my anxiety despite the seriousness of the situation.

His assistance was invaluable; he managed all our activities in this bustling city, allowing me to relax without worrying about logistics or planning.

From what I could gather, Magid was employed in Dubai as an ambassador for an Indian charity. Instead of forwarding substantial donations to those in need, he had pocketed the lion's share. When I asked him about this, he said with a shrug,

"I helped a lot of them, you know."

Biting back a terse, sarcastic response along the lines of

'Oh, well, that's alright then, as long as you let them have some of the donations meant for them.'

Still, I kept my thoughts to myself and wondered how he had persuaded them to trust him with this responsibility. However, I knew he could be very plausible when financial gain was in sight.

A black transit van with bars on the windows rolled up outside the court, and Magid was among the prisoners brought in. They ushered him into a cage-like structure to be tried and to address the judge when called upon to do so.

The proceedings in the courtroom were beyond our comprehension, and Caesar interpreted what he could, telling us it didn't look good for him. He was sentenced to eight years in Tora prison.

On our next prison visit, he looked fine; however, true to form, he began pressing me for yet more money—£10,000.

"Why do you need this?" I asked, feeling put out that he had the gall to ask for more. *"You know what for?"* he calmly responded. Intuitively, I understood that this would be a bribe to facilitate the release of some high-ranking official or to reduce his prison sentence.

Despite this man's boundless audacity and corrupt ways, I considered his request for the sake of the children. They still loved him and were unaware of the implications of his misdemeanours.

Later, I discussed it with them, and while they wanted their dad released, they were uncomfortable with the idea of bribery, though they agreed to contribute £5,000 each, money they had received from me after I sold my house.

Testing them to see how much they cared about their father's freedom, I was proud that they were selfless and willing to give up their own money to expedite his release.

Of course, I intended to reimburse them, but they were unaware of my intentions at the time, making their spontaneous decision both generous and selfless.

Dismayed and desperate to see him released from this horrendous Egyptian jail, we were introduced to Hisham, who was unofficially appointed as his mediator. He looked shifty to me, but Magid assured us he was trustworthy, adding conspiratorially that he could see it in his eyes.

Hah! He could not have been more wrong!

LONDON

When we got back home, Hisham relentlessly called and pressured us to pay this money, always emphasising it was time-sensitive. He bombarded me with constant phone calls, insisting,
"You must transfer it within 48 hours!"
The urgency stressed me out and made it feel like there was no room for negotiation. Unaware of the actual situation, I felt

pressured to comply with his demands and duly transferred the funds.

We were easy targets, innocents abroad, and Hisham took advantage of this. He, of course, pocketed it all and vanished. Filled with anger, frustration, and devastation at being tricked out of such a significant amount for nothing, I felt like a fool for once again being taken for a ride.

To make matters worse, my wallet was stolen on the train from Cairo while I was travelling to my main bank branch in Alexandria. I reported the theft to the police, but this proved futile, as I never recovered my purse. The bank clerk told me there was nothing she could do to get back the £10,000.

Although she appeared genuinely sorry, empathetic, and even somewhat ashamed that one of her compatriots had stooped to such a low level, she could not recoup this money. Moral standards are low, and crime is rampant in this country.

~

Amani steered Kerry-Ann through the vibrant market one sunny morning, immersing her in the colourful stalls brimming with exotic spices, handcrafted goods, and lively chatter.

Meanwhile, I seized this perfect opportunity to embark on a serene boat trip along the legendary Nile River with Adam and Shadia, Amani's charming friend and neighbour.

As our journey concluded, we returned to the dock, where the sturdy boat rested about eighteen inches from the wooden walkway extending towards the shore. The gap between the boat and solid ground felt daunting, especially as I peered into the deep, murky depths of the Nile below—*a dark, swirling abyss that heightened my unease.*

Caesar arrived to pick us up and deftly lifted me from the boat onto the land as though I were a small child. Shadia had already leapt across like a young goat, but he must have noticed the terror in my eyes and sensed my *phobia of deep water.*

"Did you think I would let you fall?" he exclaimed.

Later that evening, he took the kids and me to the Guesthouse in Zamalek.

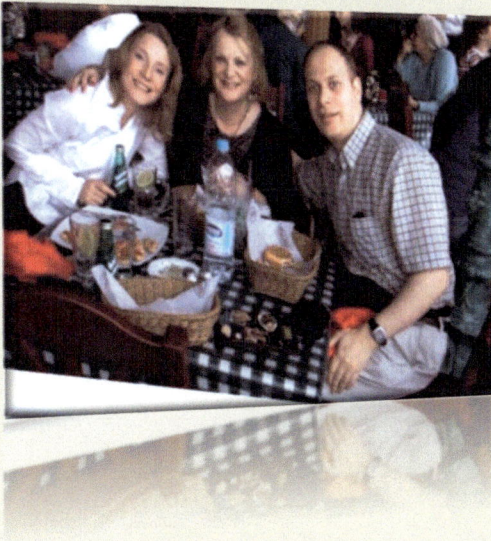

We were too late for tea there, so I took them out to dine in one of the main restaurants on 26th July Street, around the corner.

By now, I had reached the point where I was on the verge of *throwing in the towel* regarding Magid and his self-induced problems, but I knew the depth of love Kerry-Ann and Adam had for him and felt obliged to continue to help him.

Despite everything that had transpired, they still wanted their dad in their lives, and I guess they were hoping things would get back to how they were, but I knew that ship had sailed long ago…

I eventually told Kerry-Ann about her dad using her compensation money, and unsurprisingly, she metaphorically shut the door on him and severed any further contact. *Who could blame her?*

~

My strong faith in God and concern for Adam and Amani played a significant role in my willingness to continue granting him access to our lives, despite having reached the end of my tether.

"For I know my plans for you," declares the Lord, "plans, to prosper you and not harm you, to give you hope and a future" Jer. 29:11 NIV

PART TWO

RESTORATION

Chapter Twelve

LONDON – 2003 ~ A New Romance

Twelve years since my divorce from Magid, on a chilly March evening, I met Tony at the lively Water's Edge pub in the nearby district of Ruislip.

He inadvertently knocked my drink over as he passed our table, where I sat with friends from my Sports Club, and gallantly insisted on replacing it. We chatted, and our conversation flowed effortlessly. Before we parted ways, we exchanged phone numbers.

I knew from experience the issues that arise from being in an unbalanced relationship, so I laid my cards on the table and informed him from the outset that I am a Christian and, therefore, cannot be romantically involved with someone who doesn't share my faith. It took me quite some time to fully understand the importance of this principle, which led to my making many mistakes that I promised myself I would never repeat.

When the Apostle Paul says, *"Do not be unequally yoked,"* he emphasises two main points.

First, we should avoid forming close associations with unbelievers who do not live for Jesus. Second, entering into any intimate relationship or partnership with someone who does not put Jesus at the centre of their life can ultimately cause our downfall.

Hard though it is, I knew we must sever ties with anything or anyone that leads us into darkness. I learnt this the hard way.

To my surprise and relief, Tony accepted my beliefs, embraced them, and began attending church with me, ultimately resulting in his baptism at Harrow International Christian Centre.

In November 2003, after enduring months of pain when I could hardly walk, I was admitted to the Royal National Orthopaedic Hospital in Stanmore for my first hip surgery. Tony faithfully visited me most days, although it was a 60-mile round trip.

Adam also often came to see me with his friend Keiran, a lovely young police officer from our church.

Bed baths were a regular daily occurrence and a new experience for me. Due to the trauma of the operation and the inevitable pain and immobility that followed, I felt vulnerable, weepy and depressed.

A beautiful bouquet from my work colleagues lifted my spirits, and Dr Seyan, one of the main GPs in our Practice, came to visit me, which cheered me up enormously.

Following the regulatory physiotherapy, once the consultant was satisfied that I could walk up and down stairs and use the bathroom unaided, I was discharged home to begin my long recovery.

In the meantime, Adam travelled to Salem, Oregon, to visit my cousin Bill and his wife Judy for a brief getaway.

I was delighted that he had the opportunity to experience a new environment, hoping it would benefit him, and he'd make the most of it.

On his return, he eagerly shared stories about his adventures, and I was delighted to see that he had had such an exciting time. Bill generously gifted him a high-end camera, which brought Adam immense joy, and he proudly showed it off to all his friends.

Shortly after this, he sadly experienced another psychotic episode and went missing for two days. When he was eventually found, he was admitted once again to the Mental Health Unit of Northwick Park Hospital. Insisting that his name was *'Gaia'*, he refused to respond to *'Adam'*. His eyes were red, staring, and his voice deeper than usual. Alarmed, I recognised this was demonic possession and prayed for his deliverance.

Disturbed about the link to ancient Egypt, since Gaia is an ancient Egyptian deity, I invoked the name of Jesus, and he promptly regained his usual persona. The psychiatrist Adam was under discharged him two weeks after this unsettling incident, and prescribed new medication to stabilise him.

~

Shortly after my second hip resurfacing operation, while I was still teetering about on crutches, Nick, a friend of Adam's, invited us to spend Christmas with him at his sister Lorna's hotel on the Isles of Scilly. We flew across to St Mary's by helicopter from Penzance, which was a new and exciting experience.

Our time there was unforgettable as we explored the picturesque neighbouring islands, such as St Agnes, Bryher, Tresco, St Martin's, each with a unique character. Lorna accompanied us on our outings with her son Ethan, a tall, sturdy, blonde-haired young man of about nineteen. Sadly, they were not believers and didn't attend any church, so we hunted for a service to attend on Christmas Day. Lorna's cooking skills were renowned, and she refused any help, making sure I didn't have to lift a finger during our stay.

(I don't think she trusted me in her kitchen.)

Alan and Janet, their parents, also joined us at Lorna's Bijou Country Hotel for the Christmas celebrations. Alan, a very loud, extroverted character, boldly raised a glass and proclaimed during his after-dinner speech one evening that he would live to a hundred.

A sudden wave of unease washed over me when I heard him make this announcement. After all, it is God who dictates the timing of our departure from this world, not us.

It's not our place to predict or declare how long or short our lives will be.

Strangely, a month later, while on his way to a Masonic Lodge meeting, Alan suddenly stopped talking mid-sentence in the back of the car. I shivered when I was told that, despite having no prior health issues, he had passed away unexpectedly.

God will not be mocked!

HICC had been my church home for over seven years, and I also occasionally attended Ealing Christian Centre, a lively church in South Ealing with a diverse, multinational congregation where people often came and went at random during the service. They also sometimes did the conga around the church, which I found amusing and exhilarating.

In this large church, I had a golden opportunity to join a class studying the Old Testament, a subject I had previously found intimidating. It was like a big, old, dark house that I did not want to enter.

An inspirational and engaging instructor, Dr Peter Rowe, led the course. For a modest charge, Peter supplied us with the relevant thick manuals to be used in his course.

An exciting new world was panning out...

Peter earned our respect as a passionate and exceptional teacher who could transport us to every scene of the lesson's topic, encouraging us to discuss what we might have noticed if we had been there with the Israelites in the wilderness, emphasising the smells and sounds.

By bringing the Old Testament stories to life, he explained concepts I had failed to grasp. Feeling like I was on the precipice of something new and exhilarating, I was excited and hungry to learn more.

He explained that each time the Israelites set up camp, their tents were pitched in an orderly manner according to the ranking of each of the twelve tribes, with the Tabernacle in the centre.

Model of the Tabernacle

If a helicopter were to fly over the area, the occupants would see their tents pitched in the shape of a cross, a foretelling of Christ's crucifixion thousands of years beforehand...*Amazing!*

Taking it in sections, he explained that the Bible's first five books, collectively known as the Pentateuch, are equivalent to the Jewish Torah and taught us about the prophets, providing an overview of the timeline, and bringing these scriptures to life.

In our discussion, we examined the accuracy and origins of the Bible, analysing the compilation process that included various literary genres, such as history, prophecy, and poetry.

Intrigued to learn that God inspired the Bible through His Holy Spirit, and gained a deeper understanding of its content, shedding light on the significance of these elements.

Dr Rowe relished unpacking how Jesus is present throughout the Old Testament in various types and foreshadowing of Christ. This was a major and significant fact I had not appreciated or understood before.

all Scripture is God breathed

This topic is often overlooked and underrepresented in churches. The New Testament recounts these types of Christ found in the Old Testament.

Moses is a type of Christ and shares many similarities with Him.

For example:

- At the time of Moses' birth, Pharaoh cruelly ordered the death of all male Hebrew babies (Exo. 1:22).
- King Herod ordered the murder of children under two to kill Jesus. (Matt. 2:16).
- They both had to hide to escape infanticide.
- (Exodus 2:2, Matt. 2:13).
- Moses was adopted by Pharaoh's daughter (Exodus 2:10), while Joseph, Mary's husband, took Jesus into his family. (Matt. 2:14).

Neither was raised by a biological father.

He taught us principles we could use to determine whether an appearance is a genuine Christophany *(appearance of Christ)*, such as the appearance of Melchizedek, who had no lineage and no record of his birth or death. This warrants further study. He had no successor, so, like the priesthood of Christ, this is eternal.

Jesus was not descended from the *tribe of Levi*, like the other earthly Jewish priests, but from the *line of Judah, a high priest in the order of Melchizedek, King of Salem—King of Peace and King of Righteousness.*

Because there was no set formula, each incident was different.

Previously, I had read the Old Testament in black and white, but now it burst forth in full technicolour with high definition. Studying the Old Testament became a new passion, and Peter provided manuals on each topic for our reference. I learnt that:

God is in the details, and none of the facts in the Bible serve as mere garnish. Everything holds significance and often carries multilayered spiritual meaning.

The Old Testament prepares the way for Christ and points to Jesus, while the New Testament reveals and explains the deity of Jesus.

The most impactful thing I learned from the Old Testament is that Jesus' existence did not begin with his birth in Bethlehem; He was present at the beginning of time and is the Creator of the universe, alongside God the Father and the Holy Spirit. This realisation has had a profound and lasting influence on me and is certainly a game-changer from the standpoint of understanding the scriptures.

As we explore the concept of the Trinity, many of us feel confused, much like I did, as a seven-year-old discovering that the Earth is round—it simply doesn't seem to make sense.

I learned that the three persons of the Trinity are distinct, each possessing the same divine essence, like an egg, which has a shell, egg white, and yolk.

They can each be used separately and have distinct functions, yet they are one egg that, under the right conditions, will hatch, bringing forth new life.

Recognising that the Bible was originally written in Hebrew, Aramaic, and Greek underscores the importance of linguistic comprehension when interpreting its teachings accurately.

Therefore, the advantages of linguistic study go well beyond mere scholarly interest; they are essential for a comprehensive understanding of the Scriptures and their deep wisdom. Greek and Hebrew are alphanumeric languages. Hebrew has an alphabet of twenty-two letters, each with a numerical value, making it a rich language.

Numbers are equally as significant as letters in the Bible, so it's worth learning about them.

Focusing on words comes naturally, and numbers can appear unimportant to us.

Each letter has a numeric equivalent, for example, in Hebrew, alpha corresponds to 1, beta to 2, and so on.

Matthew highlights three spans of fourteen generations: one between Abraham and David, one between David and Babylon.

Between Babylon and Jesus.

1 = Unity	2 = Division Double Witness	3 = Divine Fullness Perfection
4 = Earth Material Creation	5 = Grace Favour	6 = Man/Work
7 = Completion Spiritual Perfection	8 = New Beginnings	9 = Visitation Judgment Bearing Fruit

His triple repetition underlines the significance of this number. The numerical value of David's name is fourteen.
I find languages fascinating, and my Syriac Peshitta Bible, a direct translation from Aramaic—the mother tongue of its

author, George M. Lamsa, is highly enlightening. George addresses discrepancies in various Bible translations and clarifies certain puzzling passages.

Noting that many words in Aramaic resemble each other and that punctuation and paragraphing were not yet standardised at the time of writing, this can lead to difficulties in interpretation.

For example:

"It is easier for a camel to go through the eye of a needle than for someone rich to enter the kingdom of God."
Matt. 19:24 NIV

The word for 'camel' in Aramaic is similar to 'rope,' which makes perfect sense. However, the *'eye of the needle'* in the Middle East refers to a small door inserted into a larger gate or door, allowing camels to enter with their masters. They would kneel and unload their burden before entering the gate; therefore, either explanation holds validity.

When the course ended, the church leader asked if I would share my experience of studying the Old Testament with the congregation. The Sunday it fell on was Mother's Day. As I stood on the platform, a wave of enthusiasm washed over me as I spoke about this inspirational and enlightening course the church was offering. I passionately encouraged the congregation to consider signing up for it in the upcoming term, highlighting the invaluable insights they would gain. The moment became even more special as I took the opportunity to extend heartfelt good wishes for Happy Mother's Day to all the mothers present in the congregation, mindful that among them may be women who had longed to conceive but had faced heart-wrenching disappointments.

In recognition of their experiences, I gently reminded them that some people embrace the role of spiritual mothers, endeavouring to ensure every woman felt seen and valued in this celebration.

God is with those who feel alone or are struggling, and He has urged me to help them endure.

The Bible records several instances of key women who were barren until God intervened, enabling them to bear children under miraculous circumstances.

For example, Sarah and Abraham were almost one hundred years old when their only son, Isaac, was born. Isaac's wife, Rebekah, was barren until the Lord opened her womb, and she bore twins, Jacob and Esau. Jacob's wife, Rachel, was unable to conceive, demanding that he:

"Give me children, or I shall die!" Gen. 30:1 NIV

God remembered her in His heart; she conceived and gave birth to Joseph, later followed by Benjamin. She had a hard labour with her youngest son and died soon after his birth.

Because of this trial, she called him Ben-oni *(son of my sorrow)*, but Jacob refused to accept this name and changed it to **Benjamin.** *(Bin Yameen, Son of My Right Hand).*

Jacob's name was changed to Israel after a dream in which he wrestled with God and injured his hip. Jacob *(Israel)* had a permanent limp after this incident, hence the saying:

> *'Never trust a Pastor who doesn't have a limp! (A tongue-in-cheek reference to the belief that the best pastors have wrestled with God at some point in their lives.)*

At ECC, I frequently used an electronic Bible to follow Scripture passages during the sermons. Richard Buxton, the pastor, mistakenly thought my device was a mobile phone and repeatedly requested that people put their phones away, glaring directly at me. Unfortunately, I didn't get an opportunity to enlighten him that it was a Bible.

Nowadays, many congregants use mobile phones with Bible apps, so I hope he has become more relaxed and in tune with technology; otherwise, he might find himself constantly frustrated.

A group I joined from this church was excited to embark on a weekend retreat at St Katharine's, Parmoor (Sue Ryder House), a prayer centre in the village of Frieth, Buckinghamshire, to enjoy the peace and tranquillity of this majestic house and its beautiful grounds. While in our elegant, designated lounge at this retreat, our Assistant Pastor, Tanya, asked us all to be still, focus on God, and write down what we felt He was telling us.

Below is the profound message God gave me :

"Child, I am holding you now.

My ways are not your ways.

The path I am showing you is one you would have shunned, given the chance.

Your work is not in vain.

I want you to see purpose as I see purpose.

Surrender all… Don't hold back!

Give me space to act!

Believe me, there is no other option.

My Will is My Word.

Trust Me to guide your heart.

Some will question the abundant gifts I am about to give to you,

But they will stand amazed as I contend with your challengers.

Be prepared: I am giving you what you want, not what you think you want.

I think we've both noticed you are not very good at rule-keeping...

I planned each day of your life to be infused with mercy.

Wait on Me…Keep trusting!"

TRUST

PSALM 52:8

I am filled with abundance and peace.
I am purified by the Blood of Jesus.
I am infused with God's wisdom.
I possess the power of God's Holy Spirit.
I am always flourishing, growing and hardy.
I am beneficial at all times in God's kingdom.
I have confidence always in God's Mercy.
My confidence in God never withers or dies.

∞

LONDON

Tony and I were engaged six months later and planned to tie the knot the following year.

Because I wanted us to start afresh and didn't want to live in his family home, Tony sold his house and temporarily rented a small starter home in Langley, five miles away.

My bungalow was becoming increasingly challenging to maintain due to the ever-rising cost of upkeep, leading me to reluctantly admit that I would have to sell it and move to a more affordable place. Having experienced the fallout of debt before, I wanted to avoid getting into financial difficulties again.

The downside of my lodger, Delores, living with me was that she had an inherent craving to own a similar place. Consequently, I felt she secretly envied me. This manifested destructively, as she sabotaged any prospective purchase if she were present during viewings; she exaggerated the intrusion of traffic noise from the nearby M40 motorway and mentioned any other negative points that came to her mind.

Insisting that her wealthy brother in America would give her the cash to buy the bungalow if she asked him, she begged me to take it off the market. Delores was a strict, puritanical Christian with some odd ideas. For example, she refused to touch cash, believing it was contaminated and always paid her rent by cheque.

Having once complied with her request to delay putting my home on the market, even though there was no sign of any financial commitment on her behalf, I requested that she put down a deposit.

Dithering yet again, she scrawled a note on a scruffy piece of paper, confirming her intention to buy my property, but had still made no financial commitment.

After months with no progress, I waived her objections and placed the bungalow with the local estate agency, much to her annoyance. She moved out eventually before it was sold, and irrationally, I felt slightly complicit and responsible for her shattered dreams of owning her own home. Life can often be challenging, and sometimes we need a reality check.

Putting my home up for sale sparked a frenzy of interest, making me wonder if I had set the price too low. However, upon checking the market rate, I found it was in line with the asking price of comparable properties in the area, and it sold surprisingly quickly. Now, I needed to find another place to live.

Many of the places I had viewed were unsuitable, with steep, hilly back gardens, or they needed an incredible amount of work, which wasn't feasible for me. I'd had enough of that in my last house and just wanted a place I could move into that was already presentable and liveable.

A modest ground-floor flat in Wooburn Green, Buckinghamshire, in the Home Counties, was on my list of viewings, and I decided that, while it wasn't perfect, it would suffice for now.

Professor Karol Sikora, my former boss at Hammersmith Hospital, kindly offered to help me move and transported my belongings in his large jeep, as he lived nearby but in a much more affluent area.

The River Wye ran past the rear of my flat, and because I made the mistake of feeding them once, ducks banged rhythmically on the kitchen window in the mornings, demanding to be fed.

Bossy coots, moorhens, and mallards made their nests on islands in the river. Watching the baby birds hatch in due season was a great privilege, something I didn't take for granted.

Tony and I began searching for a prospective house for our future home and attended St Peter's, a vibrant church in nearby Loudwater. We joined a small group at one of the other members' homes.

A few of the new Christians who had joined the group found some Bible teachings challenging, and it was good to expand on the parables of Jesus and examine the context further.

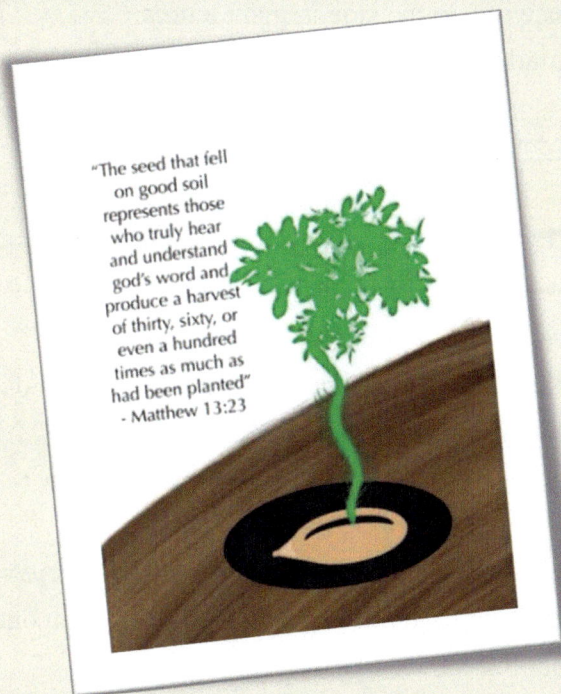

"The seed that fell on good soil represents those who truly hear and understand god's word and produce a harvest of thirty, sixty, or even a hundred times as much as had been planted"
- Matthew 13:23

Interestingly, one young lady voiced her concerns about tithing *(giving 10% of your income to the church),* citing that her limited income made it difficult for her to make ends meet.

Bring the whole tithe into the storehouse, that there may be food in my house. Test me in this, says the Lord Almighty, and see if I will not throw open the floodgates of heaven and pour out so many blessings that there will not be enough room to store them. Mal. 3:10 NIV

While driving on the motorway a few days later, a large lorry passed her with this word on the side in giant letters:
Stunned by this remarkable and timely answer to her question, she obeyed.

T I T H E

Soon after, she received an offer of a much better-paying job, which fulfilled all her obligations and more.

I have learnt over time that God doesn't always meet our needs in such a profound way, but if we persevere, we will see a breakthrough, and He gives us the grace to endure if we stay close to Him.

While leading a session at *'Connections Ladies' Bible Study Group'* one Wednesday afternoon, I was gobsmacked when one of the ladies read out this verse:

He will deliver you from six troubles; no evil shall touch you in seven. Job 5:19 ESV

It was the first time I had encountered this scripture, and it served as a powerful confirmation of the message God had revealed in my dream so long ago.

Feeling winded, as though I had been struck in the stomach by a bag of wet cement, I gasped and looked up this verse in my Bible, more than twenty years after my original dream.

From that day on, this Bible verse was pivotal for me. Here was the biblical confirmation I was seeking but had never come across before—a revelation, a powerful reminder of God's faithfulness and His divine ability to deliver us from all our troubles if we would only seek His face.

The message resonated deeply with me during difficult times, reassuring me that God is present and active in our anguish. This understanding instils a powerful sense of hope and protection that still resonates with believers today. I have personally experienced this throughout various challenges.

God didn't make everything right for me. Still, He miraculously restored my finances in ways I could never have anticipated or imagined in a million years. He was with me throughout, revealing His plan for my life as He will for every person who surrenders their life to Him. His agenda does not always align with ours. His thoughts and ways are much higher.

God's primary concern is with our eternal destiny, before our life on this earth, and He will prune away any dross from our lives that hinders the path to our heavenly home, even if it causes us pain. After all, *His beloved Son suffered horrendous* pain on the cross but ultimately won the victory over death.

We participated in an eleven-week Alpha course at St Peter's, which opened the door for discussions about faith and life. Through this course, we connected with others in the church and were given a platform to ask pertinent questions.

Although there were a few things I was unsure about, we genuinely enjoyed the experience and looked forward to the talks and delicious meals provided by the church ladies at each session. In line with the core teachings of this enlightening course, we gained further insight into the scriptures and thoroughly enjoyed participating in it.

At the end of the course, they had a Holy Spirit Day where questions such as,

'Who is the Holy Spirit?'

'What does the Holy Spirit do?'

'How can I be filled with the Spirit?'

were addressed. Some individuals reported being filled with the Holy Spirit during this event.

Another group I was involved with at St Peter's was,

'Reach a Street'.

On Saturday mornings, we visited the local neighbourhood to talk to people about God in a friendly manner and to see if they needed any practical assistance. We received a variety of reactions, some positive and some not so positive.

During this time, I met a feisty old lady named Nan, and I visited her often, sometimes helping her with her shopping. She was an interesting character and shared stories about her time as a Lollipop Lady, whose job was to help kids cross the street safely at local schools.

On one occasion, she asked me to go to the local shop to buy her a lottery ticket, a packet of cigarettes and a half bottle of whiskey *(needless to say, she wasn't a believer and had no interest in church despite my begging her to come).*

Behind me in the queue was a stern, strait-laced older lady from St Peter's church who witnessed all my illicit purchases. Her face was a picture of disgust and disapproval.

Laughing inwardly, I mischievously decided not to explain, allowing her to draw her own conclusions.

~

OUR NEW HOME

After searching for a house for about eighteen months and growing very tired of viewing unsuitable properties, we finally found one in Hazlemere, a small town three miles from High Wycombe, and decided to make an offer. However, as the negotiations progressed, the seller unexpectedly changed his mind, withdrew the property from the market, and chose to stay in his home, leaving us back at square one.

I wasn't too upset since I had had a few reservations about that one anyway. Although it was a sizable house, it felt quite dark and somewhat gloomy, and it could have benefited from some brightening up. Additionally, it stood on a steep hill on a busy road.

Following a viewing of a charming chalet bungalow in another part of Buckinghamshire that impressed us both, we found ourselves in a bit of a quandary about whether or not to make an offer. By now, I was becoming worn out and despairing of ever finding the right place.

One sunny morning soon after, as I was on my way to visit my cousin, Milly, in Chalgrove, Oxfordshire, I received a call from Tony. The estate agent had presented us with an ultimatum:

'*Another lady was a keen prospective buyer and had expressed serious interest in the bungalow*'.

He gave us until noon that day to make an offer, or risk losing the house to her. To my surprise, Tony left the final choice to me. *Wow… what an empowering moment!*

Through past experiences, I have observed instances where God conveyed a message through various channels, principally car number plates. Each number translated into Hebrew would convey a specific meaning or message.

Additionally, I noticed messages on posters and other visual cues, often conveying insights perceived as divine guidance from God. I felt strangely elated and was elevated to a higher level in this pivotal moment of decision-making. Turning again to God, I beseeched Him to guide me, even glancing up at the sky in hopeful anticipation of an answer written in the clouds. *Nothing!* … I carefully checked the number plates of the cars passing by. One had a *'Y,'* so I said,

"Lord, that's a bit tenuous; would you be more specific, please?"

The next car had the letters **YUS.**
OK, that was good enough for me!

God has a keen sense of humour.

The house purchase process was set in motion when I took the plunge and called Tony back, telling him we should proceed with making an offer.
At our House Group that evening, when I told this story, the host, Mark, a popular larger-than-life character, always ready with a joke, quipped,

"So God is from up North then?"

Our wedding was scheduled for November 5, 2005. The service was held at St Peter's Church, Loudwater.

My former pastor, Michael, from Emmanuel, valiantly gave me away and delivered a moving and inspiring speech. Youssef, a friend from Ealing Christian Centre, sang the Westlife hit, *'You Raise Me Up.'* His rendition was soulful, capturing the atmosphere in the church, much to the embarrassment of his kids, one of whom blatantly sat with his fingers in his ears throughout the performance…I hoped that, in time, he would learn to appreciate his dad's clear, soulful voice.

Dr Seyan was there, accompanied by his wife, several staff members from the GP practice, and old friends from HICC, our former church in Harrow.

Kerry-Ann had flown over from New Zealand for the occasion and looked chic in a neat, well-cut white trouser suit.

OK!

WEDDING OF JOANN STONE AND TONY THORNBY

FIRST FOR CELEBRITY NEWS
ISSUE 001 ● NOVEMBER 5 2005 ● £2 WEEKLY

A PACKED HOUSE
VIPS DESCEND ON LOUDWATER

STAR-STUDDED CELEBRATION AT ST PETER'S, EMOTIONAL CEREMONY, DESIGNER DRESS, RINGS, CAKE & WILD PARTY

THE CAKE
ALL TIERS AT THE PARTY

For two nights before the wedding, she stayed with me in my flat in Wooburn Green, and we enjoyed some much-needed girlie time preparing for the big day ahead.

Since our wedding was on 5th November, Guy Fawkes Day, Tony's Hockey Club hosted the reception at Rickmansworth, complete with fireworks.

(No excuse to forget our anniversary!)

Following our brief honeymoon in Madrid, we settled into our new house. There were a few teething problems, including alarms going off and lights and equipment malfunctioning.

Local tradesmen fixed all the niggling faults, the walls were painted, and curtains were installed, making the house comfortable. Casey, my cat, at last had own front and back garden to patrol.

~

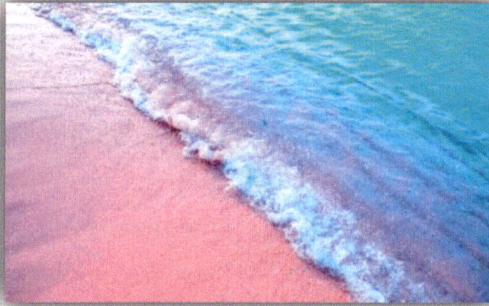

Chapter Thirteen

NEW ZEALAND

The following month, we flew to Auckland, New Zealand, stopping in Singapore for an hour and a half before continuing to our destination.

Our tight, prearranged schedule thwarted my desire to visit this fascinating country, as we couldn't leave the airport and eventually boarded a plane bound for Auckland.

Upon arriving in Auckland, Kerry-Ann picked us up at the airport and drove us to their stylish home in Mission Bay. It was great to see her, and afterwards, we proceeded to the nearby accommodation she had reserved for us.

After our tedious, long-haul flight, our primary focus was a shower and bed. Still suffering the effects of jet lag, we went into town the following day to exchange our English money for New Zealand dollars.

It took us a day or two to adjust to the time difference. Julian and Kerry-Ann took us to Ascension Vineyard for lunch, where the atmosphere was convivial and welcoming, a perfect spot for a wedding or celebration.

A vast array of hand-crafted wines was on display. Naturally, we indulged in these wines;(*it would have been rude not to.*) Julian was deeply knowledgeable about the various tipples. Kiwi wine is renowned as some of the best in the world, and visiting this picturesque winery certainly expanded our knowledge of the various wine types.

We purchased a couple of bottles at the Cellar Door and then headed to the Craft Shop, which featured a wide range of interesting wine-related gadgets. There were beautifully crafted tables made from wine casks converted into wine racks, as well as smaller items such as corkscrews, temperature gauges, and souvenirs.

We continued our journey to Oamaru, where we visited Tony's cousin, Anna, who had emigrated to New Zealand twelve years ago and now lived on a large farm deep in the countryside.

Our reunion with her and her children was very emotional. Her home was simple and rustic, a typical farmhouse with a warm atmosphere. She kept a collection of animals, some of which wandered through the house, making it an entertaining and amusing place to be.

ENGLAND *Minehead*

In April of the following year, along with a group from our church, we headed for our annual holiday at Spring Harvest, an evangelical Christian conference in Minehead, based at Butlin's Holiday Camp.

The main event occurred in the Big Top, a massive tent that served as the primary worship area.

One evening, after the main meeting, the congregation were invited to come forward for prayer.

In agony from hip pain, I hobbled to the front, hoping to receive a prayer for healing. My mobile phone was on a lanyard around my neck, which led a distressed lady to assume I was part of the prayer team.

She was upset and crying and approached me. Between sobs, she asked me to pray for her little daughter, who was about four and had a problem with one of her hands, which was perpetually closed in a fist. Despite doctors' examinations and hospital tests, they could find nothing wrong with her.

I felt the Lord was impressing on me that He had given her a supernatural gift and commanded her not to release it until He instructed her to do so.

This is the verse He gave me for this worried mother:

Then the Lord asked him, "What have you in your hand?"
"A staff," he replied. Ex. 4: 2 NIV

Her face lit up when I explained *that God had given a message to her little daughter, and He told her He would allow her to release it only in His time*.

After sharing God's message, I felt the anointing of God and could barely walk back to my seat, lunging all over the place as though drunk, under the power of the Holy Spirit.

What an extraordinary experience!

This happened during the Easter weekend.

On Easter Sunday morning, we gathered on the beach at 7 am to listen to the rich, stirring, melodious trumpet fanfare playing,

'Christ is Risen Today!'

With an atmosphere of awe and reverence, we praised the Risen Lord, with our hands in the air, in worship. That incredible moment remains locked in my memory forever.

Cliff Richard, Sue Rinaldi, Noel Richards, Sheila Walsh, Daniel Bedingfield and other Christian celebrities were frequent guests and were there with us that morning.

Later in the evening, they offered comedy shows, quizzes, sketches and other forms of light entertainment. They had a comprehensive program, but no pressure was placed on participants to attend every event. We selected those of particular interest and enjoyed interacting with the speakers at Question Time.

~

INDIA

In 2011, Joan, a loyal, close friend and the wife of Michael, my former pastor from Emmanuel, and Pam, another friend, invited me to accompany them to Kolkata *(formerly known as Calcutta)*.

They ran a charity called Compassion Service Society of India (CSSI).

At Heathrow, our luggage exceeded the guidelines permitted limit, so we prayed fervently for it to go through unchallenged. It mostly consisted of toys and clothing for the children in the slums. Our prayers were answered, and much to our collective relief, we were cleared to board the plane without any hitches.

Thank you, Lord!

Compassion Service Society of India *(CSSI)* was a Christian charity that supported poor and underprivileged communities in Kolkata.

This organisation focused on educating children and offered a women's empowerment program to equip local women with the necessary skills to help sustain their families. CSSI primarily worked in West Bengal and Kerala with a vision to empower marginalised communities in villages and slums. Their initiatives encompassed social, economic, educational, and healthcare programs, funded through donations from fundraising events and contributions from generous benefactors.

Sadly, the charity ceased operations in 2021, and its responsibilities were transferred to larger organisations, such as the Kolkata City Mission (KCM), which primarily receives support from churches in the US and Canada through The Flume Foundation.

The Charity's director, Shaji and his dear wife, Beena, welcomed us when we arrived at Dum Dum Airport in Kolkata, West Bengal. They took us to a small, budget hotel in the town centre. Though basic, it was quite comfortable. Joan and Pam shared a room, while I had a large single bedroom.

The TV reception was poor, so we called a hotel staff member to fix it. After he improved the reception, he lingered, expecting a tip. Since we hadn't exchanged our money yet, we couldn't oblige, so we explained this to him, promising to give him a tip. I was unsure of how much of what we said he understood, but he eventually left looking frustrated and discontented. Making a mental note of his name, I gave him a generous tip the following day. His demeanour changed instantly, from one of misery and resentment to joyfulness.

There was much merriment and banter when Joan mistakenly popped a mothball from a dish into her mouth, mistaking it for a Mint Imperial. We teased her mercilessly about this.

Then, it was my turn to have fun poked at me. When I washed my underwear in a basin, I accidentally caused it to be sucked down the drain with the disappearing water and ended up getting stuck in the system.

Joan had wisely packed an assortment of crispy crackers and creamy cheese, knowing that the culinary offerings would likely be limited. From past experiences, she had anticipated a monotonous menu dominated by tender chicken, fluffy rice, and yet more chicken, leaving little room for variety or surprise once we sorted it out. I was unsure of how much of what we said he understood, but he eventually left looking frustrated and discontented. Making a mental note of his name, I gave him a generous tip the following day. His demeanour changed instantly, from one of misery and resentment to joyfulness.

Kolkata is a lively and energetic city, filled with crowds, pollution, and overwhelming poverty. The people are generally gentle and wry. Hinduism is the primary religion, followed by Christianity, the third-largest religious community, and there is also a significant Muslim presence.

Mother Teresa, a Roman Catholic nun and founder of the Order of the Missionaries of Charity, was a revered figure in Kolkata. While there, we visited her organisation, which still serves the families based in the slums.
An ethnic Albanian, she lived and worked in Kolkata for nearly seven decades and eventually became a citizen of India. Her charity headquarters, the Missionaries of Charity, is a centralised Catholic religious institute recognised in the Catholic Church as the Saint Teresa of Calcutta Foundation. This

organisation honours and continues her work for the poor and underprivileged following her death in 1997.

According to traditional accounts, St Thomas travelled outside the Roman Empire to preach the gospel, reaching as far as Mylapore in South India.

Kerala is home to a huge Christian community, and CSSI also had a branch there. CSSI enabled women to attain independence by providing them with loans to start their own small enterprises, which they could repay as their businesses grew. It was a remarkably successful venture, and donors in the UK were prompted to send several sewing machines to aid this vital project.

Having sold my home in Wooburn Green, Buckinghamshire, I was in a position to make a substantial donation to CSSI.

Stipulating that the funds be used to contribute to the purchase of a minibus for the women in the outlying villages who were currently transported to the nearest hospital on the back of a motorcycle, while heavily pregnant, sometimes resulting in several tragic accidents.

Hoping to ensure their comfort and safety at this crucial and challenging time in their lives, a spacious, comfortable white minibus was purchased, and I was honoured to be invited to cut the ribbon at the opening ceremony before its first official use.

Under the guidance of Rita, one of the charity workers' wives, Joan, Pam, and I bought brightly coloured saris and silk trousers to complement them.

Seeing the cable system for transporting receipts and change in the shops was nostalgic. The bill, or the cash, was inserted into a small metal container swinging on a zip wire across the shop floor to the recipient's bench, where it was opened, the contents dealt with, and then it was sent spinning back along the wire with the change or receipt.

Dressed in our new saris, we attended major events and ministered in slum areas, providing toys and lollipops for the children. Seeing how inventive they could be in trying to obtain more than their allotted one item each was amusing. *They could be pretty crafty!* One little boy pretended he needed an extra lollipop and toy for his brother, who he claimed was at home sick. Upon further investigation, the claim was a fib—he didn't have a brother.

Many of these children looked stunning, with glowing skin, symmetrical features, big brown eyes, thick, shiny black hair, and long lashes. It occurred to me that they would have made outstanding film stars, and I wished better opportunities would come their way.

The older girls danced mesmerising local dance sequences for us, with beautiful swirling skirts and graceful, expressive arm and hand movements.

Red, gold, blue and white were the primary colours displaying the endless twisting and twirling scarves to the rhythmic beat of

the Indian drums, which was enchanting and scintillating. We expressed our appreciation by clapping loudly when they finished their performance.

Later, vainly trying to imitate them, and much to the scorn of Shaji, the director in Kolkata, we were hopeless, and they tittered shyly behind their hands at our efforts.

Shaji had a church in Midanpur, an outlying village, and held regular services where we participated in regular prayer sessions for those with special needs. Their circumstances were often heartbreaking, but the worship and prayer were enthusiastic and sincere. Funding for a medical centre and a school was successfully raised.

We sponsored wells in remote areas where obtaining water was a daily challenge. These wells significantly alleviated their burden of walking miles to the river for dirty water.

Ours was named *'Jacob's Well,'* with a plaque giving the dates and other details at the front.

The locals addressed us as *'Auntie'* after our names, so I was known as *'Joann, Auntie.'* Travelling on the back of a motorbike, side-saddle, while wearing a sari is an experience I don't intend to repeat anytime soon.

It was extremely hairy!

During my stay at the CSSI Centre in the village, I was allocated a generously sized room with a protective mosquito net over the bed. I felt privileged to have such accommodation; however, the toilet facilities left much to be desired, consisting merely of a hole in the ground and a basin filled with freezing water. Nevertheless, I'm sure this was updated later when funds allowed. It was a humbling experience to learn that approximately six people usually shared that room and willingly gave up their beds for my comfort.

Pam, a gifted teacher, cherished her interactions with the children. She organised games to keep them engaged and occupied. With a vibrant, rainbow-coloured silk parachute, she entertained them for hours as they spread it out, grasping the edges and joyfully dancing in a circle.

Pam & CSSI Friends

Hindus revere cows as sacred, which leads them to meander around often in unexpected places, such as people's backyards. As a result, beef was off the menu. The only meat provided was chicken.

Watching cows strolling around unaccompanied through the streets was a novel experience. Noticing the alarmed look on my face, a local stallholder laughingly exclaimed, *"It's OK, they know their way home!"*

Compared to Egypt, the poverty level there seemed much higher. Babies were sleeping in skips, and I saw children doing their homework on the side of the streets.

One fateful day, we witnessed a belligerent anti-Christian march of right-wing nationalist Hindus through the village, which was extremely unsettling and intimidating. There was a commotion, and they displayed violent, threatening behaviour. They intended to destroy the Medical Centre.

At the front of the mob, the dogs looked wild and vicious, with scary, glaring red eyes, snarling and baring their teeth at us. Hindu shrines set in the bushes are a familiar sight; we noticed these as we walked past. That day, they marched past, but thankfully, they did not damage anything.

God was protecting us.

The Centre Manager, Sahadeb, severely damaged his throat when these Hindus ran a steel wire across a narrow road from one tree to another on the other side of the pathway. Sahadeb's wife, Lakhsmi, told me this dramatic story:

He unwittingly rode into this trap on his bicycle, and the wire viciously sliced through the skin on his neck. It was fine wire, and he didn't see it, so he rode straight into the trap they set. She described how blood seeped through the makeshift bandages that were frantically applied, creating a chaotic scene. Those helping worked quickly, using every scrap of cloth to staunch the flow. The urgency of the situation propelled them into the waiting minibus. As they sped through the bustling streets toward the city hospital, she described that his face was pale, starkly contrasting with the crimson stains on his clothes. The medical staff sprang into action to treat his wound, but the experience understandably left deep emotional scars.

The haunting memory of that day affected him so deeply that he was hesitant to ride his bike again. The thrill of the open road for him was forever overshadowed by the memory of this trauma.

In other villages, the people welcomed us warmly and viewed us as a curiosity. We enjoyed pseudo celebrity status. One memorable lady, Jamuna, was a rare and endearing character. She lived in a stone-built house with a courtyard in the middle where they kept their goats, ducks, and other animals. Her favourite saying was, *"I'm coming to Lawndawn (*London*) with you!"* Then she would burst into uproarious laughter.
Our stay in Kolkata was eventful.
One day, I fell flat in the street, tripping over a loose stone in Dum Dum, where Shaji and Beena lived, while rushing to get into the minibus. Getting up quickly, embarrassed by my clumsiness, I tried to brush it off.

Still, Shaji was very concerned about my well-being and insisted on taking me to the local hospital, where they X-rayed my hand, revealing arthritis, which I knew was a pre-existing condition; there was no real damage to my hand from the fall. However, the staff there made quite a fuss and put me in a wheelchair. Poor Pam had to wheel me around for the rest of the day and received a lecture into the bargain for not looking after me properly, which became another subject for banter among us.

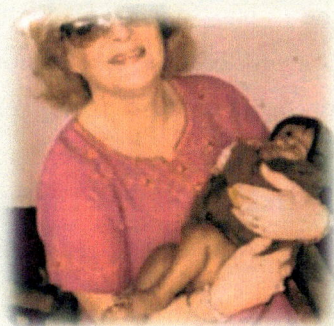

Witnessing the extreme poverty in India certainly made us appreciate the luxuries we enjoy at home, which we so easily take for granted in the West.

Yet these people, who had few material possessions, knew Jesus and were bubbling over with joy and contentment, supported by their communal ties and simple lives.

LONDON

Tony took on the charity's treasurer role and participated in regular biannual meetings at Joan and Michael's home in Ruislip, a suburb of London. During these gatherings, they discussed fundraising initiatives and monitored the supplies sent to the children in the slum.

Kind-hearted local women knitted vibrant hats and jumpers that the children cherished, ensuring they stayed warm during winter. Regular curry evenings at a church in South Ealing offered vital support for the charity. Joan and Michael often shared slides from their visits to West Bengal, showing the children proudly wearing the knitted garments, which brought great joy to the generous ladies who made them by hand.

They also highlighted the significant progress made in constructing wells, a school, medical facilities, and improved housing for the support workers and their families.

Now he who supplies seed to the sower and bread for food, will also supply and increase your store of seed and will enlarge the harvest of your righteousness. 2 Cor. 9:10 NIV

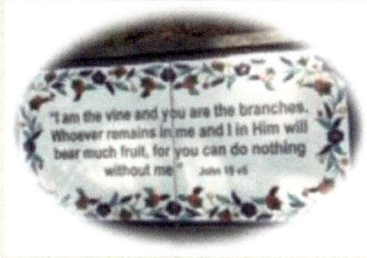

Chapter Fourteen

AMANI

Adam connected regularly with his Aunt Amani, and despite the language barrier, they enjoyed occasional phone conversations. She mentioned to him that she was still visiting Magid in the Tora Jail, telling him that, *"Something very bad has happened."*

Although she didn't elaborate *(either out of loyalty to Magid or due to a lack of language skills)*, my gut feeling about this was foreboding; I sensed it was significant and a harbinger of something catastrophic.

Soon after this, Amani was struck by a heavy lorry while crossing the busy road outside the prison shortly after visiting Magid. This collision left her in a coma for three days.

Tragically, she didn't survive and lost her fight for life soon after.

Hassan called me on my birthday, his voice heavy with sorrow as he gently delivered the heart-wrenching news.

A wave of grief poured over me, leaving me utterly shattered. In a daze, I reached out to Kerry-Ann and Adam, my first duty was to share this painful news, knowing how deeply Amani had touched our lives. They were devastated as they loved her so much.

Amani was a truly exceptional soul—sincere and genuine. She radiated kindness and warmth that drew people to her. Despite her burdens, her unwavering loyalty to her brother overshadowed her needs, as she devoted her days to catering to his every need. Amani often sacrificed her own happiness for that of her family, leading a life that was all too solitary and devoid of joy.

It seemed hopelessly unfair that someone so deserving should face such a tragic fate. I'm comforted that she is at peace now. Concerned about her eternal destiny, I prayed fervently for her while she was in a coma. On the side of my wardrobe, by our bed, is a picture of an English garden scene, and when I looked, it morphed into a touching picture of *Amani wrapped in the arms of Jesus* within the pattern. This image was a supernatural message, reassuring me that she accepted Jesus miraculously, and I sensed the gospel was supernaturally explained to her during the time she was in the coma. When I gave this testimony in our church, I'm sure most of them thought I was deluded…

I didn't mind at all, as it would have made them ponder.

EGYPT

I purchased a modest holiday apartment in Hurghada, just a short walk from the seafront, thinking it would be a good investment for my children, as they don't have any grandparents to leave them an inheritance.
Additionally, it could serve as a potential meeting place for Kerry-Ann, Julian, Adam, Tony, and me.

Unfortunately, this opportunity never materialised. While Adam stayed there a few times, Kerry-Ann and Julian never had a chance to visit, so my hopes for a family holiday spot didn't turn out as planned.

Negotiations to purchase this flat took place through meetings with lawyers at McDonald's at 9 pm on a Sunday. Although this seemed unusual, it is a customary practice in Egypt, so I had to adapt to their relaxed approach to business.

While I was in Hurghada, Tony called to give me the sad news that my beloved cat, Casey, had died. He had found her stiff body underneath the bed and told me he wasn't sure whether to call and tell me or to wait for my return.

In the end, he decided it would be best to let me know, and he buried her at the bottom of our garden. Casey had reached the grand old age of twenty-one and enjoyed a long, blissful life.

Before I had left for Egypt, she was suffering from various illnesses, incontinence, and confusion due to her advanced age, making loud, high-pitched noises and howling during the night, so her passing didn't come as a surprise.

In a way, it was a release for her. She was old, and it was her time. I would miss her desperately as she had been my loyal companion for so many years, but I was comforted by my belief that I would see her again one day in Heaven.

Within a few days, I flew back home and negotiated with the seller of my flat in Egypt to complete the purchase.

Adam and I travelled back to Egypt two weeks later to check Amani's flat and sort out anything we needed to do there. After spending a few days at my new flat in Hurghada, we boarded the Superjet, a coach with scheduled routes across Egypt, to travel to Cairo.

The journey covered approximately 500 km along the desert road, with only one stop halfway at a service station for refreshments. Getting off the coach at any road stop was perilous, as you risked being devoured by mosquitoes. Local passengers knew better and refused to budge, but foreigners like us found out the hard way.

Using the Christian Guesthouse in Zamalek as our temporary sanctuary, we hailed a taxi and headed towards Saida Zainab, a lively, established suburb of Cairo with memories of Amani's past.

The streets bustled with life as the taxi navigated through the vibrant neighbourhood, filled with the tantalising scents of street food and the sound of lively conversations.

Our mission was both poignant and practical; to sift through Amani's belongings and bring a semblance of order back to her cherished home, where echoes of her life still lingered.

Upon entering, we were greeted by an overpowering stench that hung heavily in the air. In the bathroom, damp clothes festered in the washing machine, their acrid odour mingling with the mustiness of the stale air. The oven contained remnants of spoiled food, emitting a foul, nauseating scent that turned our stomachs. The lounge was particularly distressing; a pervasive, sour smell lingered, suggesting that poor Amani had been vomiting there, bringing a grim reminder of the recent chaos in her life.

Thus, we set about restoring a pleasant ambience in her apartment. In the bedroom, I found some money stashed haphazardly at the back of her wardrobe, but I wasn't sure what to do with it, so I left it there for the time being.

During our visit, a few of her close neighbours, whom we had met during previous visits, kindly came by to express their condolences and offer their help in removing the rubbish left in the flat.

One of the priests at Saint Catherine's Cathedral arranged for us to visit Magid in prison again. Amr picked us up and drove us to the jail.

Since I believed they were close and that he genuinely cared for her, I expected to find Magid in a state of distress over Amani's death, but I was perplexed to see that he didn't seem particularly upset. Instead, his primary concern was whether I had found any money in her apartment.

"There was still cash in her wardrobe," I assured him, and he visibly relaxed at this news.

"Phew, thank God for that!" was his relieved response. Two days later, I scooped up the pile of soiled Egyptian pounds *(valued at around £800)* stashed in a black muslin bag and took them to him in jail. This served as a massive wake-up call, revealing his true priorities.

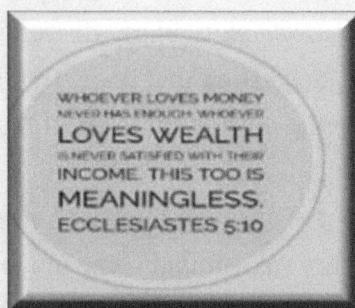

WHOEVER LOVES MONEY NEVER HAS ENOUGH. WHOEVER **LOVES WEALTH** IS NEVER SATISFIED WITH THEIR INCOME. THIS TOO IS **MEANINGLESS.** ECCLESIASTES 5:10

His next mission was to claim life insurance for her. I was certain this wouldn't succeed because there was a strong possibility that she had deliberately walked in front of that truck in her disturbed state of mind when faced with the fact that she would have to leave her flat, which was her only home. She would have nowhere to live and no money to get another place.

Unfortunately, we learned the flat was in Magid's name. I discerned that he had probably told her he would need to take it back upon his release from prison.

Her mind and emotions must have been in turmoil as she would have had nowhere to go. She loved living there, and I strongly suspected that this was *'the bad thing'* she mentioned to Adam and, indirectly, the cause of her death.

Outraged by his callousness and the injustice doled out to his only sister, who was always as kind and supportive as anyone could be to him, I abruptly ended my visit and left the building.

The insurance claim came to nothing, as I suspected they would have decided suicide was a strong possibility. Magid's obsession with financial gain blinded him to reality, which had no place in his world.

My apartment in Hurghada could have been her home if I had only known; I would have offered it to her. Being in a strange town would have been tricky for her, but she would have had a decent place to live and, in time, could have gotten used to the new place and made friends there.

Regrettably, I never had the opportunity to put this suggestion to her.

Fathi, one of the regular taxi drivers who was familiar with us from our stays at the Hilton Hotel, offered to collect us from Saida Zainab and take us to the airport. Still, I didn't trust him, having once witnessed him opening a tourist's suitcase by unscrewing it from the back when a passenger had left it behind in his taxi.

I was reticent to say anything to him about this, so I kept silent, aware there could be nasty repercussions. This was a widespread practice, I learned, and typical of a few dishonest taxi drivers in the area.

Suspicious that he had an ulterior motive for helping us and was planning a scheme to make unreasonable demands for money, I gave him the slip. Random men from the neighbourhood emerged from every doorway, pestering us to pay imaginary electric and water bills they claimed Amani owed but, as they had no legitimate paperwork to show, I dismissed them as charlatans who thought they could extract money from us because we were, in their eyes, wealthy foreigners, ripe for picking, callously using the unhappy circumstances of her death to their advantage. *Were there no depths to which these people would stoop!*

Avoiding Fathi's offer, I hailed a passing cab and told the driver to take us to the airport.

Adam, deeply unsettled by this scenario, continued to glance over his shoulder even after we entered the Departure Lounge. Gradually, he relaxed and began to take in his surroundings at the Duty-Free Shop.

A famous face caught Adam's attention; unruly light blonde hair gave him away; it was of course *Boris Johnson.*

Adam boldly approached him and asked if he could take a photograph of me with him. He was friendly and happily obliged. We chatted, and when I inquired about what he was doing in Cairo, he replied that he was working on a documentary about Egypt for the BBC.
Enquiring when it would be released, I was rather dubious when he responded with a flippant,

"Oh, not for ages yet!"
Seated a few rows away from us on the plane, he worked feverishly on his laptop throughout the flight.

~

ENGLAND/*Buckinghamshire*

Tony and I decided to check out a church closer to our new home, as attending St Peter's on Sundays and the weekly groups was proving difficult. We checked out St Birinus Church *(now Christ the Servant King),* which is only a few kilometres away.

Shortly after we began attending this church, I had a dream involving Steve, the Vicar, which I shared with him during a small group session.

He was astounded that my dream featured solutions to issues he was struggling with at that time, and he asked me to speak to the congregation when an available slot arose.

However, certain aspects of the church made us uncomfortable, such as the statues at the front of the auditorium and their adherence to doctrines we didn't support. At the right time, we moved on to a smaller church called Marlow Christian Fellowship (MCF). This was a small, friendly Bible-based church.

Community Bible Study International (CBS) was a regular Bible study program led there by Louise, the wife of one of the elders. She was introduced to it while living in the USA and believed it would benefit the church.

CBS consisted of set Bible studies on specific books and Bible themes. Initially, I struggled with it and was guilty of not completing the required homework for the lessons more than once.

As a result, Louise became exasperated with me and gave me a well-earned reprimand. After that, I buckled down, began to see its value, and diligently completed the homework for my studies. Ruth, who led the classes, was so knowledgeable about Scripture that she gained my undivided attention and admiration.

She was an inspiration. I admired her wisdom and balanced approach, as well as her knowledge of numerous backstories about Bible characters, engaging listeners and bringing these characters to life.

This marked the beginning of a long and fruitful association with Community Bible Study. Scripture from their discussions became an essential learning tool, and over time, I went on to lead Bible study classes, both face-to-face and on Zoom during the COVID-19 outbreak, with Tony and a friend, Catherine.

Whilst still at this church, I suffered further problems with pain in my joints and lack of mobility, and was advised to undergo foot surgery, eventually having a cage implanted in my left foot with screws inserted into each of my toes.

My recovery was complicated by an MRSA infection in the wound, which I believe occurred after the dressing was changed at the hospital, as it became wet several times. Luckily, it didn't spread and cleared up quickly. Due to the various implants and artificial joints in my body, my friends jokingly refer to me as *The Bionic Woman*. Airport security is an experience for which I steel myself *(pardon the pun)*.
Raising my hands, I resign myself to the inevitable thorough frisking as my metal implants set off all the alarms, so when I walk through the checkpoints, people joke that *they think they've won the jackpot*.

This can be a massive problem in third-world countries, as they don't have the necessary technical equipment to detect medical implants, and I was often frisked within an inch of my life in these places, despite having a hospital letter outlining all my metalwork.

For nine enriching years, we immersed ourselves in the vibrant community of our quaint little church in Marlow, forging deep friendships and enjoying the warmth of fellowship.

We often gathered in one another's homes for shared meals, heartfelt Bible studies, and meaningful conversations. The bonds created became incredibly meaningful, and the church family became like an extension of our own.

Despite extensive advertising, they reached a crisis point when they lacked a leader for an extended period.
A young new pastor from South Africa arrived, and they appointed him to fill the position. He seemed like an answer to prayer, tall, eloquent and good-looking with a neat family, a pretty wife and a baby boy. He wormed his way into the hearts of many in the congregation, specifically the widowed older ladies.

However, I began having serious doubts about his authenticity when he didn't keep his many promises to help members of the congregation who were in difficulty.

He began teaching a strange doctrine that didn't align with the Bible in the small groups, while enthusiastically preaching the true gospel on Sundays. Occasionally, he made mistakes when quoting verses of Scripture, and when confronted about them, he would immediately instruct the sound technician to stop recording the CD and ask them to erase it.

Long, intense phone calls to people in South Africa, speaking in Afrikaans, were a frequent occurrence, and more South Africans were joining our church, sitting in small huddles and speaking in their native tongue, which I found quite disturbing, and it began to feel like a creeping takeover by a cult.

Tony and I investigated his background online and found that he was trained at a college in Port Elizabeth, which specialised in a doctrine called Hyper-Dispensationalism, a perspective on the Bible that mainstream Christianity does not support.

Teaching that the New Testament begins with the Acts of the Apostles instead of the Gospel of Matthew was viewed as unconventional, especially since Red-Letter Bibles *(so-called because they display Jesus' words in red)*, were deemed unnecessary; they argued that Jesus' teachings were mainly directed at Jews, not Gentiles.

They believed that the foundation of the Church was established by the Apostle Paul rather than by Christ Himself. They also followed various unusual theories that deviated from mainstream Christianity and held strict interpretations on eschatology (or beliefs about the end times).

Before accepting his position, the elders were well aware of his background; however, he assured them that he had completely disowned these doctrines and claimed they no longer represented his beliefs.

Yet, incriminating video clips surfaced online, showing him mockingly discussing his upcoming role in England, making light of the seriousness of the Gospels, which painted a starkly different picture. There was one interview where, when asked how he planned to preach in the UK, he mockingly replied,

"I'll just dance around the gospels a bit before I get to the real stuff!"

The elders refused to listen when we drew their attention to this, shutting it out, as it wasn't what they wanted to hear. They were acutely embarrassed at having taken on a person who had hoodwinked them and didn't want to face the truth.

The church in Marlow was a satellite church of the mother church at Gold Hill in Chalfont St Peter. Consequently, we had meetings in our home with the elders from Gold Hill to discuss this matter further. The heartbreaking decision to leave the Marlow church had to be made, as they refused to budge on their choice to keep him on as their new pastor, but we couldn't accept this false teaching.

Over time, the leadership at MCF decided to relieve this new pastor of his duties and welcomed a new pastor, Kenn Baird, whose teachings, I'm happy to say, are firmly rooted in biblical principles.

The relief and hope that washed over us was palpable; finally, they now had an authentic, Bible-believing pastor guiding the congregation.

Though we considered returning to that church, we had already started to settle into our new community at King's Church in the nearby town of High Wycombe, and we were happy there, as it was a much larger, livelier church with lots of small groups that we could get involved in. The preaching was Bible-based, passionate and inspirational.

We had already made many new friends there, and the teaching was excellent.

After leaving MCF, we stayed in touch with a few valued friends from our previous church. One close friend, John McCollough, had moved back to the beautiful landscapes of his native Cornwall. We enjoyed visiting him at his lovely, spacious new bungalow just a few miles from the beach, where we shared delicious home-cooked dinners. He took us with him to his local church service on Sunday. It was a very different style of church from those we were used to, very relaxed, and we enjoyed meeting the people there.

Mimi was another dear friend who lived in Marlow until her untimely passing in 2023. We met regularly to pray for one another in each other's homes and often attended events

together.

Sadly, she didn't enjoy good health and was often ill. Ultimately, she bravely fought against the complications of breast cancer, spending her last days in a local hospice. I sat with her daughter, Wendy, and a few others in the Hospice when she died.

Her absence leaves a tender void in my heart, and I often think of her, missing her comforting presence, our walks, chats, regular coffee times and the laughter we shared.

~

Meanwhile, it had been several years since I'd seen my dear friends Glenn and Wills from the Harmony Christian Singles Group, and I was delighted when Adam told me he had bumped into them at a Christian event in Central London. He gave them my married surname, so they were easily able to find me on social media and got in touch.

Soon after reconnecting with them, Adam became unwell once more and was admitted to the Mental Health Unit of Northwick Park Hospital. A week later, he was discharged with new medication and appeared stable.

Glenn and Wills supported him, acting as guardian angels. This was heartwarming for me and lifted the weight off my shoulders, as I knew I could trust them to keep an eye on him and contact me if there were any problems.

Unfortunately, on another occasion, they had to call an ambulance for Adam when he displayed catatonic symptoms while in Will's flat in West London. As soon as I heard about this, I drove straight to London.

Adam was taken to St Mary's Hospital, Paddington, but on arrival, I was put on guard by the hushed conversations among the reception staff when I asked them where I could find Adam.

Their responses made me feel very concerned, as it seemed that something had happened that they didn't want me to know about. It was then that they eventually informed me that he had absconded, prompting me to rush out and drive straight to his flat several miles away in Northolt. I rang the bell, but when there was no answer, I let myself in with my spare key for emergencies.

Stumbling sleepily out of his bedroom, Adam told me, the nurse at the hospital said he could go home.

Whether this was true or not, I don't know, but I was just relieved to see him and reassured that he was alright.

~

OBERAMMERGAU, AUSTRIAN TYROL

In September 2022, my second knee replacement surgery was performed at the Royal National Orthopaedic Hospital (RNOH) in Stanmore.

The recovery process was challenging and proved to be more painful compared to my first knee operation, perhaps because this knee had borne the brunt of my weight for years. Despite this setback, I looked forward to the trip Tony planned for us.

We were scheduled to visit Oberammergau to enjoy the Passion Play, a rare and extraordinary event that occurs only once every decade. COVID-19 postponed the original 2020 performance of this play, rescheduling it for September 2024.

The history of the Passion Play is rooted in the harrowing events of 1633, when the quiet Bavarian village of Oberammergau found itself at the mercy of the Great Plague. As fear and despair gripped the community, the villagers turned to fervent prayer, pleading for divine intervention and healing from the relentless suffering surrounding them.

Their prayers were answered in a remarkable turn of events, and the plague began to subside, restoring hope for the beleaguered inhabitants. To show gratitude for their salvation, the villagers made a solemn vow; they dedicated themselves to God by staging a powerful play that recounted the poignant story of Jesus Christ's time on earth — the agony of his suffering, leading to the ultimate triumph of his resurrection.

This heartfelt commitment led to them establishing a tradition, culminating in a vow to perform this Biblical play every decade as a lasting tribute to their miraculous deliverance, a reminder of answered prayer, and the enduring strength of their faith.

The tradition of the play has endured since its legendary first performance in 1634. For over 350 years, the play has evolved into a globally renowned event, once performed in a cemetery near the graves of victims of the plague. Now more sophisticated, this elaborate production attracts thousands of visitors from around the world. Supporters travel to Oberammergau to experience it to witness this profound and captivating portrayal of faithfulness and history unfold before them.

Despite my recent surgery, I desperately wanted to see this play, and I didn't want to miss this golden opportunity, so we booked a 10-day coach tour of the Austrian Tyrol, Germany, and Bavaria.

Tony rented a wheelchair for me, but struggled to push it over

cobblestone streets in the little towns on our itinerary. Munich and Salzburg were easier to negotiate as the streets were paved, but when we reached the Bavarian Alps, I felt sorry that he had to negotiate the cobbles, though thankfully, the younger ones on our coach lent a hand.

Outside the Salzburg Cathedral on the Kapitelplatz, in a large square, Mozart's Golden Ball is easily recognisable from afar thanks to its golden sheen reflecting the sunlight.

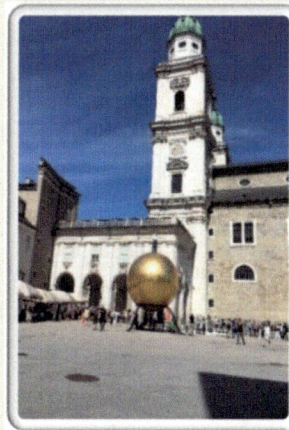

This is the sculpture, Sphaera, on Kapitelplatz, in the heart of Salzburg. It's about nine metres high and was created by German artist Stephan Balkenhol. It represents a male figure with a neutral expression on a golden sphere and has become a popular point for tourists to take photos.

Excited and looking forward to seeing this long-awaited, famous play at last in the picturesque village of Oberammergau, we joined the long queue outside the theatre waiting to be allowed inside.

The Passion Play cast comprises only local amateur actors. Although there are few speaking roles, more than 2,000 residents took part in the production. Men participating in the play need to start growing their hair and beards fifteen months before the performance to achieve a genuine appearance.

Although the performance is in German, the audience has a booklet that translates the script into English. It was a challenge keeping up with the dialogue, resulting in me losing my place several times, and I had to resort to looking over the shoulder of the man next to me to find my spot again. *(I don't think he minded.)* I couldn't glance at Tony's booklet as he was seated in the middle of the row.

As darkness fell, torches illuminated the booklets, and the auditorium's lighting was very dim. The play lasts seven hours, which is a long time to sit in one place, but there is a three-hour interval halfway through, during which you can go outside, enjoy a meal at a local restaurant, and do some shopping.

A packed auditorium arranged in ascending tiers ensured that everyone had an unobstructed view; there must have been over

4,000 people in that open-topped tent. The evening sky was visible, and the expectant atmosphere was palpable. Positioning myself at the end of a row in my wheelchair for convenience, should I need to use the bathroom facilities, I was thrilled to have secured such a good vantage point.

A unique feature of this Oberammergau Passion Play is the living montages of colourful scenes from the Old Testament, woven into the story of the Passion in the form of still-life pictures. On stage, the atmosphere was electric, featuring live animals, including majestic, well-trained horses ridden by actors in costume. This created an impressive, realistic ambience. Camels and goats on leads for optimum control graced the stage.

Toddlers could be seen running between the actors' legs and around the vast stage, dressed in appropriate attire of the portrayed era, under the guidance of their parents, adding an extra layer of authenticity. Special effects were elaborate and inspiring, with images of angels floating up to the heavens.

Many people, including us, used our phones to take several photos, although I'm not sure if this was permitted. There were no signs restricting photography. The music was invigorating and intermittently performed by a choir dressed as nuns. The collective spirit of these dear performers was enchanting.

What an unforgettable experience!

It was definitely worth the wait and the discomfort of queuing to enter the theatre. I highly recommend that anyone interested in spiritual and historical events book tickets to see this fantastic production. Afterwards, we bought T-shirts and other souvenirs to remember this powerful Passion Play.

Our next destination was Neuschwanstein Castle, which we reached aboard a vibrant open-topped train that took us through the beautiful gardens.

After exploring the castle and its grounds, we headed to Linderhof Palace, built and once inhabited by King Ludwig II. There, we visited the grotto and admired various displays, including statues, armour, and swords, as well as commanding portraits of members of the royal family in the neighbouring rooms. Near the entrance was a small, ornate chapel where we sat in reverence and prayed before leaving.

Our rather eccentric Austrian tour guide, Paulina, who at one point disappeared to visit her family who lived nearby, leaving us to get lost in one of the towns. On one such occasion, we called her to ask if she could come and pick a group of us up in her car and take us back to the coach.

She was clearly very disgruntled about this, making it obvious that she regarded it as a huge imposition.

Returning to Munich for our flight home was not easy for Tony. He had to balance the suitcases and push my wheelchair, which left me feeling helpless. I hated being the cause of such logistical difficulties, but we managed to get through. Despite the mobility problems, it was a valuable experience I wouldn't have missed for the world.

Tony's parents, Bet and Ray, lived in an upstairs flat in Harlesden, a busy area of Northwest London. When Tony took me to their home and introduced me to them, she was disgruntled and clearly unhappy. She was fond of his ex-wife, Judy, who used to take her out for meals and cater to her every whim.

His father, Ray, a retired police sergeant, was a tall, friendly, tolerant man, and he was much more accepting of our relationship.

Following a stroke, Ray was advised by the hospital to move down to their bungalow in St Mary's Bay, Kent. It was their holiday home in the form of a modest three-bedroom bungalow, a stone's throw from the seafront. Living in their flat in Harlesden was no longer viable as the stairs there were extremely steep.

Since they both originally hailed from Kent and had siblings living nearby, we took them on the long journey there and assisted in settling them into their bungalow.

However, Bet hated it; it was too quiet for her, and she missed the bustling streets of Harlesden as well as the constant activity in the area. She used to look after the *'old lady'* across the street, where they lived, who was, in fact, much younger than her, bringing her cakes and other treats she had baked. Bet deeply resented being so far away from the area she knew and irrationally focused the blame on us, as we were the ones who took them to Kent.

Bet was a complex character who phoned us obsessively, several times a day.

She continued to call me Judy, the name of Tony's ex-wife, for around six years after we got married. Reaching the end of my tether, I told her that if she called me Judy one more time, I would hang up. *She did, and I did!*

Tony's children, Mark, Lucy, and Adam and Lucy's young son, Yaseen, experienced a unique relationship with their grandmother. Rather than treating them as her grandchildren, she behaved as though she were their mother.

This dynamic resulted in her becoming increasingly involved in their lives, frequently stepping in to offer unsolicited advice and direction, which looked more like control than care.

As time passed and she lived farther away from her grandchildren, opportunities to see them in person became scarce. This distance was a source of deep frustration for her, intensifying her desire to maintain her influence from afar.

Lucy found it challenging to manage her grandmother's constant calls and text messages, which often disrupted her own family life. The frequency of these communications became a significant annoyance for Lucy, leading her to ignore or avoid her grandmother's calls altogether. This pattern created tension between her and her Bet, as well as within the family, as they navigated the complexities of love, loyalty, and independence.

Due to her diabetes, her sight had severely diminished, leading to her being registered as partially blind. Her mobility deteriorated rapidly, leaving her increasingly immobile and confined to their home, which made her even more bitter about the situation.

Ray and Bet argued frequently, causing alarm among the neighbours, who occasionally called the police out of concern. They also contacted us, seeking our intervention, which was challenging due to the distance between us. However, Tony did contact them regularly to try to reason with them and bring about some peace.

Visiting them meant a 240-mile round trip, but we travelled to see them as often as possible.

Sadly, Ray became ill again and was hospitalised in Ashford, the nearest large town. Bet insisted that he be brought home, as she seemed irrationally jealous of the attention the nurses were giving him *(at 92),* so a hospital bed was installed for him in the living room of their bungalow.

They held rather loose religious beliefs, and, at one point, Ray told us he had had what sounded like a near-death experience, telling us he went to heaven, but declaring disparagingly that he didn't think much of it, as everything was foggy and grey.

Interestingly, after that experience, he began to recite the Lord's Prayer doggedly, repeating it until he got it right.

The Lord's Prayer

Our Father who art in heaven,
hallowed be thy name.
Thy kingdom come,
thy will be done,
on earth as it is in heaven.
Give us this day our daily bread;
and forgive us our trespasses
as we forgive those
who trespass against us.
And lead us not into temptation
but deliver us from evil.
For thine is the kingdom,
the power and the glory,
for ever and ever.
Amen.

Shortly after this incident, he passed away and I would like to think he had a spiritual experience that led him to go to a better place.

At his funeral, he was afforded full police ceremonial protocol with a flag over his coffin and a guard of honour, which would have made him proud. He would have relished it. This was very moving, and many of us were in tears at the loss of this sweet man.

Bet managed to live independently in her bungalow for the next three years, relying on occasional assistance from local carers. During the final months of her life, she occasionally employed live-in carers to help with daily tasks.

Unexpectedly, one evening, we received a call from one of her neighbours informing us she had been taken to the hospital and had subsequently died following two heart attacks. We were told she was resuscitated from the first attack, which was rapidly followed by a second attack that unfortunately killed her.

Tony and I were shocked, upset and outraged that the carer hadn't told us she was in this state, so that we could drive down to be by her side at this crucial time, and that we had to hear this devastating news from a neighbour.

Bet's sister, Jean, and other local family members and friends from Harlesden, where they used to live, attended her funeral. Tony's eldest son, Mark, flew over from New York to be there. It was good to see him after such a long time.

The wake was held at the local pub, but disappointingly, few people turned up, so we had to return most of the food to them.

~

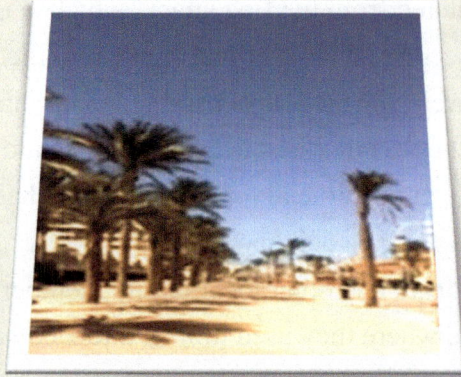

Chapter Fifteen

SPIRITUAL TRAVELS ~ *Egypt, Turkey, Israel, Malta*

EGYPT

Hurghada, on the Red Sea, the location of my flat, became a regular holiday destination for Tony and me. Several people, mostly expatriates, formed lasting friendships there, including those with Russians and Poles, some of whom lived on the same building block.

We often joined them for meals at the Marina, where the breathtaking view was calming and relaxing.

An evangelical church we attended on the outskirts of town always intrigued me; it was guarded by the Egyptian Army, who were exclusively Muslim, and patrolled the grounds, wielding rifles and machine guns.

There was a sprinkling of Egyptians, Germans, British, Russians, and Turks, forming a multinational congregation. Wild dogs roamed outside, and one of them had given birth to a litter of cute little pups on the grounds. They were so alluring that we were tempted to pick them up and stroke them, but refrained as they likely could have had fleas or lice.

A young Egyptian trainee doctor, Shadi, was studying orthopaedics and later came to London to work. Coincidentally, I met him again at the Stanmore Orthopaedic Hospital during my next admission there. He was delighted to see me, but he wasn't on the spinal team I was under, so unfortunately, he was unable to give me any information about my treatment.

In the home of one of the congregation in Hurghada, we initiated a Community Bible Study class despite the significant risk posed by the militant Muslim presence in the area.

This effort was a considerable achievement for our small group, demonstrating our commitment to faith and community, even in challenging circumstances. Although the meetings were conducted clandestinely to ensure everyone's safety, the joy and sense of fellowship we experienced each week were truly rewarding.

Our gatherings were primarily led by our pastor, Seth, an American from Boston, who brought a unique perspective and depth to our discussions. His wife, Cindy, often joined him, contributing her warm, enthusiastic spirit and insightful reflections.

Together, they guided us through Biblical topics, encouraging us to explore and deepen our understanding of the Scriptures. Each session culminated in an inspirational wrap-up talk, during which Seth and Cindy shared meaningful takeaways and personal anecdotes that resonated with our daily lives. These moments of shared faith strengthened our bond as a congregation and fortified our resolve to practice our beliefs in a challenging environment.

In Hurghada, the Christian community is predominantly Coptic, and one of the noteworthy landmarks is the Cathedral of St Shenouda, situated in a bustling square near the town centre. Although not particularly spectacular in its architectural design, this charming church offers a serene atmosphere that makes it well worth a visit. Whether you're drawn to its simple beauty or the peaceful environment, it's a lovely and quiet place to explore. We found navigating through this local church's spiritual and historical significance fascinating, although it can't compare to the majesty of Western cathedrals.

TURKEY

Tony and I have travelled extensively, yet our most treasured memories stem from places steeped in Biblical history. Our journeys took us to Turkey, Israel and Malta, each with rich historical significance.

Exploring the vast ruins of Ephesus, we navigated through expansive areas, often treading on uneven and sometimes prickly surfaces.

Ephesus is mentioned numerous times in the Bible; it is one of the seven churches in the Book of Revelation, where St John received a divine message in a city where the Apostle Paul lived and carried out his ministry.

The subject of the Book of Ephesians was next on our agenda. It is also said to be where Mary, the mother of Jesus, lived in her final years, and we saw her tiny house with the nearby tomb of the beloved saint, John. Our tour guide had a wealth of knowledge about the region, though strangely, he seemed obsessed with communal latrines, elaborating profusely on the workings of the sewage drainage systems everywhere we went. This became a standing joke. Everyone on the coach found it quite comical, and we waited eagerly for him to launch into his favourite subject at every stop.

He didn't disappoint!

Ephesus is an ancient city in Turkey's Central Aegean region, near the modern town of Selçuk. The excavated remains reveal a rich history spanning from classical Greece to the Roman Empire, during which it served as the Mediterranean's primary trading port.

For Christians, the district holds particular significance, as it features St John's Basilica. This continues to capture the attention of visitors. The region is widely recognised as a notable Biblical location, attracting those interested in its historical and religious heritage.

ISRAEL/*Jerusalem*

In 2019, we were privileged to be invited on a customised tour of Israel led by Steve and Janet Gaukroger. The coach driver was a friendly English-speaking Israeli guy named Neif.

Our party consisted of around thirty-five Christian pilgrims from churches around Oxfordshire and Buckinghamshire. We bonded well during the trip and appreciated that this journey to Israel was more than a holiday; it was an exploration of sites mentioned in Bible stories, and we were walking where Jesus walked, seeing things that impacted our lives and faith.

A trip to Israel for a Christian brings a deeper understanding of the environment in which the Bible was written and where Jesus walked, taught and revealed His Heavenly Father's nature to mankind. Being in the land where these things happened brought the Bible to life in ways nothing else could, and this reinforced our faith.

Following the flight from Gatwick to Ben Gurion Airport in Tel Aviv, we disembarked from the aircraft and proceeded through security without incident. Emerging into the distinctive atmosphere of the Holy Land, the air was heavy with the glorious scent of orange blossoms.

Among our eclectic group, we were particularly captivated by an intriguing American couple, Claudette and Ridgley. Both impressively tall and blessed with distinctive first names that lingered in the air like a melody, their warm and inviting personalities made our conversation entertaining and truly memorable.

As we exchanged stories and discovered they were members of Gold Hill, a charming church in Chalfont St Peter's, in Buckinghamshire, a few miles from our home.

We knew this church as it happened to be the mother church of our smaller satellite congregation in Marlow, which had been an integral part of our lives for nine enriching years. This unexpected connection resonated deeply with me as I reminisced about the Bible course I had participated in, the engaging events and classes.

I occasionally attended Gold Hill and appreciated the superb pastors, such as Jim Graham and David Pawson, who have written numerous Christian books, as well as the congregants I had known there over the years. Both these men are sadly now deceased, but have left a lasting legacy in that church and throughout the wider Christian community.

As we wandered through the vibrant markets and the bustling, notorious Jimmy's Bazaar in East Jerusalem, rich aromas and colours filled the air, creating an enchanting atmosphere. We excitedly browsed the stalls and selected beautifully crafted olive wood crosses and fragrant frankincense oil, each a perfect souvenir to bring home, anticipating the joy these treasures would bring to our friends and bless them with these thoughtful gifts.

Transported by coach from Tel Aviv, we climbed into the hill country to arrive in the ancient City of Jerusalem, where we checked into a charming boutique hotel.

The following morning, we went to the top of the Mount of Olives and walked down to the Garden of Gethsemane, which was surprisingly smaller than I had imagined. The original site would be buried over time under mounds of earth.

We were dismayed to find we could not enter the garden because of a cordoned area around the entrance. This restriction was necessary to protect the foliage, as some guests inevitably tried to take souvenirs from such a sacred place.

When we visited a tomb said to be the tomb of Jesus, I noticed a large stone outside, like the one described in the Bible. Whether or not this was the actual site of Jesus' tomb didn't matter, as it provided us with unique insight into how His actual tomb may have looked. Seeing the Western Wall, the remaining wall of the Ancient Temple, where Orthodox Jews were rocking back and forth, praying, and inserting rolled-up papers with prayer requests into the brickwork, was intriguing. Steve explained that this was common practice.

The Old City is divided into four distinct quarters; the Muslim Quarter, the Christian Quarter, the Armenian Quarter, and the Jewish Quarter.

The following day, we walked around the city walls and visited the Pool of Bethesda, a place where local people with disabilities and other significant ailments gathered during Jesus' time. They hoped to be healed by entering the water when it was 'stirred up by angels'.

Another breathtaking Biblical site on our journey was the Church of St Anne, the best-preserved Crusader church in Jerusalem. This location marks the home of Jesus' maternal grandparents, Anne and Joachim, as well as the birthplace of the Virgin Mary.

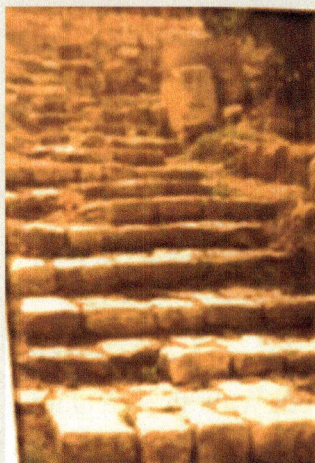

Walking along the Via Dolorosa *(its very name gives me goosebumps)* was an emotional time. Once a dirt road, it is now paved with steps.

Along the path are fourteen plaques and markers detailing the significant events that occurred on the day of Jesus' Crucifixion.

The sound of the vendors calling us to inspect their wares faded out as I began to fixate on the gravity of the significance of my surroundings.

Shopping is one of my favourite pastimes *(as my long-suffering husband will testify).*

However, we weren't there to examine the goods on sale, but on a pilgrimage in the place where the Lord walked on His way to Calvary, and my heart and mind began to connect with that horrific scene over 2,000 years ago. Jesus was beaten beyond recognition, mocked, and forced to carry His heavy cross on His shoulders to His crucifixion.

Visualising his savagely beaten body with open scars and wounds, the crown of thorns pressed on His head *(to remove the curse God put on the ground, Gen. 3:18),* piercing His skin, causing blood to trickle down His face, I was firmly immersed in the moment.

The hot sun would have been scorching, and the wooden cross weighed Jesus down so much that He collapsed, with Simon of Cyrene lending a hand.

Being there brought it all into powerful perspective, rendering me and others in our group to be overcome with emotion and gratitude to our Lord and Saviour for what He endured for our sakes, to purchase our salvation.

Groups of Jews passed us by on the street, the women dressed in filmy white dresses and headscarves. We assumed they were Ashkenazi Jews or another such Jewish sect, and I desperately wanted to ask them to tell us who they were, but couldn't summon up the nerve to do it.

Claudette was also too reserved to approach them, so we remained in ignorance.

And when they came to Golgotha (which means Place of the Skull), they offered him wine mixed with gall, but after tasting it, he refused to drink it. When they had crucified him, they divided up his clothes by casting lots.
And sitting down, they kept watch over him there.
Above his head, they placed the written charge against him:

Two rebels were crucified with him, one on his right and one on his left. Those who passed by hurled insults at him, shaking their heads and saying,

"You who are going to destroy the temple and build it in three days, save yourself and come down from the cross if you are the Son of God!"
In the same way, the chief priests and the teachers of the law mocked him among themselves. "He saved others," they said, *"but he can't save himself! Let him come down now from the cross, and we will believe in him."* Matt. 27: 33-42 NIV

Steve and Jan had visited the historical sites numerous times before, making them exceptionally well-versed in the rich tapestry of their histories.

As we explored each landmark, Steve captivated us with his knowledge and fascinating, detailed talks, weaving stories of ancient civilisations and pivotal events that had shaped the region. By pointing out specific architectural features or artefacts, he explained their significance in a way that brought the past to life.

Every evening, as we gathered around the table in our accommodation, we had the chance to ask questions and engage in lively discussions about the places we had seen. These conversations deepened our understanding and fostered a sense of connection to the history and culture we were experiencing firsthand, making our journey all the more enriching.

Each day, we read the relevant Bible passages on our way to the locations where momentous events took place, using the microphone located in the front section of the coach. As we had an hour to spare before dinner each evening, we sang God's praises and listened to a Bible message expertly delivered by Steve.

The Garden Tomb is tranquil, starkly contrasting with the bustling Old City of Jerusalem. In this beautiful garden, an empty tomb and a cliff face resembling a skull's features, hence its name, Golgotha, meaning *'Place of the Skull.'*

It is an inspiring place to reflect on the Lord's horrific crucifixion and the ultimate triumph of the risen Lord Jesus. As we read the Scriptures, we were transported to the incredible events of the first Easter and attended a momentous communion service held there.

Hallelujah!

I began to worship and praise my Saviour for sacrificing His life for me.

Interestingly, *Hallelujah* is the only Hebrew word commonly used in English.

Some members of our party elected to miss lunch to visit the Dome of the Rock, a prominent Islamic shrine at the centre of the Al-Aqsa Mosque compound on the Temple Mount, as it was nearby but not part of our itinerary.

After lunch in a quaint little café near the Jaffa Gate, we visited Caiaphas's  house at St Peter Gallicantu. In the courtyard, a statue of the rooster which crowed three times as Jesus predicted, signifying Simon Peter's denial of Christ, which he later bitterly regretted and was forgiven by Jesus.

"But I have prayed for you, Simon, that your faith may not fail. And when you have turned back, strengthen your brothers."
But he replied, "Lord I am ready to go with you to prison and death."
"Truly I tell you," Jesus answered, *"This very night before the rooster crows, you will deny me three times."*
Luke 22: 32- 34 NIV

Descending into the dungeon underneath Caiaphas's house, where Jesus was lowered by rope and kept overnight before his trial, was a joyless excursion. What a dark, sombre, desolate, comfortless place that was.
Bizarrely, it was there that I felt the presence of the Lord the most, in that depressing, dank cavern of bleak nothingness. Despair permeated the walls.

Two days later, we were taken to Bethlehem Bible College, a place steeped in history and purpose. There, we listened intently to a heartfelt talk from a Palestinian resident who shared the poignant story of how the loss of his parents' property had a devastating impact on their livelihood.

He told of the suffocating restrictions that prevent Palestinians from entering Jerusalem, a city that holds deep significance for them. His words, laced with emotion, vividly depicted their struggles. As he recounted these hardships, we were moved to tears, deeply affected by the loss and longing in his narrative. He added defiantly that they could still enter Jerusalem using the underground tunnels.

In the afternoon, we visited Shepherd's Field, where the ancient shepherds received a divine revelation that a Saviour would be born in Bethlehem, and we proceeded to the Nativity Church.

Since at least the first century AD, people have believed that the site where the Church of the Nativity now stands in Bethlehem is the birthplace of Jesus.

One of the caves over which the first church was built is traditionally assumed to be His actual birthplace.

And an angel of the Lord appeared to them and the glory of the Lord shone around them and they were filled with great fear. And the angel said to them, "Fear not for behold I bring good news of great joy that will be for all the people. For unto you is born this day in the city of David a Saviour who is Christ the Lord. And this will be a sign for you. You will find a baby wrapped in swaddling cloths and lying in a manger."
Luke 2: 9-20 ESV

The trip included a compulsory visit to Yad Vashem, the Holocaust memorial and museum, which contains reams of heart-wrenching historical pictures and information about the Jews who were victims of Nazi oppressors.

Over 3,000 of the approximately 8,000 shoes belonging to children murdered in Auschwitz were carefully preserved and returned from these vile camps to be displayed at the memorial

museum. The exhibition was a poignant, thought-provoking, and sad experience.
We could scarcely imagine what these poor children had endured.

QUMRAN

Upon checking out of our hotel in Jerusalem, we travelled to Qumran, where the Dead Sea Scrolls were discovered in an ancient clay jar, although we didn't get to visit the actual location.

Swimming in the Dead Sea was a unique experience; it was an odd sensation to have to struggle to stand upright in the water, and it was quite unsettling. We were cautious not to get seawater in our eyes due to its high salt content. A few unfortunate individuals got splashed and quickly poured bottled water over their eyes to rinse out the salt. Then they were given over-the-counter eye drops to relieve the horrendous stinging sensation.

Of course, we covered ourselves with Dead Sea Mud, believed to have cosmetic benefits for deep cleansing and skin stimulation, as well as having a rich mineral content. This is often marketed at a high price by the cosmetic industry.

Next was the historic, renowned city of Capernaum, located on the northwestern shore of the Sea of Galilee. Capernaum was not only Jesus' second home during his earthly ministry but also functioned as a garrison town and an administrative centre.

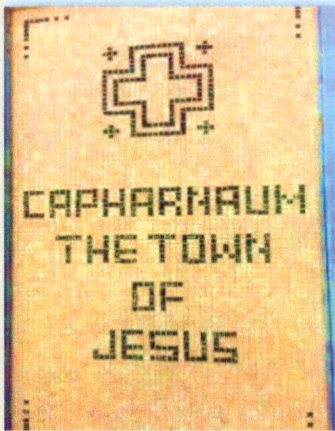

Here, Jesus chose his disciples, Peter, Andrew, and Matthew and here he performed numerous miracles.

Startled to see a cross-dresser, mincing on high heels, as he strutted down the main street, I thought about the stark contrast in our modern-day culture that has developed over the centuries, and I found it difficult to imagine such a scene taking place in Jesus' time.

Magdala, recognised as the birthplace of Mary Magdalene, was next on our agenda. A church in the village, said to be the house of Mary Magdalene, where it is recorded that Jesus cast out demons from her, proved to be a worthwhile visit.

The Jesus Boat Museum is an intriguing and historically significant site, located on the shores of the Sea of Galilee.

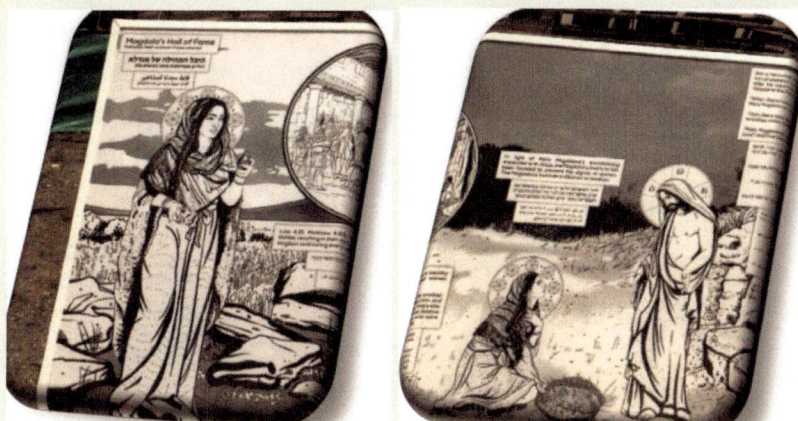

This museum displays the remains of an ancient fishing vessel, dating back to the first century, a time when Jesus and his disciples were known to have traversed these waters.

This boat was discovered in 1986 by two brothers who stumbled upon it while searching for ancient artefacts in the mud of the Galilee.

The preservation of this vessel offers a remarkable glimpse into the maritime culture of the region during that era, providing insight into the types of boats that fishermen used in ancient times.

The museum itself features informative exhibits detailing the boat's discovery, its archaeological significance, and the life of the fishermen who once relied on these waters for their livelihood. Visitors can not only admire the well-preserved remains of the boat, but also explore the interactive displays that delve into the historical and cultural context of the time, making it a memorable experience for anyone interested in the history of Jesus and the early Christian era.

The boat appears small and delicate, offering little protection against turbulent waters. It is no surprise that the disciples felt frightened when sailing in it.

During the fourth watch of the night, Jesus went out to them, walking on the sea. When the disciples saw Him walking on the sea, they were terrified. "It's a ghost!" they said and cried out in fear. But Jesus spoke up at once: "Take courage! It is I. Do not be afraid." Matt. 14: 25 – 33 BSB

A boat trip on the Sea of Galilee, where this famous incident took place, was a memorable occasion and a highlight for one couple, Margaret and Peter, who got engaged when Peter went down on one knee to propose on the boat amid the sea.

What a romantic and memorable location for a proposal – something they will never forget.

Cheering enthusiastically for them, we wished them all the very best for their future together.

In the evenings, we were suitably entertained by another of the guests, affectionately known as Mr. Brown (even his wife called him that), who thoughtfully brought along complex games to keep our minds active. This exercise was fun and a terrific opportunity to interact with the others on the trip.

Continuing to Tiberias, we spent the night there. The next stop was the Mount of Beatitudes. The River Jordan surprised me, as it wasn't how I'd imagined. An unappealing yellowish-brown colour, it was cloudy and dirty-looking, as though it contained a lot of mud.

On the banks of the Sea of Galilee at the foothills of the Mount of Beatitudes, Tabgha holds a special place in our faith, commemorated as a holy site. This is where the miracle of the loaves and fishes took place.

Blessed are they who mourn, for they will be comforted

Inside the small *Church of the Fish and the Loaves*, the floor is adorned with mosaics depicting this miracle, with various icons, including the *Virgin and the Child*, making it an absorbing experience. At midday, we all enjoyed a delicious fish lunch at the famous St Peter's Restaurant, followed by a scenic sunset boat trip before spending the night in Tiberias.

The following day, after checking out of our hotel, we stopped to visit Mt Carmel and Haifa on our way back to the airport, and we explored the neat terraces on the north slope of Mount Carmel at the *Bahá'í World Centre.*

These terraces are beautifully maintained with manicured gardens sloping down to a large shrine. This shrine took seventy years and 250 million dollars to build. Filled with a variety of flowers, I pondered the huge maintenance they would require. Although regarded as a horticultural wonder, it was beautifully neat but exuded a flat, dormant, artificial look.

A brief stop at Caesarea was next, to view the aqueduct and a cave north of Caesarea Philippi, claimed to be the birthplace of the Greco-Roman god Pan *(Lucifer)*, which once stood as a sanctuary used as a base for pagan rituals.

Human sacrifices, mostly babies, were thrown into the river flowing out of the cave, a tributary of the River Jordan. This dark place has many names:

The Temple of Zeus, Banias, the cave of the fertility god Pan, the gates of a spiritual underworld kingdom, a kingdom of darkness, literally, *the gates of Hell.*

An enormous invisible stop sign loomed before me, causing my heart to race as I instinctively recoiled, unwilling to step into this pagan site where countless malevolent rituals had taken place. I waited outside with Steve.

"Who do people say the Son of Man is?" was the crucial question Jesus posed while gazing down at the cave of Pan?

Simon Peter responded, *"You are the Messiah, the Son of the living God,"* a profound revelation given to him by God the Father. Jesus then replied—

"On this rock, I will build my church, and the gates of Hades will not overcome it." Matt. 16:13 NLT

Jesus was not referring to a specific place, but to a person —the Apostle Peter, whose name means *'stone'* or *'rock.'* He made this profound declaration at the gates of the underworld to proclaim his ultimate superiority and dominion over evil.

This location was the base of Mount Tabor/Herman, the *Mount of Transfiguration*. The purpose of Jesus' transfiguration was to instruct the apostles to see Him as He truly is, the Son of God, in all circumstances, even when His body hung on the cross, and He would appear least like the Messiah.

Inspired by this breathtaking view, I immersed myself in the scene that unfolded at the transfiguration, an awe-inspiring, life-changing experience for the disciples.

Gazing at the top of this snow-clad mountain, I tried to imagine what they must have felt.

As the men watched, Jesus' appearance was transformed. His face shone like the sun, and his clothes became as white as light. Suddenly, Moses and Elijah appeared and began talking with Jesus. Matt. 17: 2 - 3 NLT

As we gazed out the coach windows, the magnificent snow-capped mountain captivated us, stirring visions of the profound events that unfolded there many years ago.

Oh, to have been there at that time…

This pivotal moment marked the conclusion of our brief tour of Israel, and we were sad, but strangely refilled by our experiences there.

Upon our arrival at Ben Gurion Airport, we checked in for our return flight, determined to return one day to delve deeper into this remarkable country, where our Lord Jesus walked and where the stories of the Bible spring vividly to life.

.

Chapter Sixteen

CLOSURE

Four years later, Tony and I took a trip to Malta and stayed in a hotel on the main street in St Julian's Bay, which proved to be an excellent base to explore the rest of the island. A beautiful view of the harbour was visible from our hotel room window.

Armed with weekly bus tickets, we explored the island. Conveniently located nearby, there was a bus stop serving the route to Valletta, the capital, and other interesting destinations along the way, which was very helpful and made travelling around the island much easier.

Although the service could be slow and sporadic at times, for example, we once found ourselves stranded for several hours when the bus failed to appear. We eventually gave up and caught one going in the opposite direction to the nearest big town to get the right bus back to St Julian's Bay, so it's worth checking if all routes are running.

Valletta, renowned for its museums, historical edifices, and remarkable architecture, serves as the cultural epicentre of the Maltese islands. Visitors to Malta should be aware that most establishments close around 4 pm, which can lead to inconvenience if this isn't taken into account.

St Paul was famously shipwrecked on this island, and in memory of this event, a church imaginatively named *'St Paul's Shipwreck Church'* was built.

The island's interior has small, picturesque alleyways, and we strolled around the twisty, narrow back streets. As we walked through these ancient alleyways, we sensed that this place hid many secrets yet to be uncovered.

St Paul's Catacombs in Rabat are Malta's earliest and most significant specimens of archaeological evidence of Paul's presence on the island. Statues of St Paul in the caves, where he resided for a time, decorated the entrance area.

Steps down to the bowels of these caves are narrow and worn. The dark, winding corridors made me feel claustrophobic. These steps were excavated in the last century. Looters had already taken anything of value, so there wasn't much left behind.

Gozo, the neighbouring island, is beautiful and characterful with an imposing statue of Christ on a hill overlooking Ir-Rabat *(Victoria),* the main town.

The shuttle ferry carries passengers between the two islands, and locals told us that some Gozitan residents commute daily to Malta to work, as there isn't enough employment for them on this small island.

In Victoria, there is much to do, from shopping and visiting historical sites to soaking up the vibes of this historic town, which in places seems to have stopped in time, blending the charm of the past with the best that modern technology has to offer.

At St Paul's Bay, Malta, we took a boat trip to see the Blue Grotto, a stunning and rare sight, revealing a deep turquoise sea. This was a highlight of our trip.

Though I have a healthy respect for the sea *(bordering on fear),* being in a small boat a few feet above the deep ocean made me feel vulnerable and nervous, even though we were wearing life jackets. I was very relieved to step back onto dry land.

The sea belongs to him for he made it. His hands formed the dry land too….. Ps. 95:5 NIV

St Paul's Bay is a charming place, and reminders of his presence are punctuated throughout.

On a tiny rock off the coast, there was a statue of this fruitful saint who brought Christianity to the Maltese islanders.

We read in the Acts of the Apostles that Paul spent three months in the area, deeply committed to spreading the gospel and ensuring the salvation of everyone he met. Many locations bear his name.

During his stay, he was bitten by a snake while gathering brushwood for a fire. The local inhabitants superstitiously perceived this as a sign of his guilt as a murderer. However, when his limbs didn't swell and he survived this deadly snakebite, they marvelled and hailed him as a god.

Paul In Malta

After we were brought safely through, we then learned that the island was called Malta. The native people showed us unusual kindness, for they kindled a fire and welcomed us all because it had begun to rain and was cold. When Paul had gathered a bundle of sticks and put them on the fire, a viper came out because of the heat and fastened on his hand.

When the native people saw the creature hanging from his hand, they said to one another, "No doubt this man is a murderer. Though he has escaped from the sea, justice has not allowed him to live." He, however, shook off the creature into the fire and suffered no harm. They were waiting for him to swell up or suddenly fall down dead. But when they had waited a long time and saw no misfortune come to him they changed their minds and said that he was a god.

Now in the neighbourhood of that place were lands belonging to the chief man of the island named Publius who received us and entertained us hospitably for three days. It happened that the father of Publius lay sick with fever and dysentery. And Paul visited him, prayed, and, laying his hands on him, healed him. And when this had taken place, the rest of the people on the island, who had diseases, also came and were cured. They also honoured us greatly and when we were about to sail they put on board whatever we needed.

Acts 28: 1–10 ESV

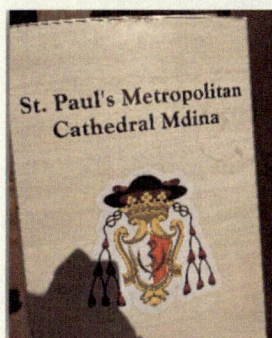
St. Paul's Metropolitan Cathedral Mdina

Another unmissable tourist attraction is the walled city of Mdina. The Normans once occupied the tiny golden building, which the Knights of Malta later managed, rumoured to be another one-time home of St Paul.

The surrounding streets have preserved their ancient charm, remaining almost unchanged for centuries, complete with traditional street lamps illuminating the area as darkness falls.

While we were there, I noticed a missed call from Egypt on my phone, which seemed odd. I didn't recognise the number, and I hadn't been in contact with anyone from Egypt for some time. It gave me a strange sense of foreboding.

Shortly after this, I received a text from Ahmed, a relative of Magid's, informing me of *'Magdy's current health problems.'*
Prostate cancer had been diagnosed and had spread to his bones. He had recently experienced a fall in his flat, which resulted in a broken hip. He underwent surgery to replace the joint.
I was saddened to hear this news, knowing that the medical expenses in Egypt would be substantial, as only minimal free

medical care is provided there, and his health was deteriorating quickly.

Ahmed urged me to invite Adam and Kerry-Ann to reach out to him to lift his spirits. Kerry-Ann attempted to speak with him but received no answer, and frustratingly, Adam had no success either.

When I rang, I was told, *"He is sleeping a lot, please call back later,"* by the nurse, who couldn't speak English, but fortunately, I understood what she said.

~

ENGLAND 2023

When we got back home from Malta, I called Magid again, and this time managed to speak with him. Of course, true to form, *he begged for money.*

Despite his serious condition, I felt no compulsion to help him, particularly considering the devastation he had caused to our family. I also felt he should have had savings and have established an income by now to support himself. His unending irresponsibility made me reluctant to 'open my chequebook'.

Instead, I suggested he contact his ex-wife, Heike, and his two grown-up daughters in Germany for assistance. I suspected he had already done so and got a negative response, which made me even more hesitant to step in.

He was unprepared for emergencies yet again, and while I felt a bit sorry for him, my doubts were more substantial. A

message played on my iPad, and his voice sounded strained and
desperate.

"If I don't get some money, I will die!"
He pleaded; his words laced with urgency and resignation.
An unfamiliar wave of apathy washed over me; I hadn't spoken
to him in what felt like aeons. It was as if I were watching a
distant storm unfold, aware of the inevitable destruction it would
bring while remaining unaffected by the chaos. His audacity in
reaching out for help was striking; it was clear that he
functioned without any apparent shame or moral compass, still
expecting people to jump to his aid while utterly disregarding
the fallout from his past actions.

Despite my detachment, a flicker of hope remained in my
heart that he could garner support to meet his immediate needs
and relieve his dire situation without my help.

With that in mind, I contacted Nathan, a familiar
acquaintance based in Cairo who was on the board of directors
of an international charitable organisation devoted to assisting
families in distress across the region. Explaining Magid's
predicament and emphasising the urgent need for funds to
provide medication as well as medical care, I told him about the
situation, hoping he would intervene.

Nathan contacted Ahmed, who provided him with context
and helped him assess the situation. However, his response was
disappointingly harsh.

Rather curtly, he decided not to extend any assistance,
leaving me to grapple with the weight of my mixed emotions
about the ordeal.

Having contributed significantly to the company recently, I found his decision particularly disappointing, considering the organisation's stated commitment to altruistic and charitable principles.

Still, I recognised that he might have compelling reasons rooted in his deep understanding of the culture and the specific circumstances. He might have perceived mitigating factors which had eluded me, so with a heavy heart, I accepted his judgment.

~

On 16th November 2023, I received the news of Magid's *(Magdy's)* death. He passed away at 10 am and was buried later that day at 2 pm.

The swiftness of the events felt somewhat jarring. While relieved that his suffering had ended and a sense of closure had come, I found myself strangely detached emotionally. I surprised myself *and didn't cry.*

The absence of Magid in our lives felt surreal. He was always a significant, albeit ethereal, presence in our family's lives. However, any potential grief was eclipsed by a profound resentment stemming from his treatment of me, our children, his siblings, and countless others unfortunate enough to be connected to him.

His life was driven by insatiable greed and a blind, unrelenting pursuit of wealth. He justified his despicable actions with an overwhelming sense of entitlement and an obsessive need for material gain. He was a deeply flawed individual, and part of me believes the world is ultimately better off without him. He is now in God's hands. I lack the energy to continue harbouring resentment.

I would like to think that he found peace with his Maker before he passed away, but somehow, I doubt it.

Do I have any pleasure in the death of the wicked? declares the Sovereign LORD. Instead am I not pleased when they turn from their ways and live? Eze. 18:23 NIV

Magid's family in Egypt are all gone now, and it's strange to contemplate that a whole generation has passed away.

~

Tony is truly an extraordinary person. Although it took time to develop, the bond we share is powerful.

We consistently support one another through life's ups and downs, although we inevitably need to manage the baggage from past relationships that is bound to affect us from time to time.

Throughout my challenging journey of recovery following multiple orthopaedic surgeries, Tony has been my unwavering support, encouraging me without hesitation, and I value his integrity, especially given my past experiences.

Recently, I reflected on the situation involving my ex-husband, which was undeniably sorrowful. However, I felt emotionally detached from it, accepting that it no longer fell within my sphere of concern or responsibility.

Magid's cousin, Ahmed, contacted me again. He informed me that *'Magdy had left debts to be settled.'* Ahmed was seeking a financial contribution from us, citing that *'honouring the deceased by clearing their debts was essential for their peace in the afterlife.'*

It's a customary belief in Islamic culture that when a person dies with outstanding debts, their soul will not find rest; consequently, it falls upon the eldest son to settle these obligations.

A strong stance was called for on this matter, as there was a risk it could cause Adam a serious setback with his mental health, so I told Ahmed emphatically that *nothing we do on earth can affect those who have passed away,* and he should not ask Adam, *his only son,* for money.

I emphasised that Adam should not be burdened with these financial responsibilities as, under these circumstances, *it wasn't his duty to settle his father's debts.*

A long and drawn-out debate ensued over our differing religious beliefs.

How ironic that even beyond the grave, we were being pressed for money on his behalf!

Ahmed furtively hinted that there were rumours of a large payment about to be made to Magdy due to an ongoing dispute with a bank. This was typical of Magid, he would fabricate these scenarios to entice and manipulate people to do what he wanted; but of course, it was wishful thinking.

He would dangle a carrot before those he needed to support him, telling them he was in line for a big payout to whet their appetites and motivate them to keep paying his bills and supporting his luxury lifestyle, relying on a substantial reward once the elusive funds finally arrived.

He was judging them by his own materialistic standards.

Over time, I have forgiven Magid, even though it was difficult, as he caused a great deal of pain and destruction in my life and the lives of my children. Holding on to grievances is not God's way, and, as Nelson Mandela once wisely declared,

"It's like drinking poison and expecting the other person to die."

We can *conquer evil with goodness* and aim for r*estoration* whenever possible. Although some days are still a struggle, I have found healing and freedom from bitterness and resentment through God's unending, limitless and outrageous grace.

God instructs us to love and forgive
one another, just as He forgives us.

Instead of resenting God's teachings or viewing His ways as a burden on our lifestyle, I rejoice in them and let them guide me to victory with God's help. If we do not forgive others, God cannot forgive us.

Forgive us our trespasses, as we forgive those who trespass
against us.

Tony and I have now been married for almost twenty years.

~

In January 2024, I had my second major back surgery, my tenth orthopaedic operation, and by far the most extensive and complex one, explicitly mentioning the possibility of death as a potential risk on the consent form. The procedure took nine hours and was carried out in two stages.

After the operation, I was moved to ICU for three days. The room had no windows, making it feel dark and gloomy. I was relieved when they moved me to the central ward because the constant monitoring of my vital signs and the persistent beeping of the machines was overwhelming.

When the nurse held my hand during the night, I mistakenly thought she was being kind and supportive, but later it dawned on me that she was checking my pulse to ensure I was still alive.

The Royal National Orthopaedic Hospital in Stanmore is approximately five miles from Pinner, West London, where Adam lives, making it convenient for visits. He came to see me regularly, brightening my day.

Tony visited me almost every day, even though the hospital was thirty miles away, which resulted in a sixty-mile round trip.

A lovely couple, friends from King's Church, Lynda and Brian, unexpectedly made the journey to surprise me with a visit, which lifted my spirits.

Following surgery, I was left with two scars on my lower back and side, along with a swelling the size of a football, which took several months for the swelling to go down, prompting my friends to ask: *"How's your football?"* during my recovery.

Having new implants (scaffolding) in my lower back, hip resurfacing, knee replacements, a cage in my left foot with screws in every toe, and a silicone implant in the big toe of my right foot, I can honestly say I am well acquainted with incapacity and pain, and admit I often find it difficult to count it all as joy as St Paul suggests.

Nevertheless, I don't feel sorry for myself.

Be joyful in hope, patient in affliction, faithful in prayer.
Rom. 12:12 NIV

However, questions that never seem to go away are:

1) *"If God wants us to be healthy, and Jesus' body was given for us, why are some Christians suffering from physical disability and ill health?*

2) *Where is God when it hurts?"*

God is with us in our suffering; that's the whole point. Things that cause us pain bring God even greater pain.

Christ's suffering on the cross challenges any self-pity we may feel about our suffering, but we can cling to the joy and hope of eternity.

God's eternal plan is paramount and overrides any pain we endure on this earth.

> *"He will wipe every tear from their eyes. There will be no more death or mourning or crying or pain, for the old order of things has passed away."* Rev. 21:4

God is loving, good, holy, wise, and all-powerful.
We live in a fallen world where the devil roams and evil prevails. Unfortunately, we often become desensitised to this evil.
The devil causes suffering, particularly among the people of God, who pose a threat to his ambitions of becoming *like, or even greater than, God.*

Evil is temporal…

Heaven and earth will pass away,
but My words will never pass away. Matt. 24:35 NIV

None of us willingly endures pain or suffering, yet the reality is that most of us encounter health challenges and trials at some point in our lives. It's entirely natural to experience doubts and fears during these times.

In His infinite wisdom and compassion, the Lord understands the confusion and anguish we endure, but here lies the essential truth:

He is with us throughout every struggle.

He equips us with invaluable resources—spiritual weapons and divine strength—empowering us to break free from even the most formidable demonic strongholds.

Suffering can lead to profound transformation and ultimately salvation, opening the gates of Heaven before us.
The Lord uses our hardships to mould us into something new and breathtaking.

Throughout this journey, suffering cultivates endurance, shaping a strong character and obedience to God's Word and gives birth to hope. This hope is unwavering and never disappoints us, for God's love has been abundantly poured into our hearts, granting us the strength to greet each day with renewed purpose and resolve.

During a pre-op consultation at the hospital, pounding the desk, the Senior Registrar explained,

>*"We want to* **do the right thing, in the right way, at the right time**.*"*
>*"That's an awful lot of rights!"* I flippantly responded.

Following our church service, the next Sunday, we all had an opportunity to chat with one another before the second service began. A dear friend, Joan, asked if I had been given a date for my operation yet.

When I told her *I had and told her the details*, she immediately reached out and put her hand on my shoulder to pray for me.

>*"Lord, we pray for your guidance for the surgeons and staff during Joann's operation. We pray that* **the right thing will be done, in the right way, at the right time**.... *"*

My ears pricked up when she prayed this last sentence. I expected to hear a heartfelt prayer, the kind said in tough times, but I was shocked when I heard Joan's words.

I couldn't believe she was repeating the exact words spoken by the doctor at the hospital, confirming that God was with me. What I had understood before in my head, I now sensed in my heart. *Wow!*

He was present at that consultation, and this realisation assured me he'd be with me in the operating theatre.

The spinal surgeon knew my friends were praying for me, for him, and the robot. *(Robots are used routinely during these procedures.)*

He added with a confident, cheery smile, *"It's good that people are praying, but they needn't worry about the robot; I'll look after that!"*

I'm happy to say he did. Christians will inevitably attract conflict; the person of Jesus challenges those in power. It would be kind of odd if we didn't provoke those in power.

But if we confess our sins to him, he is faithful and will forgive us and cleanse us from all wickedness.
1 John 1:9 NIV

EPILOGUE

It brings me immense sorrow to report that my former
pastor, Michael, who once led our community at
Emmanuel, is now experiencing the challenges of
advanced vascular dementia.

Thankfully, he resides in a compassionate facility,
Christian Assisted Living Accommodation, in Bedford,
where he is lovingly cared for by his devoted wife, Joan.
Together, they find solace in the daily rhythms of life,
participating in uplifting services, engaging in Bible
studies, and surrounding themselves with prayer. Their
family makes it a priority to visit as often as possible,
providing support and connection.

On one summer visit, Tony and I went to see them, but
my heart sank when he looked at me, his eyes filled with
confusion. Then he asked,

"Where do I know you from?"

I was dismayed and disappointed to see that, although he is still alive, much of him has been lost to this cruel, demonic disease. It feels like we have been prematurely robbed of the essence of this dear and remarkable man, who has played a crucial role in my salvation and the salvation of many others.

A deep concern about the immense burden on his beloved wife, Joan, hangs over me. The daily struggles she must endure are incomprehensible, but I am heartened to know they still have some good days. Living in this Christian community, sustained by daily prayer and regular spiritual guidance, is ideal for them, and the love and support of their family are added blessings.

Encouragingly, Joan tells me that his spiritual life remains intact, as does his musical ability. Recently, I watched a video of him playing the hymn. *'I Cannot Tell Why He Whom Angels Worship'* to the haunting tune of *'Londonderry Air.'*

It was truly inspirational!

He often played that hymn for me, acknowledging my birthplace, Londonderry, so it always felt special. Its haunting melody, *'Danny Boy,'* is a well-known Irish lament, a popular choice at funerals.

Adam's current diagnosis is 'residual schizophrenia,' although at times this shifts to 'schizoaffective disorder.' I'm uncertain about the distinctions between the two. Still, he is managing well without medication or support from medical services and continues to express his artistic talents in numerous ways, including writing poetry, photography, and occasional acting.

Adam strongly believes in the Lord Jesus, which brings me immense joy. Although he may not always incorporate Biblical principles into his thoughts and lifestyle, he, like me, is a work in progress.

Another familiar grievance is that:

'God keeps us waiting too long before answering our prayers.'

Recently, in our small church group, someone remarked that we were all waiting for something we had been praying about for a long time.
One prayed for healing, another for her unbelieving husband, another for a housing problem, and finally, another needed their work conditions to improve —
All everyday prayer requests.

In the Bible, Mary and Martha desperately wanted Jesus to come and heal their brother Lazarus, who was extremely ill, but Jesus delayed and arrived *too late*.
His dear friend had died.

Jesus wept bitterly, revealing his humanity and empathy for Mary and Martha, and then raised Lazarus from the dead by the power of his divinity.

Jesus wept. (The shortest verse in the Bible.)
Then the Jews said, *"See how he loved him!"*
John 11:35-36 NIV

He had been in the tomb for four days.

After three days, the decomposition process starts. At that time, a common misconception was that the spirit would leave the body after three days, which may also have contributed to this deliberate timing.

Jesus called his friend by name and instructed him to come out of the grave.

He raised him from the dead! ... *(full story in John 11)*

Jesus was four days late, but just in time; God's timing is perfect. He is never early and never late.

God's wisdom is profound, embodying a deep understanding consistently rooted in kindness. When life's challenges cloud our vision and we find it difficult to grasp His intricate plan or recognise His guiding hand, I encourage you to trust His loving heart, which always seeks our ultimate good.

Over the past several years, I have dedicated myself to nurturing and deepening my relationship with God. Although I often stumble and fall short of my best intentions, I find comfort in the fact that I am no longer in the bleak, despairing place I once was.

Each slip-up serves as a lesson, and while perfection remains elusive, I strive for a heart attitude that aligns with the core values of love, compassion, and integrity—principles that truly matter in this life and the next, shaping the eternity that awaits us.

Throughout my life, like many folks, I have encountered significant losses—personally, emotionally, and spiritually. Yet, I have gained from these experiences an invaluable, deeper connection with God and assurance of my place in eternity.

These challenges, rather than weakening my faith, have given me insight into His purpose amid the trials and have strengthened me, bolstering me to fulfil my godly purpose…

—a divine setup? ... I think so!

> He will wipe every tear from their eyes, and there will be no more death or sorrow or crying or pain. All these things are gone forever."
>
> Revelation 21:4 NLT

Prophecy	Old Testament	New Testament Fulfillment
He will be born in Bethlehem.	*Mic. 5:2*	*Matt. 2:1-5*
Son of God	*Psalm 2:7* *Prov. 30 - 40*	*John 3:16-17* *Heb. 1:5*
From the Tribe of Judah	*Gen. 49:10*	*Heb. 7:14*
Born of a Virgin	*Isa. 7:14*	*Matt. 1:18-22*
A Prophet like Moses	*Deut. 18:15*	*John 7:15-17*
The King of Israel	*Zech. 9:9*	*Mark 4:1 - 10*
He will be riding on a Donkey	*Isa. 53:3*	*John 1:11*
He will be Rejected	*Isa. 53:3*	*John 1:11*
He will be Beaten	*Mic. 5:1*	*Mark 15:19*

Prophecy	Old Testament	New Testament Fulfillment
He will be Betrayed	*Mic. 5:2*	*Mark 14:17-20*
He will be Tried and Condemned	*Isa. 53:8*	*Matt. 27:1-2*
He will be Crucified	*Ps. 22:16*	*Matt. 14:17-20*
He will be Pierced	*Zech. 12:10*	*Luke 23:33-34*
His Garments will be Divided	*Ps. 22:18*	*John 19:23-24*
He will be Given Vinegar & Gall	*Ps. 69:21*	*John 19:28-29*
His Bones will not be Broken	*Ex. 12:46*	*John 19:31-36*
The Messiah is Our Sacrifice	*Isa. 53:5- 61*	*1 Pet. 2: 24-25*
He Will be Raised from the Dead	*Ps. 16:10*	*Luke 24:1-7*
God will Create a New Covenant	*Jer. 31:31*	*Heb. 8:7-13*

NB. These are just a few examples; there are many more.

The Armour of God

Finally, be strong in the Lord and his mighty power. Put on the full armour of God so that you can take your stand against the devil's schemes. For our struggle is not against flesh and blood but against the rulers, against the authorities, against the powers of this dark world and against the spiritual forces of evil in the heavenly realms.

Therefore, put on the whole armour of God so that when the day of evil comes you may be able to stand your ground and after you have done everything, stand.

Stand firm then with the belt of truth buckled around your waist with the breastplate of righteousness in place and with your feet fitted with the readiness that comes from the gospel of peace.

In addition to all this, take up the shield of faith with which you can extinguish all the flaming arrows of the evil one. Take the helmet of salvation and the sword of the Spirit which is the word of God. And pray in the Spirit on all occasions with all kinds of prayers and requests. Be alert and always keep praying for all the Lord's people.

Pray also for me that whenever I speak, words may be given me so that I will fearlessly make known the mystery of the gospel for which I am an ambassador in chains. Pray that I may declare it fearlessly as I should.   Eph. 6:10 – 20 NIV

JABEZ

The Bible character, Jabez, in 1 Chronicles, stands apart from us; he didn't live amid our modern materialism. His prayer cannot be directly applied to our lives unless we understand how it relates to his unique situation and Jesus Christ.

> *God promises us provision, not prosperity, as some mistakenly believe. Jesus warns us that we will have trouble in this life.*
> *Jabez lived in a time when God had foretold destruction because of the people's rebellion against Him, so he had much to fear. From his perspective, provision was prosperity.*

The essence of the Prayer of Jabez centres on transforming our hearts to align with God's intentions, empowering us to confront life's challenges.
God answers our prayers through His divine will, rather than merely fulfilling our desires. While we perceive only a limited view, He sees the whole picture.

"I am the Alpha and Omega, the beginning and the end, the first and the last." Rev. 22:13 NIV

Jabez exemplifies this principle through his enduring legacy of faith, which transcends mere familial lineage. Instead of being granted material wealth as a direct reward for his fervent prayers, Jabez received the essential resources required to fulfil God's purpose throughout his life.

His prayer is not merely a plea for personal blessing; it is a heartfelt cry for God to bless him in his role as a member of His Covenant People.

Jabez sought divine empowerment to expand his influence and stewardship, reflecting a deep understanding of the responsibilities that come with being part of a larger spiritual community.

His request for protection and abundance demonstrates a desire not just for individual prosperity but for the well-being and advancement of his people, displaying a profound commitment to the covenant relationship* between God and His followers.

The name Jabez means pain and sorrow.
Imagine having to navigate life with such a name.

He may have lived in constant dread that this name could become a self-fulfilling prophecy, driving him to pray for God to expand his territory—not in the sense of physical land, but in terms of spiritual influence over others.

God granted his request. Jabez studied and adhered to the law, trusting God to steer his life.

His deep understanding of the law led to the city where he resided being named in his honour. His legacy endured through the many disciples he left behind.

AUTHOR'S *COMMENTS*

I am sorrowful and concerned for those who reject Jesus Christ.

The sorrows they will face are far-reaching and heartbreaking, but avoidable if only they would repent, accept Jesus, who is the Way, the Truth and the Life, and seek His forgiveness.

When someone is reunited with God and fellow Christians, the demons scream in anguish while the angels rejoice in celebration!

We inhabit the natural world and yet coexist with the supernatural realm. An invisible dimension exists more real than our own.

While we possess physical bodies, there are also beings in spiritual form.

The Bible mentions angels more than three hundred times. They exist and move between Heaven and Earth to serve God.

But you are not controlled by your sinful nature. You are controlled by the Spirit if you have the Spirit of God living in you. (And remember that those who do not have the Spirit of Christ living in them do not belong to him at all.) Rom. 8:9 NIV

Reflecting on my past, I wish God had been present in my early life so I could have avoided the many mistakes I have made. However, His ways and timing are perfect, and if He didn't give up on me, He won't give up on you either. His Hand is always there, guiding you.

He knows your name.

Suffering leads to refinement and growth and is God's method of purifying and humbling us.
Therefore, do not flee from suffering.

> *Many will be purified, cleansed, and refined by these trials. But the wicked will continue in their wickedness, and none of them will understand. Only those who are wise will know what it means.*
> Dan. 12:10 NASB

The stories of important Bible characters illustrate that having faith in God does not guarantee safety or comfort in a world influenced by Satan. God's purpose is to lead us into His Kingdom. Even during times of suffering, these individuals trusted in the Lord and held onto the hope that He would ultimately save them. The central theme of the Bible centres around the concept of sin.

Sin occurs when we attempt to take God's place and control our own lives. Yet God turns this on its head by taking our punishment and judgment upon Himself. This reversal is what represents the Gospel…

Good News!

We all carry burdens from our past: some with deep, painful memories, leaving profound regrets, emotional scars, and wounds weighing us down, hindering us from fully embracing the abundant life that God has in store for us.

However, I want to encourage you today that our Heavenly Father is a God of redemption who desires to liberate you from the chains of the past...
It's time to let go now!

God is calling us to a new season of freedom. His mercies are new every morning!

Regardless of our trials or sorrows, when we recognise that *the Lord's mercies never cease*, we find comfort in Him.

My past actions do not define my worth. By keeping my focus on Jesus, I maintain a thankful heart, knowing that I am forgiven for my wrongs.

We can experience freedom and joy by walking daily in step with the Holy Spirit.
Jesus paid the price in full for our sins. Therefore, if we refuse to forgive ourselves for past transgressions, we diminish Jesus' sacrifice on the cross.

We are not defined by our past sins or shortcomings but by our identity as children of God. Let's not confine ourselves to a mindset of unworthiness or self-pity.

God has a plan and a purpose for you.

God has intricately woven my mistakes and experiences into the very fabric of my life, reshaping me into the person He intended me to become.

Like all, I am a work in progress, still on a journey of growth and discovery. However, I can now move forward with a renewed sense of purpose and passion, fully aware that I have a clean slate and am firmly grounded in my new identity in Christ.

~

In the Old Testament, God's people adhered to strict laws and regulations to draw into His presence, regularly offering sacrifices as expressions of confession and gratitude.

These rituals acted as a crucial framework for atonement and maintaining a relationship with God. However, a significant change occurred in the New Testament.

Jesus willingly paid the ultimate price for our sins, becoming the perfect sacrifice that forever transformed our connection with God.

This profound gift of grace means we no longer need to rely on rituals to seek forgiveness, but instead, we can confidently approach Him, knowing that we are fully accepted and loved.

If you are reading this and feel like you are beyond help or too broken, remember that Jesus wants you, not to shame you, but to bring you home.
He loves you more than you can imagine.

∞

He will sit as a refiner and purifier of silver, and he will purify the sons of Levi and refine them like gold and silver, and they will bring offerings in righteousness to the Lord.

Mal. 3:3 ESV

Jesus said, *"I promise that I will never leave you helpless or abandon you as orphans---I will come back to you!"*

John 14:18   TPT

A group of women doing a Bible study were puzzled by a verse in the Old Testament that states God would sit as a Refiner and Purifier of silver and gold. They pondered on what this passage implied about His character and nature. One of the women offered to investigate the process of refining and report her findings back to the others.

That week, she called a goldsmith and asked if she could observe him at work without mentioning her reasons, except for her curiosity regarding the refining process. He agreed, and she attended.

As she watched, he held a piece of gold over the fire and allowed it to heat up. He explained that to refine gold, it has to be held in the middle of the fire, where the flames are hottest, to burn away the impurities.

The woman contemplated God. She considered the idea of God holding us in such a fiery spot, and then reflected again on the verse. He sits as a Refiner and Purifier of silver and gold, and she asked if it was true that he had to stay there the whole time when the piece was being refined.

'Yes', he replied, asserting that even a moment's delay would cause damage.

Then she asked: *"How do you know when the gold is refined?"*

He smiled and replied,

"That's easy, when I can see my image in it."

Send the Holy fire! Send the Holy fire!
Send the Holy fire!

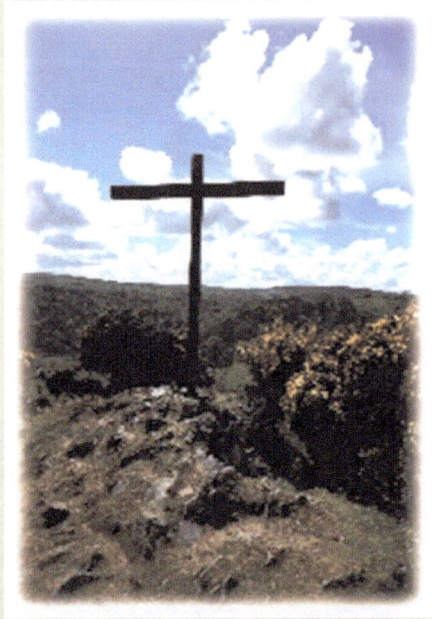

Ffald y Brenin, Wales

(A Place – where the line between heaven and earth is thin. Many have had spiritual experiences there.)

So is my word that goes out from my mouth: It will not return to me empty but will accomplish what I desire and achieve the purpose for which I sent it.
Isa. 55: 11 NIV

Life is fragile and precious; savour every moment and stay close to the Lord.

The best is yet to come!

ACKNOWLEDGEMENTS:

Firstly, I thank our Heavenly Father for saving me through the blood shed by His precious Son, Jesus, for speaking to me in a dream and for inspiring me to produce this book.

I want to express my gratitude to Sandra Carter, a retired journalist and accomplished author, for her support and for reviewing this book.

I also want to thank her husband, Roger Carter, for his invaluable help with the cover design. Their guidance, encouragement, and support were essential in creating this work.

Thanks also to my dear friends, Samantha Shaw and Angela Sutton, for their loyalty, encouragement and helpful feedback and for believing in me.

∞

REFERENCES/SOURCES:

Scripture taken from various translations of the Holy Bible ~ NIV, MSG, NLT, ESV, AMP, ASB.
Some travel info is taken from TripAdvisor.
The Book of the Prayer of Jabez – Bruce Wilkinson

(The Root of an Asparagus Plant)

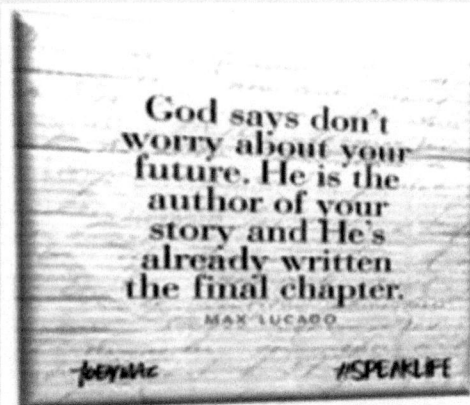

God says don't worry about your future. He is the author of your story and He's already written the final chapter.

MAX LUCADO

JOANNAC   #SPEAKLIFE

Underwritten by God.

Never will I leave you, never will I forsake you.

-Hebrews 13:5

To all my dear readers:

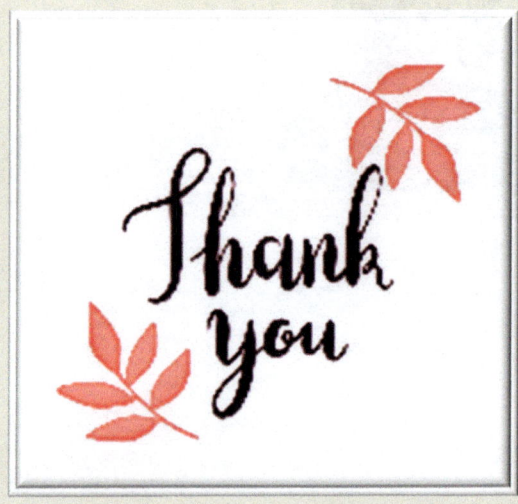

Thank you